Female Sex Offenders

Female Sex Offenders

What Therapists, Law Enforcement and Child Protective Services Need to Know

Julia Hislop, Ph.D.

A subsidiary of Idyll Arbor, Inc., PO Box 720, Ravensdale, WA 98051
www.IdyllArbor.com 425-432-3231

Editor: joan burlingame

ISBN 1-930461-00-3

Library of Congress Cataloging-in-Publication Data
Hislop, Julia
   Female sex offenders : what therapists, law enforcement and child protective services need to know / Julia Hislop
     p. cm.
   Includes bibliographical references and index.
   ISBN 1-930461-00-3 (alk. paper)
   1. Female sex offenders – Services for. 2. Female sex offenders – Identification. 3. Female sex offenders – Mental health. 4. Adult child sexual abuse victims – Services for. 5. Child sexual abuse – Prevention. I. Title

HV6657 .H57 2001
362.2'7—dc21

00-054162

Contents

Introduction

The purpose of this book is to help to reduce the number of victims of child sexual abuse through a levelheaded approach to the topic of women who sexually abuse others. Research is limited on this topic and the studies that do exist are often difficult to find. This book is an attempt to organize existing knowledge on female sexual abusers for the people who are responsible for keeping children safe and to begin to examine mental health treatment strategies for these women.

Few programs exist which specialize in the treatment of female sex offenders. Recommendations for treatment discussed in this book have drawn from the studies published by therapists who have treated these women and from the implications of studies that have examined the backgrounds of female sex offenders. Because these women have often been severely victimized themselves, recommendations for their treatment have also drawn from research in the area of victimology. Knowledge concerning the treatment of female sex offenders is in its infancy. It is hoped that the treatment recommendations addressed in this book will serve as a starting point for the further discussion, research and empirical investigation that is so needed on this topic.

In this book the terms perpetrator, offender and abuser are used interchangeably to refer to individuals who have had inappropriate sexual contact with others. They are not meant to reflect legal definitions, which may vary from location to location.

The book begins with a fictional account of the development of a girl into an offender. While it borrows from the real life experiences, which many female sex offenders have described to researchers and to therapists, it is not a biography. It is meant to paint a picture of the human side of trauma and the impact that it can have upon the girls who become offenders. That the offenders are also human beings with their own histories can often be lost in the numbers and percentages found in the research on this topic.

It is my hope that this book will contribute to an increased awareness of the existence of female offenders. While they are much fewer in number than male sex offenders, they are significantly harming the lives of many children. It is my hope that the information presented here will assist those who are devoted to the protection of children, and will be used to assist in the identification and treatment of female sex offenders and their victims.

1. Development of a Female Sex Offender

Debbie as an Infant

"Finally, someone who will always love me." Sara held her new daughter, Debbie, all the way home from the hospital. She loved the smell of her infant and the way that her daughter looked at her. "There's no love like that of a daughter for her mother," she beamed. Her husband, Max, grunted. He was exhausted and would be working overtime the next day, and well into the next month, to pay for the baby supplies. Sara patted his arm, "Don't forget to stop for beer." Max pulled over and bought two cases.

Sara's felt as if her life were finally coming together. For years, she had lived with her mother and with her uncle who sexually abused her. Her father had left the family when she was in grade school, leaving her mother and four children dependent on the uncle's support. Until she became a teenager, she often felt as if she were a prisoner. At fifteen she began to defy her family by staying away from the home in the evening until she knew that her uncle would be asleep. By sixteen, she was a frequent visitor of the local bars.

At nineteen, she had met Max, who was also a regular in the bars. Like Sara, he was escaping the misery of a troubled home-life. His stepfather was a raging, violent man, who battered him throughout most of his adolescence. Sara and Max were married within six months of meeting.

The evening that Debbie was brought home from the hospital, Sara held her for hours on the porch. She and Max shared their ritual six-pack. She watched his typically irritable demeanor become more calm and felt some of her ever-present sadness subside into a quiet contentment. She had escaped from her family. She had a tiny house with a man who seemed to understand what it was like to be different and alone. She had pleasant evenings drinking beer on their porch. And now, she would have someone who would always love her.

No friends came by to see the baby. No family. None ever did. The baby cried a great deal during her first week. And the next. And the next. Sara felt tension begin to escalate in her home. Max was tired from work when he came home and it was harder for her to control his anger. When the baby would cry, Sara would see the veins in his forehead bulge as he sat alone at the empty table guzzling his beer from the can. She would hurriedly try to quiet her child, "Shhh.

Shhh. Shhh." She would carry her to the second bedroom of their tiny house.

One evening, her husband had had a particularly trying day at work. Debbie, who had contracted a fever, had been difficult to quiet and was whining incessantly. From inside of her daughter's room, she could feel her husband's temper escalating. He began pounding loudly on the wall in the kitchen. "Why don't you shut up that God damned screaming wench?!" Debbie's crying became louder. Sara felt her pulse race. Max was beginning to sound like her uncle did, as he escalated into a rage over the course of several days before he would molest her. She bounced her baby on her knee, as his shouting got louder and more insistent.

Dinner was late. Sara began to berate herself. She was not taking care of Max and he was under pressure from his job. He always got angry when she did not take care of him. No one else had ever taken care of him. She knew that he depended on her. She thought about how she looked. She had not showered and her hair was a mess.

Panic shot through her. What if he left her? If she lost him, who would take care of her? Would she have to return to her uncle? In exasperation, she screamed at her child, "Why do you treat me like this, you stupid brat!! Don't you see what you make him do? Why don't you love me?"

This scene repeated itself several times before Max began to slap Sara. Each time it would throw her into a panic.

What if he should leave?

Debbie as a Preschooler

At two, Debbie was forming one and two word sentences. Her father Max, in a company lay-off, lost his job. His drinking became heavier. His life felt out of control and disorganized. He hated when things felt out of control. It brought back the feelings of his stepfather's rage, which there had been no stopping.

Sara began to notice that the veins on his forehead were constantly pulsating. With him at home, at the same time with Debbie, her life was constant tension. Max put Sara on a schedule of daily chores and was constantly slapping her for not being able to stick to it.

"Why do you have to spend so much time with that spoiled little brat? Her damn nose is running! Can't you take care of shit?" The slapping would start again. It was getting harder. If she stuck to the schedule, she was ignoring him. If she tended to him, she was ignoring the schedule. Her life was a constant state of vigilance to his mood, and was constantly tense. She developed painful ulcers. When her husband would go out, she would lock Debbie in her room and curl up in the fetal position in her bed, trying to relax her stomach. With the pillows over her head, she could almost tune out her daughter's cries. She would pretend she was in Italy. She had heard about Italy in the third grade. When her uncle was molesting her, she had learned to go there in her head. She would try to drink enough to fall asleep but still keep one ear open so she could hear her husband's return as he drove his truck up their gravel road.

Other children of preschool age were beginning to develop their words through conversations with their parents. They were beginning to express feelings and to be taught how to manage them. They were turning to their parents for comfort and were beginning to learn the basic skills of self-soothing and self-regulation. Other parents were taking their children to preschools, to Sunday schools, to day care and to friends' homes where they would play with other children. They were teaching their children to share, not to hit, and to master the basic skills for negotiating their worlds.

Debbie stretched the tops of her tiny fingertips to the bottom of the door-knob, and screamed at the top of her frantic lungs, "OPEN!!!"

Debbie at Seven

Debbie, at seven, started a new year at school. By now her father had entered a vicious cycle. His alcohol abuse had created a series of legal and financial problems that left his world spinning out of control, like a cyclone that had torn open his rage. His drinking no longer calmed him but ripped away the lid that contained his violence. He had become violent towards his wife and child and, full of rage, had sexually assaulted both of them.

He molested Debbie the night before her first day of second grade. Brutally. He was full of rage and had been drinking for most of the week. He ordered her to her room for spilling water on the floor. He was yelling at her in echoes of his stepfather, "You bitch! You don't know how to do shit! How many times to I have to fucking tell you!" His speech was slurred and he was staggering. He grabbed her arm hard and pulled her into her room. Debbie was panicked. She was screaming, and he covered her mouth. He slapped her face several times. Hard. Her heart was racing. She was panicked and tried to pull away, as his fingers dug deeper into her arm. He pulled off his belt and pulled off her under-pants. He hit her backside several times, but missed and hit her head once. Twice.

Her screaming enraged him, "I'll give you something to cry about, you stupid bitch!" He lowered his jeans and shoved his penis into her face, grabbing her hair. His penis took up all of the room in her mouth. The corners of her mouth felt as if they would rip. He had not bathed during the past two days of his drunken spree and the smell of the sweat on his genitals nauseated her. The curled hair on his genitals was matted and oily. She was disgusted. Sickened. She gagged and felt waves of nausea run through her. One of his hairs caught in her mouth and then in her throat. She couldn't breathe. Then there was slime running over her tongue. It reminded her of blowing her nose. She vomited.

Her father fell asleep. She called quietly for her mother, not wanting to awaken him. Sara had fallen asleep from drinking hours beforehand and did not answer. Debbie crawled under her bed, listening for the sound of her father's possible return for as long as she could, until she fell asleep near three in the morning. Before sleep overtook her, she crawled out, terrified, to set her alarm clock. If she did not get herself up on time, she would miss the bus and would have to stay at home with the two of them the next day.

She had not had enough sleep. She had not had breakfast. Debbie had dressed quickly and combed her own hair into a messy and lopsided ponytail. She was shaky from hunger, fear and lack of sleep. Irritable. Outraged. On edge. She spent the classroom morning devising a plan of places to spend the afternoon after school. There was a neighbor who would sometimes let her visit, if only she could think of a reason to go there. She would ask to play with the dog or to see the neighbor's flowers. Maybe she would crawl under her porch and sleep. The teacher was asking a question. "What?" The students were laughing at her.

"Debbie is not paying attention." It was the teacher's voice calling her to the board. "Perhaps you would like to solve this math problem." The symbols did not make sense. She had seen addition before, but not arranged like this. The students were laughing. She felt her cheeks burn. A boy called Bobby made fun of her hair. Her anger overtook her and she spun around and yelled at the child, "Shut up!" The teacher reprimanded her but Debbie's fury had well exceeded her ability to contain herself. The tidal wave of rage and indignation was breaking and she could not begin to stop it, "That fucker just made fun of my hair!"

The teacher was livid. She grabbed Debbie's arm, just as her father had done the night before. Adrenaline shot through Debbie like fire. The teacher had her hand on her hip. Debbie's brain interpreted that she was going for her belt. "Stop it!!" Debbie was screaming. "Get off of me, you bitch!!" The teacher took Debbie by the arm into the principal's office, where her hands were slapped hard with a ruler. The principal instructed her firmly that she must learn to obey adults if she wanted to have fewer problems in life.

As she was returned back to the classroom, she heard the children talk about her, "She's bad. I bet she got spanked." Debbie's head was spinning. Her body hurt. She was humiliated, enraged and exhausted. The other children pointed and talked about her all afternoon.

She did not learn well that day.

Debbie in Junior High

By age eleven, Debbie had experienced numerous similar incidents. She was barely passing her classes and had been assigned to some remedial courses. Debbie had alienated most of her teachers. Few of the children would speak to her. Most thought that she was slow. And strange. Debbie always went to school.

She had been through a period when she had not wanted to attend and had pretended to be sick to stay away from the teasing of the other children. On one of those days, her father had vaginally raped her.

Debbie began to create a fantasy school in her head. In the beginning, she knew it was a fantasy. In order to get herself to school in the mornings, she would imagine that she had lots of pretty girlfriends and that she was the smartest child there. She began to talk to her mother about "Bella," her new best friend, and the fantasy became increasingly real. "Bella loves it when I braid her hair. I put ribbons in her braids at recess." Her mother seemed pleased for her and would sometimes engage her in conversations about the friend. Debbie dialed pretend phone calls and spent half hours chatting with Bella. One day her mother called her to the phone, saying that it must be "Bella" who had asked for her. Debbie went to the phone, fully expecting her friend to be there. It was a wrong number.

At the fringe of her awareness was the knowledge that if she decided to realize that school was bad, she would have to stay at home and would be hurt. One day when a classmate shoved her into a wall and then walked away, awareness tapped her shoulder and she experienced a sickening feeling. Then, like a magic spell, she heard a thought in her head, "That didn't just happen." Her anxiety dissipated, and she felt surprisingly calm. Her thoughts continued, "I never have problems, only good friends who love me. Once I get through this next class, where none of my good friends have been assigned, I'll be able to go to my favorite class, where my good friends are, and we will show off our A's." She would tell herself this before every change of class. Increasingly, she was able to keep the knowledge of her home life and her school life out of her awareness.

Debbie as a Teenager

As a teenager, Debbie was expected to change for gym class. On the first day, the sweaty smell of the locker rooms, combined with the sight of so many people undressing, threw her into a panic. The smell reminded her of being orally sexually assaulted by her father. Debbie became nauseated and was excused from class at first. She was glad for the vomiting, to avoid the terror that she felt when she undressed with someone present. Eventually, however, she began to skip gym class. She would slip out of the school door and into the woods nearby. Other teens, troublemakers, were often there smoking.

"Want a cigarette?" It was one of the boys who was skipping class. She accepted and engaged in nervous chatter with him.

"Do you like to go roller skating? My friend Bella and I go all the time." Her longing for friends was becoming particularly strong, as it was with the others of her age. Before long, she was skipping other classes to engage in awkward conversations with some of the teens in the woods. Once she and Bella were invited to go roller skating and she accepted. "We got invited to party instead," she told the boy the next day.

One of boys in the woods began to take an interest in her. He did not force the issue, but asked if he could "feel her out." Debbie had never been taught the possibility of declining sex. She did not have the social skills to change the topic of conversation to something else. There was no place for her to go; she could not return to class before it ended. She was a physically developing teen who was beginning to feel sexual arousal. She allowed herself to be touched.

The sensations overwhelmed her. During her first encounter, she was lying on the ground with a boy's hand in her jeans, looking at the sky. Her sexual feelings began to nauseate her. As the sick feelings overtook her, she stared at the sky and was reminded of playing outside as a child, looking for pictures in the clouds. New magic words came to her, "This is not happening." The nausea ceased. Debbie concentrated on the shapes that the clouds were making and believed that she was staring into the sky with the boy next to her, playing picture games. She was vaguely aware that she was having sexual feelings. Some of the feelings felt affectionate, which puzzled her. Sex having always been associated with brutality. She began to fantasize that the boy must be her boyfriend.

By the end of the month, she had been "felt up" by six different boys. The episodes were surreal, and Debbie was never sure whether they had actually happened.

Some days, particularly after a sexual episode at school, she would return home feeling "not all there." Sometimes she felt as if she were watching herself from the outside. She did not have friends to distract her from herself, and she carefully avoided her parents. One quiet evening she was sitting in her room, unable to shake a feeling that she was not real. Her clock was quietly ticking, the only noise in her room. She was feeling outside of herself. She stared at her hands, which did not seem to be her own. In one of them was a safety pin. She pressed the sharp tip into her arm. She could feel nothing. She had long ago begun to divorce herself from pain. She thought about all of the ways that she disgusted herself and poked again. Harder. Nothing. Suddenly, she saw blood and she startled. Like a cold splash of water on a sleeping child, it jolted her awake.

She returned to herself.

The First Offense

Nothing much came of the relationships with the boys in the woods. She was a difficult girl to interact with, desperately awkward and irritable. Some of the boys had interacted with her with the sole goal of sexually experimenting. Without ever becoming fully aware of her motivations, Debbie began to engage the boys in a sexualized fashion. The emotions that she felt from the boys during the encounters were something akin to affection. The sexual feelings, though largely tuned out, were pleasurable when she could eliminate the nausea. She began to pretend that she had boyfriends.

When she was seventeen, she was asked to baby-sit for a neighbor with an eleven-year-old son. She sat next to him on the couch where they were watching TV. In one scene, there was a prolonged panorama of the sky. Debbie began to become aroused and to tune out much of her environment. She entered the "only half there" state where she went when she was being touched in the woods. She told the boy that she wanted to show him how to "make out." He was a curious child, who had begun to hear something about this from his friends. Debbie taught him how to kiss and to touch her. She told him to say, "I love you," and to say that he was her boyfriend. It was the first time that she had ever felt in charge of a sexual experience.

No one ever found out.

Early Adulthood

As Debbie grew older, she learned to find places to go that were not at home or school. Her parents continued to drink and her father continued to be abusive. Sometimes the boys would take her to fast food restaurants during school hours. This caretaking had an irresistible appeal for Debbie; she skipped classes whenever she was invited to go. Always a distracted and preoccupied student, she began to do even more poorly and did not graduate. In some ways, she was relieved to have been forced to remain in high school another year. She did not wish to stay at home all day and other options had not occurred to her. Her father had always had work-related problems and her mother had never worked. She had never had a friend close enough that she might observe how other families managed to find or keep jobs.

One of the boys who had touched her sexually, who had graduated, began to fight with the other boys who attempted to engage her in sexual contact. He hit them brutally. At a very primal level, Debbie had always craved someone strong who would protect her from others having sex with her. From her earliest days, sex was a brutality and, at some level, would always be, no matter how gentle the initiator. Debbie was instantly in love. The boy, Leonard, had a job. He fed her at lunchtime. When he asked her to live with him, Debbie was thrilled. Leonard slapped her when he was angry. It was a small price to pay.

He gave her love for which she had been starving. Caretaking. Protection. Escape. Social interaction that she craved, as a choking victim craves air. Debbie quickly forgot the times that Leonard hit her. She was an expert at forgetting. Besides, he was not nearly as brutal as her father and she was an expert at tuning out pain. He had also been molested by his father. When Debbie learned this, she felt that they were the only two in the world who knew what it was like, and that they were meant for each other. Leonard sometimes drank heavily, but only on the weekends. He liked sex that seemed unusual, but was affectionate and appreciative of her while it happened. Debbie did not notice whether she liked sex or not. Leonard began to sell drugs to supplement their income. Debbie did not notice that either.

Leonard's niece and nephew were left at their home for a long weekend. The niece was pubescent. She was being molested by Leonard's father and by his brother. She behaved in a very sexualized fashion towards Leonard while he was drinking and smoking marijuana. The nephew had also been molested and behaved in a sexualized fashion. Leonard approached Debbie. "They seem to want it, but they don't really know what it's all about. Let's help them." Debbie initially demurred, to which Leonard responded with anger. Debbie did not want to be hit. The weekend was going so pleasantly. The request was not so unusual to Debbie. They were not going to physically hurt the kids. The kids were already about the age of Debbie's first "boyfriend," whom she had molested only two years ago while babysitting. It wasn't as if they were raping seven-year-old children, the way it had happened to them. The children did seem to want it.

Leonard had done so much for her. Surely she could compromise her own preferences for an afternoon. In the back of her mind, panic flashed like an explosion. She did not know what she would do if Leonard left her. Life without Leonard was a lonely insanity in which clocks ticked, pins pierced the flesh and thoughts of her father's angry penis intruded into her mind like a never-ending violation. She had never lived on her own, had not finished school and did not have the expectation that she would ever be chosen as an employee. She would surely continue to be brutalized in her parents' home, should Leonard ever leave her.

Leonard called his niece over to him and told her what was going to happen. He held her wrists above her head and ordered Debbie to undress her. The niece looked resigned and detached. She was thinking to herself, "It is better to be seductive and to encourage the man to molest you when you get ready, than it is to sit around until he gets ready and feel scared the whole time." Debbie obeyed, glancing out the window to the sky. "It's okay," she thought. "This isn't really happening."

2. What Harm Can Be Done Without a Penis?

It is widely believed that females are not capable of committing sexual offenses. However, females of all ages have been known to sexually harm others. The sexual abuse of children by females has been documented with abusers as young as four years of age,[1] and by women who are grandmothers[2] and even great-grandmothers.[3] Finkelhor & Williams[4] had in their sample a 77-year-old female sexual abuser. Not only have children and teenagers been documented as victims of these women, but infants as well.[5] Both male and female children have been victimized by female sexual abusers.[6]

Many individuals have difficulty picturing the acts that might be committed by female sexual abusers. The idea of women committing sexual offenses runs contrary to the commonly held notion that sexual abuse is synonymous with rape. Rape is commonly defined as the forceful presence of a penis in a vagina. And, without a penis, what sexual crimes can be committed?

The sexually abusive acts committed by women against children are as varied as sexuality and abuse themselves. They run the gamut from the seduction of, or sexual acquiescence to, a willing but illegally underage pubescent partner, to the violent, forced sexual penetration of infants with objects. They may include acts that are disguised as caretaking, or more overtly sexual activities. Female abusers may directly take part in the sexual acts, force sexual acts to take place in which they themselves do not participate or may procure victims for a second or third party. They may initiate the sexual acts as primary offenders or may unwillingly take part in the abuse under duress from a co-offender.

Sexual Acts Committed Independently by Females

Females, in some cases, engage in overtly sexual acts with children, independently and of their own initiative. In many cases, acts of sexual abuse committed by females closely resemble acts of sexual abuse committed by males.[7] The obvious exception is that women do not force their penises into victims. One study, however, found that sexual penetration of victims with objects might be more commonly engaged in by female sexual abusers than by males.[8] Another researcher also found this type of abuse to be commonly reported by victims of female sexual abusers.[9]

Aside from this, females commonly engage in the same sexual activities with children, as do male child molesters. According to at least one study, females are just as likely as males to engage in intercourse, fondling and oral stimulation with their victims. They are just as likely to use threats, coercion and physical force.[10] In at least one study, sexual abuse has been found to be equally severe with either males or females as perpetrators.[11] Allen[12] found evidence that in some cases, the abuse committed by female sexual abusers may be more severe than that committed by males.

Among Allen's sample of 65 female sexual offenders, 30% engaged in vaginal or anal intercourse with victims. Manual or oral sexual stimulation occurred with 42%, and exhibitionism or voyeurism with the remaining 28%. Among a similar population of males, only nine percent reported vaginal or anal intercourse and only nine percent engaged in exhibitionism or voyeurism. For most male offenders (80%) the sexual activity included manual or oral sexual stimulation. Of course, it is possible that only the more severe cases involving women were noticed by those in positions of authority.

Evidence is only beginning to trickle in concerning the female offenders. Children who report that females have sexually aggressed against them are probably not as likely to be taken seriously as those reporting sexual offenses committed against them by males. Information concerning female offenders is largely unavailable to researchers. For this reason, it is premature to draw conclusions based upon existing evidence concerning comparisons between the sexual crimes committed by males and females.

However, the sexual acts in which females participate with children are being increasingly documented. It has been well documented that some female sexual abusers engage in sexual intercourse with younger male adolescents.[13] In some cases this has been known to result in the pregnancy of the female offender.[14] Simulated sexual intercourse and related activities have also been documented. Johnson[15] noted that among female children who were sexually abusive towards other children, some simulated sexual intercourse and some had genital contact with no penetration. Russell[16] also noted similar activities.

Female sexual abusers may also use objects or fingers to penetrate victims' vaginas[17] and rectums.[18] Similar penetration has also been noted by Russell.[19] Any number of bizarre items have been used by females to sexually penetrate children, such as sticks,[20] candles,[21] knives, metal toys, a crucifix, a toothbrush, crochet needles, lit matches or candles, a bottle brush, a knife handle, a plunger handle,[22] a whiskey bottle,[23] a knitting needle, a potato masher, a bath brush, pencils, lit cigarettes, coat hangers, an ice pick, thorny rose stems,[24] surgical knives, hair rollers, keys, light bulbs, hair brushes, fruits and vegetables, wooden spoons, religious medals, goldfish, vacuum cleaner parts, dildos and vibrators.[25] In one case study, the object was a metal screw, which was found in the vagina of a four year old.[26] Females may also be penetrated by their victims.[27] Hislop,[28] for example, noted the case of a woman who had been penetrated by a dildo that her female child victim had been made to wear.

Anal stimulation may occur as a form of abuse. Anal penetration may occur as a form of abuse between female offenders and their victims.[29] Female sexual abusers may also manually or orally sexually stimulate the anal regions of the child or make the child stimulate them in this fashion.[30] Anal intercourse can occur with male victims, although there is presently less documentation of this in the literature. Analingus may also occur.[31]

As with the male offenders, female sexual abusers may engage in oral sexual stimulation of genitals with children and adolescents of both genders. They may both stimulate the children and have the children stimulate them.[32]

Female sexual abusers may fondle or aggressively stimulate the breasts or sexual organs of their victims.[33] The child's body may also be rubbed against the female in a sexually stimulating way.[34] Victims may also be forced or coerced into stimulating the female.[35]

Other behaviors have also been described. Yorukoglu and Kemph[36] discussed the case of a woman who had her male and female children suck her breasts while she masturbated herself with a vibrator. Mitchell and Morse[37] noted bestiality had been involved in female perpetrated child sexual abuse in eight percent of cases (these were not differentiated into independent and co-offender cases).

Occasionally, less overtly sexual activities will be included in descriptions of sexual abuse initiated by women, such as sexualized hugging and kissing, inviting a child to do something sexual or exposing the genitals of the offender or child.[38] French kissing has also been described.[39] Rosencrans[40] described a woman's report of sexualized fondling on the buttocks and legs by her mother.

More violent or degrading activities are sometimes described on the part of women who independently offend against victims. Pinching genitals, breasts and nipples, and biting genitals[41] have been described in the literature. A case was described by Rosencrans[42] in which a girl was given beer and also beaten and burned to ensure her compliance. Elliott[43] relayed the account of a female whose mother cut the edges of her vaginal opening with scissors. Wulffen[44] described cases of caretakers who beat their charges for sexual gratification. Chideckel[45] also discussed the existence of teachers and policewomen who had beaten children for sexual gratification. de Young[46] described the case of a maternal abuser, who herself had been violently, sexually abused by her own mother. Her (the mother's) childhood abuse had consisted of being placed in scalding water, after ritualistic prayers were chanted, and included the placing of clothespins on her nipples and various objects in her rectum or vagina. Ramsey-Klawsnik[47] reported upon cases of female sexual abusers that included sexual sadism. Cases involving bondage and sadism and masochism were noted by Davin.[48]

Rosencrans[49] reported that of 93 women molested by their mothers in childhood, 70% indicated some degree of physical violence along with their abuse.

Sometimes, the acts committed by the female abuser are particularly bizarre. In Canada, The Committee on Sexual Offences Against Children and Youth[50] reported upon the case of a woman convicted after her husband found her with blood dripping from her mouth and hands, while her daughter lay bleeding from the genital area. Mitchell & Morse[51] reported that women in their sample had reported beatings, burnings, being held or tied down, hung upside down, being locked in enclosed places and abortions being performed at home by female abusers, in some cases with co-offenders. Douching and being urinated and defecated upon were among the activities described by participants in a survey of 80 females who were sexually molested by females in childhood.[52] Silber[53] described the case of a mother, who, in the course of sexually abusing her very young son, would forcibly run his face against her genitals and frighten him by spreading her vulva and making growling sounds.

In some cases, the sexual activities between the females and their child victims may include group sex[54] with other adults or children involved. Wulffen,[55] for example, described a case of an eighteen-year-old female who encouraged sexual acts between an eight-year-old boy and an eleven-year-old girl and herself.

Females may also solicit under-age prostitutes. Juvenile prostitutes of both genders in Canada have reported being solicited by females.[56]

While not commonly found in the literature, there is at least one report of a woman sexually assaulting two 18-year-old females in the course of committing another crime. The *News Sentinel*[57] in Fort Wayne, Indiana reported on the case of a twenty-five-year-old woman who robbed and sexually assaulted two females at gunpoint.

Among emerging reports in the literature are such cases, in which the sexual activity between the female and the child or adolescent is overtly sexual. However, in some cases, the sexual abuse is subtler and is disguised as caretaking.

Direct Sexual Contact Disguised as Caretaking

One of the reasons that females do not come to the attention of authorities is that their sexual activities with children may be disguised as acts of caretaking. For example, Myers[58] reported that, while others in her sample of eleven female victims of female perpetrated child sexual abuse had been more violently abused, two in her sample had been abused while being put to bed, bathed or dressed.

Females may sexualize activities such as bathing, bedtime rituals, caressing, dressing, play, enemas, spanking, toileting, inspections and similar behaviors that easily elude detection. Stirling[59] described the case of a woman who would masturbate while breastfeeding. Kasl[60] noted that women might kiss or hug children in a highly sexualized fashion, expose themselves, voyeuristically watch children or comment in a sexual fashion about changes in their bodies during puberty.

It is sometimes difficult to draw the line concerning what constitutes the inappropriate touch of a child, particularly when the person touching is a woman. In some cases, sexualized activities that occur during the course of caretaking are part of a pattern that includes more overt forms of sexual abuse. In others, the sexual activities are limited to those that are disguised as caretaking rituals

Several authors, for example, have described cases of children who are sexually abused during bathing. Miletski[61] reported that several authors have described cases of women bathing their teenage sons, women bathing with their sons and women who excessively cleaned their sons' penises. Bachmann et al.[62] similarly reported on the case of a man who had been sexually abused in childhood by his mother while he bathed. Stevens[63] revealed the case of a woman bathed by her mother until she was 16. Elliot[64] revealed the case of a man who, as a child, had been made to wash his aunt's genitals, or to wash his own in her presence, or have his washed by her; spankings and powdering were components of the abuse, which also included oral, anal and vaginal intercourse with the youth before he was 13. Two cases of females being sexually abused by their mothers while they were bathed were reported by Ogilvie & Daniluk.[65] In one of these cases the female was also offended against while being powdered and while having lotion placed on her. Stirling[66] described similar cases.

Inappropriate fondling has been noted in case studies. Lawson[67] reported upon the case of a mother who would sleep with her son during his adolescence, and stroke his penis to soothe him. Cooper and Cormier[68] reported upon the case of a mother who was obsessed with the genital cleanliness of her daughter and would rub her daughter's vagina with cream ostensibly to prevent odor and discharge when the daughter was between the ages of six and fourteen. Stevens[69] also described a case in which a female victim had cream rubbed into her genitals by her mother. Elliot[70] noted the case of a man who described his mother's occasionally sleeping with him, placing his hand on her breast and her hips against his erection; the mother also walked in on him in the bathroom and made comments about the size of his penis. Less overtly sexualized fondling has been described by authors such as Kasl,[71] who noted that women might sexualize their relationships with children by continually caressing a neck or back. Sexualized kissing and touching by female offenders has also been noted by Ramsey-Klawsnik.[72]

Intrusions into private activities or intrusive inspections have been described in cases of women who sexually abuse children. Kasl[73] noted that women might sexualize their relationships with children with intrusive questions regarding bodily functions or with other invasions of privacy. Rosencrans[74] reported that some of the women in her survey had reported vaginal exams, given by their mothers during their dating years. Berry[75] reported upon the case of a man who had shared his mother's bed during adolescence; she had exposed her genitals to her son and had frequently inspected his genitals, ostensibly to see if they were growing properly. Holubinskyj & Foley[76] reported upon a mother, who in addition to committing other more overtly abusive sexual acts, would watch her daughter use the toilet, dress and bathe.

Several authors have commented on the inappropriate or compulsive use of enemas on children for the sexual gratification of sexually abusive women.[77] Sexualized medical or cleaning rituals have also been reported,[78] as has the use of a rectal thermometer through the age of ten.[79] These activities may be particularly difficult to identify as abusive, particularly when they occur exclusive of activities that are more overtly sexual.

Sexual Acts Committed with a Co-Offender

While some women commit their sexual offenses independently, others sexually abuse children and adolescents in the company of another abuser. Sexual abuse of a child by a female who is in the company of a male co-offender has been documented by several authors.[80] The sexual abuse in such cases may include all of the forms of sexual contact that a woman might have with a child, as well as other forms of sexual contact with the male offender, such as vaginal or anal intercourse. Co-offenders may also force children to have sexual contact with each other, to watch sexual activity or to be watched by others as they are sexually abused.[81]

Numerous examples of such cases have been documented. In Canada, The Committee on Sexual Offences Against Children and Youth[82] documented the case of a woman, who with her common law husband would entice young males into their home. Following "seduction and coercion," the boys would have anal intercourse with her. The two boys in this case were twelve years old. The same committee described a case in which a married couple recruited young boys through a volunteer organization. The boys would engage in intercourse with the female while being "buggered" by the husband; other sexual acts, sometimes photographed, also occurred. The committee also described a case in which the male and female offender, in addition to other types of sexual activity, forced bestiality with a dog upon a victim. A case of child sexual abuse was also described by this committee, unusual in that it involved explicit, sexual photography of a girl, without either direct sexual contact or distribution of the photographs. A couple photographed their female daughter's genitals and took photos of the girl wearing lingerie and assuming suggestive poses. Others have documented photography occurring or videos being made,[83] with photos sometimes taken by one partner of the other engaging in sexual contact with children.[84]

Rowan, Langelier & Rowan[85] described the case of a female who would vaginally penetrate her young daughters in the company of her boyfriend. They further described the case of a couple that would engage their children in games that would result in the father sodomizing them, or with the children performing oral sex on the parents. Faller[86] documented the case of a woman who would procure latency age children, dress them according to the preferences of a male offender and fondle them to arouse them for the offender.

In some of the cases the sexual contact to which the child is exposed is perpetrated by more than one offender.[87] For example, Etherington[88] described a case in which a mother sexually abused a child, while herself engaged sexually from behind, with a male co-offender. Multiple victims as well as offenders may be present. In some such cases, the woman may hold or restrain a child while the partner engages in the sexual activity, without engaging in the sexual activity herself. In some cases, juvenile prostitutes, both males and females, have been approached by women who solicited them for group sex.[89]

As indicated by currently available research, the second abuser is almost always a male partner who has a sexual relationship with the female. In many, but not all such cases, the women are coerced or forced into the sexual contact with children by this male, who may also be physically or sexually abusive towards the female offender. In many cases, the woman is a reluctant participant, particularly in the beginning. In some cases, however, she later goes on to offend against the victims independently.

Wolfe[90] described the case of a woman who sexually abused with a partner; the woman had initially refused to participate, and was shocked by her partner with a cattle prod. Wolfe[91] commented that the women's participation in the sexual abuse of children in these circumstances is an extension of their own victimizations. Under these circumstances, some argue that the woman should be held accountable for the abuse because of their choice of partners and their failure to protect the children. Others argue that blaming such women or labeling them as mentally ill is inappropriate.[92]

It is unlikely that all cases involving a female offender and co-offender include an unwilling female, however. For example, Myers[93] described the case of a female who reported having had sexual contact with a variety of men and women when her parents were living in a commune. The commune was described as involving children in sexual practices, in the context of the sexual revolution of the 1960's and 1970's. The sexual activities involving children were described as non-violent but inappropriate manipulations of prepubescent sexual curiosity. Saradjian and Hanks[94] also described two cases in which women sexually abused with males as equal partners.

In what appear to be rare cases, the female co-offender may take the lead role in abusing and may physically or sexually abuse the co-offender. Saradjian and Hanks[95] described a case in which a woman pressured her husband until he raped a 14-year-old girl, while she watched. Apparently the woman had been obsessed with trying to understand how her own mother felt, when she, herself, was being sexually abused by her father. Finkelhor and Williams[96] similarly noted that a woman may sexually abuse her son and solicit his participation in the sexual abuse of others. In some such cases she may benefit financially from allowing others to pay for participating in the sexual activities or from photographing the activities for sale as pornography.

Apparently unusual cases involve dual female perpetrators, although virtually nothing has been written about the dynamics of such cases. One such case was documented by Crewdson[97] who described an incident in which a sexually abusive mother involved her son's maternal aunt (her sister) in his sexual abuse. Elliot[98] described the case of a male who, prior to age 13, lived with an aunt and her female friend who spanked him in a sexualized fashion and required him to engage in a variety of sexual acts with them. Lane[99] reported that there have been cases of juvenile females co-participating with other females in the forcible rape of same-age male peers. Finkelhor and Williams[100] described sexual abuse in day care settings and found that, of cases involving multiple sexual abusers, 17% involved females exclusively. In some such cases an initiator with a more deviant social history engaged a more isolated or dependent follower. Sometimes the follower later became an independent offender. Kaufman and his colleagues[101] found that among 53 female offenders, 23% had offended with another female.

Very little has been written about females who offend with others in different contexts.

Other apparently unusual cases about which little has been written include sexual assault by women in gang rape situations. For example, Sarrel and Masters[102] described the case of a 17-year-old who was threatened with violence and sexually molested by two men and three women; additionally they described a case in which four women bound, threatened and forced sex upon an adult male.

It also seems likely that some women may offend in the context of being forced into sexual contact with children by their own childhood offenders, as opposed to their mates, but virtually nothing has been written about such cases. In Canada, The Committee on Sexual Offences Against Children and Youth[103] documented the case of a father who had sexually abused his daughter since she was six. The daughter was later used to procure girls to be her father's sexual partners; in one case she held the hand of a frightened girl while her father used the girl to achieve orgasm.

Finkelhor and Williams[104] found that among women who abuse children in the context of day care settings, the women were more likely to be involved in multiple perpetrator cases, resulting in their being more likely to have more victims and more frequently occurring abuse. In multiple perpetrator cases, the abuse was more likely to involve pornography or ritualistic, extended or bizarre practices. They noted that in day care settings, the co-offenders might be exclusively childcare workers, childcare workers and family members, childcare workers and outsiders or exclusively individuals who do not work as child care workers (for example support staff).

Females who Indirectly Participate

Some women who are prosecuted as sexual offenders have no direct sexual contact with the victims at all. They have nonetheless allowed the child to be sexually abused by another. Some procure children for a male who is a mate, or allow him to sexually abuse their children. Some women prostitute children or procure them for pornographic pictures. Some observe the child in sexual activity, in which they do not participate. In some cases, women are charged with sexual crimes when they allow a child in their care to be used sexually by another person or when they fail to protect the children in their care from sexual abuse by another person. Some women, who may or may not engage in more overt forms of sexual activity with children, engage them in highly sexualized interactions that do not involve direct physical contact.

The phenomenon of men using women to procure sexual victims is not necessarily new. Banerjee[105] in researching "sex delinquent women" in India in 1945-46, stated

> In ancient literature we find that kings had sex relations with women other than those in their household. On special festival days women of the town used to come to their palaces and spend the whole day there. A king sent his special maid servants to make contacts with a woman whose company he sought. The maid servants brought the woman to the royal palace under the pretext of showing her the palace, garden, tamed animals, etc. After the arrival of the lady, they used to disclose to her that the king was desirous of her company. If after repeated efforts they were unsuccessful in making the woman agree to the proposal, they used to call the king and the latter managed the affair himself (p. 5).

Cases of women prostituting children are occasionally noted in the literature.[106] Walters[107] notes that in some cases parents or stepparents prostitute their children out of financial necessity. Such is not always the case, however. Some children are prostituted for financial gain or to support drug habits. Kercher and McShane[108] reported upon cases including, among others, ones in which victims of women were prostituted, made to give a sexual performance or used in erotic material. The Committee on Sexual Offences Against Children and Youth[109] described related cases of women who solicited either male or female juvenile prostitutes for sexual activities with others. In one case, the son of a prostitute was sexually exploited by his mother's clients.[110]

Other cases have been documented in which females actively procured children for the sexual purposes of another individual. Rosencrans[111] discussed a case of a woman who was turned over to her sexually abusive uncle by her mother when she was a child. Wulffen[112] reported upon the case of a 44-year-old female allowing her 13-year-old daughter to be used for intercourse in the service of enticing the man involved and a case of a 52-year-old woman who prostituted a seven-year-old boy. Two cases of a wife cooperating in her husband's rape of a younger girl (in one of the cases her own daughter) were also reported by Wulffen.[113]

Faller[114] noted that her sample of female offenders included women who allowed others to sexually abuse children. Ogilvie & Daniluk[115] described a case in which a mother actually allowed her daughter to be used sexually "as a carrot" in order to attract men. The *San Diego Union-Tribune*[116] documented the case of a woman who allowed her twelve-year-old son to be used for sex by his principal (also a woman) for money.

Other cases in which a partner is present, but in which there is no direct sexual activity with the child on the part of the woman, include those in which the female and male engage in sexual activity in front of the children. To some extent, the notion of engaging in sexual activity in front of children as harmful may be culturally dictated. Certainly there are cultures in which the lack of housing space prohibits privacy for sexual activity.

However, cases have been documented in which the adult involved appeared to be actively exploiting or harming the children. Groth,[117] for example, reported that of sex offenders who had been sexually abused, three percent had witnessed upsetting sexual activities, usually on the part of their parents.

Some authors have described cases of children being made to watch the sexual activities of others or of being made to participate in sexual activities with others by a female. In Canada, The Committee on Sexual Offences Against Children and Youth[118] documented the case of an 18-year-old woman who had two male accomplices restrain a 14-year-old boy and threaten him with a broken bottle in a hotel room, while she masturbated. Paiser[119] noted cases of women who had been made to watch the sexual activities of others in childhood. Henry Lee Lucas, a noted serial rapist and serial killer, by one report was raised by a prostitute who would engage in sexual activity with customers in front of her children.[120] Faller[121] noted cases of children being forced to watch sexual activities between adults, as well as cases of the children being made to engage in sexual activities with each other. Photographs were taken in some cases. Rosencrans[122] noted that among 93 women who had been sexually molested in childhood by their mothers, 26% had been made to take part in sexual activities with others while their mothers watched. In other cases the daughters were made to watch the mother expose herself, disrobe, masturbate, have sex, bathe or go to the bathroom.

In some cases, while the offender does not have direct sexual contact with a child, she forces, encourages or allows the child to have inappropriate sexual contact with children or animals. Cases of female perpetrators forcing children to have sex with other children have been documented by Ramsey-Klawsnik.[123]

Others documented cases of female offenders forcing a child to watch the abuse of another child.[124] Stirling[125] described the case of an adolescent female babysitter who allowed preschool-aged children to engage in a sex play that included the vaginal insertion of clothespins. Mitchell & Morse[126] described the case of females in their sample who had been made to have sex with animals in childhood by females.

Females may also engage in other highly inappropriate sexualized behaviors with children, without having direct sexual contact. Mitchell & Morse[127] described the case of a mother who, in addition to more overt forms of sexual abuse, would take her daughter for vaginal exams with a physician. She would watch the exam and talk about it for several days afterwards.

Etherington[128] described cases in which mothers humiliated children sexually by rejecting, mocking or emasculating their male children, often as a reaction against their own male-perpetrated abuse. Groth[129] described the case of a sex offender who had been circumcised by his parents at age 14 because he handled himself too much. Women may make pornographic pictures of children,[130] which may or may not occur in the context of sexual behavior with others.

Indirect Sexualized Acts Noted in the Literature

Some authors have noted sexualized interactions that women have with children that, while less sexually explicit, have been confusing or distressing to a child. These often do not involve direct sexual contact, but rather highly sexualized solicitations. Because the sexuality of women may be seductive rather than aggressive, behaviors such as flirting or dressing in sheer clothing may not be recognized as sexually aggressive.[131]

Women may engage in a wide variety of sexualized behaviors for the purpose of arousing themselves, or of arousing or sexually intruding upon their victims. Several authors cite examples. Miletski[132] noted cases in the literature involving women who engaged in behaviors such as walking around nude, leaving bathroom doors open, commenting on a boy's genitals and masturbating in front of a male child. Mathews[133] described behaviors of sexually abusive women, such as leaving doors open while disrobing or bathing or walking in on a child who is dressing, bathing or toileting.

In a case described by Elliot[134] (which later came to include a variety of direct sexual activities) an aunt who was a caretaker wore underwear or a nightdress and laughed at her victim's embarrassment. She forced him to watch her dry herself and hit him when he had an erection. Paiser[135] noted cases of women who, in childhood, had been exposed to voyeurism, exhibitionism and sexualized talk with females. Mitchell & Morse[136] included inappropriate conversations, exhibitionism and inappropriate inspection of the child's sexual development as among the activities reported by women abused in childhood by females.

James and Nasjleti[137] discussed activities such as sexualized verbal interactions at night ("you're the man in my life now," or "you're just like me when I was a little girl") with intimate stroking, as falling along a continuum of sexually abusive behaviors. The same authors also discussed intense body contact, such as sleeping together as similarly falling along this continuum. Other authors have noted that placing the male child in the role of the "man of the house" following a divorce, or other types of separation of the mother from the father, constitutes a type of incestuous relationship.[138] Kasl[139] also noted that women may place a male child in the role of a husband, sleep with him, share emotional problems with him and so forth.

These quasi-sexualized acts may occur apart from more overt and direct sexual behaviors and, while they typically do not break laws, they may be experienced with a great deal of discomfort in those children whom they were intended to arouse or harm. They may also be a symptom of a larger pattern of boundary violation that occurs in the context of additional, more overtly sexual acts. Often, however, these sexualized behaviors towards children may be explained away as inappropriate affection[140] rather than as abuse.

Ritual Sexual Abuse that Includes Female Perpetrators

Cases of ritualistic abuse have appeared in the literature.[141] Group sexual abuse, in the context of Satanic rituals, has commonly been observed to include female participants. For example, Weir and Wheatcroft[142] wrote an article in which they described several such cases. In one, a 27-year-old man, who pled guilty to a large number of sexual offenses, admitted that he, his wife, his sister-in-law and her husband had participated in the sexual abuse of their own and other children during satanic rituals. The abuse included penetration of the victims with knives.

Crewdson[143] also reported upon two married couples in Bakersfield, California who were convicted after having ritualistically abused their own and each other's children; he also reported upon other cases. Finkelhor and Williams[144] also reported upon such cases, and Saradjian and Hanks[145] interviewed women who had participated in these rituals. Dr. Joel Norris,[146] biographer of serial killer Henry Lee Lucas, recounts Lucas's description of having participated in similar rituals.

In this category are bizarre accounts of sexual abuse that are typically accompanied by satanic worship. Many of the cases that have occurred in the literature are remarkably similar, although they have occurred in different locations. Among the commonalties found among cases of group sexual abuse of children in the context of satanic abuse are

- physical and emotional abuse of children or torture, as well as sexual abuse[147]
- active threats against those who disclose[148]
- the creation of a magical atmosphere though the use of
  - drugs[149]
  - ritualistic paraphernalia (swords, alters, candles, bowls)[150]
  - chanting or dance[151]
  - rituals, which may include symbols (inverted crosses, pentagrams, "magic circles," etc.)[152]
  - the presence of, smearing of, or ingestion of body wastes and blood[153]
  - the sexual penetration of victims with various items[154] including such items as a ram's horn[155] and knives[156]
  - ceremonial human (often child, infant or fetal) or animal sacrifice or torture, often followed by eating the flesh of the sacrificed being[157]
  - ingestion or other use of insects,[158] for example, to terrorize participants[159]
  - religious rituals at specific times of the year[160]
  - robes, masks and costumes[161]
  - mock wedding ceremonies[162]

The children are sometimes told that Satan or other cult members are always watching and can always see when the children are disclosing their abuse.[163]

This particular type of sexual abuse by females is largely under-researched. Several of the authors who have begun to uncover such cases have commented that victims are particularly unlikely to disclose because of the terror associated with both the abuse and the threat of disclosure. Some have also alluded to victims who have been discouraged by legal advocates from testifying concerning the ritualistic aspects of their abuse due to fear that including this information would cause the sexual abuse cases to be lost in court. Some have commented that the bizarre nature of the cases may create a stigma for researchers investigating them.

Summary

Documentation that some females engage in sexual behaviors with children is being increasingly found in the literature. The documented behaviors may be overtly sexual or may be disguised as caretaking. They may occur with the female under duress from a co-offender or on the woman's own initiative, with or without a partner. They may at times occur under the bizarre circumstances of ritualistic, satanic abuse.

The types of sexualized behaviors that women engage in with children are tremendously variable and run the gamut from exhibitionism to sexual penetration with objects to pornographic photography. The activities may be engaged in with willing adolescent participants or be violently forced upon children. At times, women may sexually victimize children by making them available to another party or by forcing them into sexual activity with another adult, child or animal. At times they involve the victimization of children through sexualized intrusions of an elusive nature. The varieties of sexual activities in which women engage children are only beginning to become understood.

Notes ———————————————————

[1] Johnson (1989); Wulffen (1934)

[2] Barry & Johnson (1958); Briggs & Hawkins (1995); Burgess, Hazelwood, Rokous, Hartman & Burgess (1988); Condy (1985); Cupoli & Sewell (1988); Faller (1987); Fromuth (1983); Goldstein (1992); Goodwin & DiVasto (1979); Kempe & Kempe (1984); Myers (1992); Petrovich & Templer (1984); Mitchell & Morse (1998); Rosencrans (1997); Wulffen (1934)

[3] Ramsey-Klawsnik (1990)

[4] Finkelhor & Williams (1988)

[5] Chasnoff, Burns, Chissum & Kyle-Spore (1986); Ogilvie & Daniluk (1995); Williams & Finkelhor (1988)

[6] Hislop (1999)

[7] Allen (1991); Kaufman et al. (1995)

[8] Kaufman et al. (1995)

[9] Rosencrans (1997)

[10] Kaufman et al. (1995)

[11] Rudin, Zalewski & Bodmer-Turner (1995)

[12] Allen (1991)

[13] Allen (1991); Berendzen & Palmer (1993); Condy (1985); Crewdson (1988); Davin (1999); de Young (1982); Elliot (1993); Faller (1987); Forward & Buck (1978); Johnson (1989); Justice & Justice (1979); Kempe & Kempe (1984); Koss & Risin (1987); Krug (1989); Margolis (1984); Meiselman (1978); Ramsey-Klawsnik (1990); Shengold (1980); Wahl (1960); Wolfe (1985)

[14] Knight Ridder News Service (1998)

[15] Johnson (1989)

[16] Russell (1983)

[17] Davin (1999); Faller (1987); Fehrenbach & Monastersky (1988); Johnson (1989); Mayer (1992); Myers (1992); Ogilvie & Daniluk (1995); Ramsey-Klawsnik (1990)

[18] Bass (1991); Elliot (1993); Johnson (1989); Mayer (1992); Mitchell & Morse (1998); Neisser (1997); Ogilvie & Daniluk (1995); Rosencrans (1997); Schoenewolf (1991)

[19] Russell (1983)

[20] Bass (1991); Rosencrans (1997)

[21] Elliot (1993); Rosencrans (1997)

[22] Mitchell & Morse (1998)

[23] Schoenewolf (1991)

[24] Elliott (1993)

[25] Rosencrans (1997)
[26] Holubinskyj & Foley (1986)
[27] Etherington (1997)
[28] Hislop 1999)
[29] Etherington (1997)
[30] Rosencrans (1997)
[31] Faller (1995)
[32] Bachman et al (1994); Condy (1985); Crewdson (1988); Davin (1999); Etherington (1997); Faller (1987); Faller (1995); Freel (1995); Fromuth & Conn (1997); Hislop (1999); Holubinskyj & Foley (1986); Johnson (1989); Kercher & McShane (1985); Mayer (1992); Mitchell & Morse (1998); Paiser (1992); Petrovich & Templer (1984); Ramsey-Klawsnik (1990); Wolfe (1985)
[33] Bachmann et al. (1994); Crewdson (1988); Davin (1999); Faller (1987); Fromuth & Conn (1987); Hislop (1999); Holubinskyj & Foley (1986); Johnson (1989); Kercher & McShane (1985); Mayer (1992); Mitchell & Morse (1998); Myers (1992); Paiser (1992); Petrovich & Templer (1984); Koss & Risin (1987)
[34] Etherington (1997); Hislop (1999); Silber (1979); Stirling (1994)
[35] Davin (1999); Mitchell & Morse (1998); Silber (1979)
[36] Yorukoglu & Kemph (1966)
[37] Mitchell & Morse (1998)
[38] Fromuth & Conn (1997)
[39] Stirling (1994)
[40] Rosencrans (1997)
[41] Rosencrans (1997)
[42] Rosencrans (1997)
[43] Elliott (1993)
[44] Wulffen (1934)
[45] Chideckel (1935)
[46] de Young (1982)
[47] Ramsey-Klawsnik (1990)
[48] Davin (1999)
[49] Rosencrans (1997)
[50] The Committee on Sexual Offences Against Children and Youth (1984)
[51] Mitchell & Morse (1998)
[52] Mitchell & Morse (1998)
[53] Silber (1979)
[54] Davin (1999); Faller (1989); The Committee on Sexual Offences Against Children and Youth (1984); Wolfe (1985)
[55] Wulffen (1934)
[56] The Committee on Sexual Offences Against Children and Youth (1984)
[57] *The News Sentinel* (November 18 (1996)
[58] Myers (1992)
[59] Stirling (1994)
[60] Kasl (1990)
[61] Miletski (1997)
[62] Bachmann et al. (1994)
[63] Stevens (1996)

[64] Elliot (1983)
[65] Ogilvie & Daniluk (1995)
[66] Stirling (1994)
[67] Lawson (1991)
[68] Cooper & Cormier (1990)
[69] Stevens (1996)
[70] Elliot (1993)
[71] Kasl (1990)
[72] Ramsey-Klawsnik (1990)
[73] Kasl (1990)
[74] Rosencrans (1997)
[75] Berry (1975)
[76] Holubinskyj & Foley (1986)
[77] Kasl (1990); Miletski (1995); Mitchell & Morse (1998); Paiser (1992); Quintano (1992); Rosencrans (1997); Schoenewolf (1991)
[78] Paiser (1992)
[79] Mitchell & Morse (1998)
[80] Davin (1999); Etherington (1997); Faller (1987); Faller (1995); Koss & Risin (1987); Knopp & Lackey (1987); Larson & Maison (1987); Mathews, Matthews & Speltz (1989); McCarty (1986); Ramsey-Klawsnik (1990); Reinhart (1987); Rowan, Langelier & Rowan (1988); Wolfe (1985)
[81] Davin (1999)
[82] The Committee on Sexual Offences Against Children and Youth (1984)
[83] Davin (1999)
[84] Rowan, Langelier & Rowan (1988)
[85] Rowan, Langelier & Rowan (1988)
[86] Faller (1995)
[87] Davin (1999)
[88] Etherington (1997)
[89] The Committee on Sexual Offences Against Children and Youth (1984)
[90] Wolfe (1985)
[91] Wolfe (1985)
[92] Forbes (1992)
[93] Myers (1992)
[94] Saradjian & Hanks (1996)
[95] Saradjian & Hanks (1996)
[96] Finkelhor & Williams (1988)
[97] Crewdson (1988)
[98] Elliot (1993)
[99] Lane (1991)
[100] Finkelhor & Williams (1988)
[101] Kaufman et al. (1995)
[102] Sarrel & Masters (1982)
[103] The Committee on Sexual Offences Against Children and Youth (1984)
[104] Finkelhor & Williams (1988)
[105] Banerjee (1950); Banerjee (1959)
[106] Freel (1995)

[107] Walters (1975)
[108] Kercher & McShane (1985)
[109] The Committee on Sexual Offences Against Children and Youth (1984)
[110] Harper (1993)
[111] Rosencrans (1997)
[112] Wulffen (1934)
[113] Wulffen (1934)
[114] Faller (1989)
[115] Ogilvie & Daniluk (1995)
[116] The San Diego Union-Tribune (October 27, 1996)
[117] Groth for example in ATCOM (1980)
[118] The Committee on Sexual Offences Against Children and Youth (1984)
[119] Paiser (1992)
[120] Norris (1991)
[121] Faller (1989)
[122] Rosencrans (1997)
[123] Ramsey-Klawsnik (1990)
[124] Mitchell & Morse (1998)
[125] Stirling (1994)
[126] Mitchell & Morse (1998)
[127] Mitchell & Morse (1998)
[128] Etherington (1997)
[129] Groth In ATCOM (1980)
[130] Myers (1992); Faller (1989); Freel (1995); Ramsey-Klawsnik (1990)
[131] Kasl (1990)
[132] Miletski (1997)
[133] Mathews (1997)
[134] Elliot (1993)
[135] Paiser (1992)
[136] Mitchell & Morse (1998)
[137] James & Nasjleti (1983)
[138] Kempe & Kempe (1984)
[139] Kasl (1990)
[140] Lawson (1991); Saradjian & Hanks (1996)
[141] Ramsey-Klawsnik (1990)
[142] Weir & Wheatcroft in 1995
[143] Crewdson (1988)
[144] Finkelhor & Williams (1988)
[145] Saradjian & Hanks (1996)
[146] Norris (1991)
[147] Coleman (1994); Cooklin & Barnes (1994); Faller (1995); Saradjian & Hanks (1996)
[148] Crewdson (1988); Faller (1995); Norris (1991)
[149] Crewdson (1988); Faller (1995); Norris (1991); Saradjian & Hanks; Weir & Wheatcroft (1995)
[150] Coleman (1994); Crewdson (1988)
[151] Crewdson (1988); Norris (1991); Saradjian & Hanks (1996)

[152] Coleman (1994); Colver (1994); Crewdson (1988); Finkelhor & Williams (1988); Norris (1991); Weir & Wheatcroft (1995)
[153] Coleman (1994); Crewdson (1988); Finkelhor & Williams (1988); Norris (1991); Saradjian & Hanks (1996)
[154] Saradjian & Hanks (1996)
[155] Norris (1991)
[156] Weir & Wheatcroft (1995)
[157] Colver (1994); Coleman (1994); Cooklin & Barnes (1994); Crewdson (1988); Faller (1995); Finkelhor & Williams (1988); Hale & Sinason (1994); Norris (1991); Saradjian & Hanks (1996); Weir & Wheatcroft (1995)
[158] Coleman (1994)
[159] Saradjian & Hanks (1996)
[160] Saradjian & Hanks (1996); Weir & Wheatcroft (1995)
[161] Coleman (1994); Crewdson (1988); Finkelhor & Williams (1988); Norris (1991); Saradjian & Hanks (1996)
[162] Crewdson (1988)
[163] Finkelhor & Williams (1988)

3. Why Don't People Talk About Female Sex Offenders?

Women exist who are sexually abusing children. Appalling, unfathomable and incongruent with societal notions of femininity, this statement is nonetheless true. It is well supported by legal and social science research.

While preliminary documentation has been available for decades, it has been difficult to find and has been widely ignored. Child sexual abuse is unpleasant to consider, much less discuss, and the notion of women molesting children is particularly abhorrent. Societal silence on this topic has allowed women who are molesting children to remain well hidden. It is only recently that the existence of female sexual abusers has been occasionally considered by individuals who are not victims.

Cases of women having sexual contact with children have begun to trickle into newspapers and into legal and social science research. Society is developing a tentative awareness that women can and do sexually molest children. The phenomenon itself is not new, however. Cases have been documented since at least the 1930's.[164] Kinsey and his fellow researchers made brief comments concerning women who engage in sexual contact with children, based upon their landmark research done in the 1940's. They wrote:

> Older persons are the teachers of younger people in all matters, including the sexual. The record includes some cases of pre-adolescent boys involved in sexual contacts with adult females, and still more cases of pre-adolescent boys involved with adult males. Data on this point were not systematically gathered from all histories, and consequently the frequency of all contacts with adults cannot be calculated with precision (p. 167).[165]

At a snail's pace, similar reports have inched their way into public awareness. For example, descriptions of single cases of female sexual abusers have been described by therapists, reporters and individuals in the criminal justice system. Occasional comments or observations, frequently buried in research concerning more general topics such as incest or male sexual abusers, have similarly begun to appear. By and large, however, it has only been since the mid-

1980's, that the small groups of female sexual abusers have begun to be described. It has generally only been since the 1990's that these small groups have even begun to be subjected to systematic empirical investigation and study. As a consequence, the women who have sexually abused children have remained largely ignored. Mathis[166] in 1972, summarized common assumptions concerning female sexual abusers, which are generally still present today, stating:

> ...female pedophilia comes to light either long after the fact, or if it is detected earlier, it is lightly dismissed. The usual case consists of a babysitter, maid, or female relative, who, if caught, is either discharged or strongly reprimanded, and that is that! (p. 55).

Investigation into the potential harm to the victims of female sexual abusers has been widely neglected. Although the sexual abuse of children by females has been associated with serious consequences for some, sexual abuse by women is rarely taken seriously. The sexual crimes that women commit against children are well cloaked. Most females who harm children with sexual abuse remain undetected, unpunished and untreated. More disturbingly, the children whom they harm remain undetected, untreated and unprotected.

It is widely believed, and supported by currently available research, that the women who sexually molest children are a drop in the bucket, in comparison to the men who offend against children. However, by one estimate,[167] 1.5 million females and 1.6 million males in the United States may have been sexually abused by a woman. A British researcher[168] estimates that one in each hundred males and one in each hundred females has been sexually abused by a female. Significant numbers of children have had sexual contact with older or more forceful females.

Furthermore, as pointed out by Craig Allen,[169] for those children who have been sexually harmed by women, it does not matter that theirs was a rare event! If these children are to be adequately protected, society must be able to identify, treat and appropriately manage female child sexual abusers, and must also be able to identify, protect and treat their victims. It must, further, begin to develop the means of preventing sexual abuse on the part of those women whose histories, behaviors and mental health problems place them at risk. Sadly, there are a number of factors impeding the study of women who sexually molest children.

Most importantly, the sexual abuse of children by females is not being discussed.

Reluctance of Victims to Report Female Child Molesters

A number of factors conspire together to silence the voices of those who would address the topic of female sexual abusers. Child sexual abuse rarely involves witnesses who are not either victims or perpetrators. For child sexual abuse to surface for study, therefore, the participants themselves must come forward and identify that the abuse has occurred.

Research commonly reveals that victims only rarely disclose their sexual abuse. For example, in 1983, Diane Russell[170] surveyed 930 women and found that of those who had been sexually abused in childhood, only two percent had reported their sexually abusive family members and only six percent had reported sexual abusers outside of their families. In these cases, the majority of abusers were men. When women are the perpetrators, many believe that victims are even less likely to reveal the abuse.

Many of the reasons that children who have been sexually molested by women do not speak up are common to all children who have been sexually abused. They may fear reprisal, humiliation or disbelief, and may not want their private stories opened to public inquiry, as occurs when agencies and courts become involved. They may love or fear their abusers. Quite realistically, children may fear dissolution of their families if the offender is a family member and fear retaliation if the abuser is violent.

Additionally, some children cope with sexual abuse and other trauma by putting it out of their minds, in some cases using denial and repression so that they are only vaguely aware that the events have occurred. Sexual abuse is a difficult life event that some children prefer not to re-live through remembering.

Children do not like to identify themselves as unusual. Children who disclose sexual abuse open themselves up for negative appraisal from others, who may react with disgust or disbelief. Because sexual abuse by a woman is a relatively uncommon experience, victims may believe, often accurately, that they will be viewed as bizarre following the disclosure or will simply not be believed.

Adults who are in positions to be of help to children often have difficulty fathoming the notion that adults may take a sexual interest in children. The notion that women, and even mothers, may be sexually abusive can be inconceivable. James and Nasjleti[171] point out that children themselves do not view mothers as sexual beings. Children may misjudge their responsibility for participation in the sexual activity and fear punishment for disclosing it to others.

Furthermore, the child victim may simply have no one to tell, particularly when the offender is a mother. Children are dependent upon adults and parents to shape their world views. Some children are unaware that incestuous abuse is an atypical experience. Referring to victims of familial sexual abuse, McMullen,[172] in his book on male rape victims, summarized, "Young victims, especially those who have suffered repeated abuse from whatever age, are unlikely to recognize that an offence has taken place because it's always been like this (p. 120)." Even when the children do recognize that maternal sexual contact is unacceptable, they lack the option of turning for help to the one person most responsible for ensuring their safety.

James and Nasjleti[173] also point out that if the mother is the only adult in the child's life, it may be too threatening for the child to believe that she is not a loving, caring person; the child may not wish to lose her or to harm her through disclosure. When children are dependent upon their female abusers for survival, in the form of emotional or financial support, it may be difficult to seek help when abuse has occurred. In those situations in which expressions of affection or esteem occur only during episodes of sexual contact, children may be ambivalent about that contact discontinuing.

Reluctance of Male Victims to Report Female Child Molesters

A number of additional factors are believed to keep boys from talking about sexual abuse by a female. Available research indicates, perhaps not surprisingly, that when boys are abused, especially by a female, they tend to keep quiet about it. Some sexually abused boys feel emasculated. They perceive that they have not lived up to societal expectations that they be, at all times, strong, sexually eager and able to defend themselves. Boys do not eagerly share experiences in which they have been made to feel "less of a man," especially since the sharing of emotional distress, in and of itself, may be experienced as further emasculation.

Males are not socialized to know how to disclose when they have been sexual abuse victims. Boys are not socialized to reveal doubts, weaknesses and fears;[174] to express vulnerability or helplessness;[175] or to admit having played a "passive" sexual role.[176] Victimization may be experienced as a role violation by males. Briggs and Hawkins,[177] for example, in explaining why males don't report sexually abusive experiences describe victimization as "the antithesis of the western definition of masculinity (p. 20)."

While some males don't report female sexual abusers because they recognize that they have been victimized, others do not report because they do not recognize this. Sexual experiences that would be clearly labeled abusive by females are often confusing for the males who experience them. Males are socialized to be interested in sex of all kinds. It may be difficult for them to discern whether a sexual experience with a female, however distressing, should be perceived as an incident of abuse or as a "lucky score." Since it is widely believed that boys cannot be sexually victimized or harmed by women,[178] they are unlikely to receive useful help from others during the process of sorting this through.

Males may tend not to view themselves as having been "abused" subsequent to sexual experiences that others would perceive to be abusive. When a family service agency, for example, tried to find participants for a study by running an advertisement for men who had been "sexually abused" in childhood, they received few replies. When they changed the wording to request information from men who had "sexual experiences" in childhood, over one hundred men responded. Most reported experiences that they had had with a woman.[179] Briggs and Hawkins[180] also reported that males are more likely to report upon abusive experiences in childhood when asked about childhood sexual experiences, rather than childhood sexual abuse.

In addition to finding abusive experiences confusing because of societal expectations that they enjoy all kinds of sex, males may also find sexually abusive experiences confusing for another reason. Many will respond to sexual stimulation with erection and ejaculation, even in circumstances in which they are being traumatized. As Hindman[181] commented, physiological arousal and orgasm is much more obvious in males and, hence, less easily denied and more confusing in an abusive situation.

Macchietto[182] noted this in a case study involving a 15-year-old boy who was coerced into sexual activities with a 19- or 20-year-old female. While he experienced fear, shame and reluctance during the activities, and was continuing to have sexual difficulties some four years later, he did not consider the experiences to have been abusive, because he had experienced erections and ejaculations.

Sarrel and Masters[183] were among the first to note cases of males who had responded physiologically when sexually abused by a woman. Despite panic, fright and confusion, the men and boys had erections, and several ejaculated when molested by women. Several cases were described including one in which an intoxicated man was bound, blindfolded, gagged and assaulted by four women, who held a knife to his scrotum and threatened him with castration.

Rentoul and Appleboom[184] reviewed two small studies and concluded that it is common for men to ejaculate when they are being raped. They observed that men often confuse the issues of consent and arousal. McMullen[185] similarly made this point, based upon case observations. He added that penile erection is not always within conscious control and that anxiety-provoking situations may lead to genital responses.

When a male has responded physiologically to sexual stimulation, it does not indicate that he was not coerced or forced into the sexual activity. It does not mean that he was attracted to the second party or that he agreed to be a partner. Furthermore, it does not mean that the second party was legally appropriate as a sexual partner.

Paradoxically, while some believe that if a male has an erection, sexual abuse cannot have taken place, others believe that if a male does not have an erection that sexual abuse cannot have taken place. For many, "sex" denotes a penis in a vagina and "sexual abuse" denotes a penis forced into a vagina. If a male has not had an erection, following this line of thinking, there cannot be sex and, therefore, there can be no sex that is abusive. Obviously, these notions distract from the fact that a variety of activities of a sexual nature may be forced upon an individual against his will, many of which do not require an erection. Common sexual practices such as oral sex, manual genital contact, anal penetration and so forth do not require an erect penis. Further, when the sexual abuser emphasizes the "abuse," rather than the "sexual," seeking to degrade or to cause pain rather than to arouse, the necessity of an erect penis is even less relevant. Societal preconceptions concerning sex and sexual abuse make it very difficult for males to recognize when they have been sexually abused, let alone explain it to others.

Two researchers asked male sexual abuse victims directly why they had not reported their childhood victimizations. Briggs and Hawkins[186] surveyed 194 men who had been sexually abused in childhood by either male or female offenders or by both. Among the reasons given for not having reported the abuse were having no one to tell; associating the abuse with positive emotions, such as love, adult approval, or safety; fearing punishment or violence; doubting that the report would be believed; not knowing that the sexual abuse was unusual; believing that others already knew; shame; fear of being labeled homosexual; and having enjoyed the early stages of sexual initiation. Among those who did report the abuse, some did meet with violence in the form of punishment for lying or in the form of further sexual abuse at the hands of those to whom they disclosed.

Rentoul and Appleboom[187] commented that when men are sexually abused they might question their masculinity and fear the scorn of others. Unrealistic gender expectations placed on males, that they should at all times prevent themselves from being harmed, even by individuals who are stronger, more cunning and in positions of authority, keep males from speaking up when they have been sexually harmed.

Males are not generally raised to consider that to be strong, sexually eager and able to defend themselves in all situations is unrealistic. Finkelhor[188] believes that the societal factors that contribute to the silence of sexually abused males are less of a concern to very young children. He believes that this partially accounted for his finding that a larger ratio of males to females disclosed having been abused in day care centers than is typical among older groups of children. As boys grow older, their understanding of gender expectations becomes more firmly established and they may become less likely to report their abusive experiences.

Males are perhaps less likely than sexually abused females to enter the mental health system where laws that require therapists to report abuse to authorities might provide them with some degree of protection from their abusers. Many males cope with abusive experiences by denying that they ever occurred. Even when they acknowledge that sexual acts took place, they may deny or fail to recognize that the incidents occurred in an abusive context. As Froning and Mayman[189] pointed out, even when males acknowledge that sexually abusive acts occurred, they may deny having been harmed by them or deny the need for help to recover. All of these factors keep sexually abused males from coming to the attention of mental health professionals[190] who might learn from the study of their cases. Furthermore, the behaviors that males exhibit following sexual abuse may not prompt their referral into mental health treatment by others. Because their symptom presentation may consist of "acting-out" or externalizing behaviors, they may be viewed by professionals as simply behaving "as boys."[191] In addition, as pointed out by Mezey and King,[192] many rape crisis centers may not accept male clients.

Preliminary studies that have begun to identify male victims of child sexual abuse have generally found that the abuse is frequently unreported. Johnson and Shrier[193] discovered eleven boys, sexually abused by females, who came to their attention during research interviews administered during the course of routine physical exams. Only two of eleven boys had reported their abuse. They found evidence that boys may have difficulty disclosing recent sexual abuse. The average age of the boys admitting the abuse was much higher than the average age of the boys at the time that they were actually abused.[194]

Similarly, Risin and Koss,[195] in 1987, identified 216 college men who had been sexually abused in childhood. The men were abused prior to the age of 14, and in almost half of the cases were abused by a woman. Eighty-one percent of these 216 men had told no one about the sexual abuse.

In cases in which the sexual abuser is the mother, male victims may be even less likely to disclose the abuse. Mother-son incest is often viewed as the most taboo form of incest[196] or the most abhorrent.[197] Incestuous mothers may be viewed as infringing not only upon the son's masculinity but also upon patriarchal rights[198] and sons may wish to protect their mothers from societal reactions. Rosencrans[199] reported upon nine men who had been molested by their mothers. None had told anyone about the abuse during childhood, and 89% reported that the abuse was the most hidden aspect of their lives. None of the mothers had been investigated by child protective services.

Boys who have been sexually abused by their mothers have a host of additional obstacles to overcome in revealing their abuse. Mothers are generally viewed neither as sexual beings nor as capable of harm towards their children. Lawson[200] asserts that in cases of mother-son incest, the sons themselves may view themselves as "guilty victors," rather than victims. Boys molested by their mothers may assume responsibility for the sexual contact or may fear that the incest is indicative of their having a mental illness.[201]

The complex tapestry of emotions between a mother and son may also cause the son to be reluctant to report his mother. In describing a case of mother-son incest, Hindman[202] reported that the otherwise positive relationship, and the son's memories of his mother's caretaking and sacrifice, made it difficult for him to view her as an individual who was guilty and responsible. de Young,[203] for example, described the case of a boy who felt that the sexual relationship with his mother was special and private, and did not disclose the relationship because he felt protective towards her. This particular mother was also mentally ill and he believed that to disclose the relationship would be to disclose her mental illness.

Boys are unlikely to report incidents in which females have behaved in a sexually exploitive or abusive fashion towards them. They are likely to be confused by the incidents and may take responsibility for them. Alternately, they may feel emasculated or humiliated and chose not to acknowledge their degradation. When the abuser is a mother, they may be particularly reluctant to report the abuse. Given the current lack of societal awareness of the dynamics of the sexual abuse experienced by males at the hands of females, they may realistically fear that they will not be believed or be taken seriously by those responsible for their protection.

Laws are Less Likely to Recognize Males as Potential Victims of Sexual Abuse

Laws regarding sexual misconduct vary from location to location. For example, different states define concepts such as rape, sexual abuse, child molestation, age of consent and so forth in different ways. Laws also differ in different countries. Several authors have commented that some laws do not recognize that males may be the victims of sexual crimes. Some laws may consider the crimes against males to be less serious sexual offenses. Kasl[204] observed that criminal sexual contact is commonly associated with penetration, rather than with such factors as power and consideration of which party's needs are being met. Rentoul and Appleboom[205] pointed out that in the United Kingdom prior to 1994, males were not legally recognized as potential rape victims. They note that while the law now recognizes that anal rape may be perpetrated with a penis (and therefore, that males may be raped), it does not recognize anal penetration with other objects as rape. Therefore, females are not recognized as potential rapists and may only be charged with crimes that carry lesser sentences. Macchietto[206] similarly pointed out that while most states recognize as rape the scenario in which an intoxicated woman consents to activities that she would not agree to while sober, intoxicated men who engage in such activities are more likely to be viewed as rapists than as victims. de Young[207] reported that in 1979 a New Jersey Superior Court ruled that no woman could be prosecuted for "carnally abusing" a boy under the age of 16. According to the author, the court reasoned that while girls can become pregnant or be physically damaged by actual or attempted intercourse, boys cannot. The Court also expressed concern that girls who are physically harmed by such acts may experience emotional or psychological harm that impacts upon their outlook on sexuality.

Reluctance of Female Victims to Report Sexual Abuse by a Female

Female victims also have special reasons for not reporting female sexual abusers. Females who have sexually abused by women must admit not only the unusual experience of having been sexually molested by a female, but must also acknowledge having engaged in homosexual activity. Confusion about same-sex sexual contact may create anxiety for females about their sexual identity or sexual orientation,[208] which may interfere with disclosure. Female victims may realistically believe that their reports of women not only sexually molesting but also engaging in homosexual activities will be deemed unlikely.

Physical intimacies between females are well accepted and are among the least likely to be viewed by others as sexualized, particularly when they occur between a younger and an older female. Females are commonly perceived as both nonsexual and nonaggressive. Many find it difficult to imagine that there might be sexual contact, let alone abusive sexual contact, between them. Furthermore, if sex involves a penis in a vagina and sexual abuse involves a forced penis in a vagina, then it stands to reason, for some, that no possible sexual abuse can take place between females. For girls who have experienced this not to be true, anticipated difficulties in explaining their experiences may cause them to remain silent.

Society has only just begun to consider the possibility of women having sex with children. As research develops, it becomes clear that researchers don't know the right questions to ask in order to identify the activities that take place when women sexually abuse children. They have problems enough figuring out what women do with boys, and it seems even more difficult with girls.

Hislop,[209] after using a checklist of common sexual practices for the women to describe their sexual behaviors with children, found that some of the women had to write their experiences in the margin. The checklist did not include all of the activities in which they had engaged with children. One woman had taken a small child and rubbed him on herself in a way that sexually stimulated her; another had been sexually penetrated by a young girl wearing a dildo; another had had genital/genital contact (not intercourse).

Rosencrans[210] described physical intimacies that occurred between females and their sexually abusive mothers that might not readily be recognized as sexual. For example, for a daughter and mother to sleep together or to be present when the other is dressing, bathing or using the toilet is typically normal, healthy, and socially acceptable, which may not be the case for a son. However, in Rosencrans's sample of 93, these activities were often part of a larger pattern of sexualized intrusion that included more overt forms of sexual abuse. For some, these activities, in and of themselves, had been made sexual by the mothers; they took place for the sexual arousal of the mothers, at the cost of a sense of violation by the daughters. But how does a daughter report that her mother has committed the crime of being in the bathroom when she showers? And who would think to ask? In commenting about mother-daughter sexual abuse, Goodwin and DiVasto[211] wrote that social tolerance for physical intimacy between mothers and daughters may cause it to be particularly difficult for daughters to recognize that incestuous contact has occurred.

When the victims are lesbian, the abuse may raise additional issues that negatively impact upon the likelihood of disclosure. Mathews[212] noted that lesbian victims of sexual abuse by a female may have concerns that their sexual identity will be revealed during disclosure, and added that many therapists may be uncomfortable managing such cases. Myers[213] similarly reported that a lesbian in her study struggled with the problem of whether to identify her sexually abusive mother as a lesbian, as she wanted to protect the lesbian community from censure.

When the offender is not a lesbian, or is not obviously a lesbian, it may be particularly difficult for others to imagine that sexually abusive acts have transpired between the victim and offender. When girls are sexually abused by their mothers, others may believe that, by the very nature of her having had a child, the offender cannot be lesbian and that, if she is not a lesbian, she cannot have engaged in same-sex sexual abuse. Many are not aware that sexual preference often occurs along a continuum or that some female sexual abusers are "omnisexual" in their approach to sexuality.

When girls are abused by their mothers, they may have additional reasons for not reporting. As stated by Rosencrans,[214] "...children only get one biological mother, and even if they can get some nurturing needs met by others, they are loathe to risk totally rupturing the mother/child relationship (p. 33)."

Rosencrans[215] also found that 71% of the 93 maternally sexually abused females in her study were also sexually abused by someone else. Mitchell & Morse[216] similarly found that 84% of females disclosing sexual abuse in childhood by a female (a mother in 84% of cases) reported having had multiple perpetrators. Paradoxically, those experiencing the multiple trauma of being abused not only by a mother but also by others may be ill equipped to withstand the further emotional upheaval of disclosure. They may find it too difficult to risk losing even an inconsistent or weak source of support. Female children, who may be the more likely to be multiply sexually abused, may be particularly reluctant to lose the emotional connection to a maternal figure, even if the nurturing from that figure is tenuous or if she is abusive. Who needs a mother more than a traumatized child?

Preliminary research indicates that females do not tend to report sexually abusive experiences that have occurred at the hands of other females. Rosencrans[217] collected surveys from women molested by their mothers. Over 95% of the women told no one about the abuse during childhoods. Almost all eventually found someone with whom they were able to share their secrets; however, none had informed her spouse/partner, children, clergy, colleagues or self-help/therapy group members. There was also evidence to suggest that while 81% of the women were in therapy, only three percent discussed the sexual abuse by their mothers with their therapists. None of the women reported that their mothers had been investigated by child protective services. Together with nine men who were included in this study, 81% reported that their sexual abuse was the most hidden aspect of their lives.

Myers[218] noted that of eleven women who were sexually abused in childhood by females, none of the victims in her study had told anyone about the abuse at the time that it was happening. All but one (unusual in that it was the only case in which the mother had turned herself in) kept the abuse to herself until many years after it had ended. Though some received support when they later disclosed their abuse to members of their support network, negative reactions in the form of disbelief, discounting, silence, verbal abuse and inability to manage the disclosure were not uncommon. Further compounding the secrecy was the fact that many had repressed the abuse; only two reported that they had "always remembered" it.

Mitchell & Morse[219] reported that the majority of the 80 women in their sample who had been sexually abused in childhood did not tell anyone about the abuse during childhood and that the few who did were not believed. Seventy percent had told no one about the abuse while it was occurring. Of those that told, only 21% were believed. Only nine percent reported the abuse to have been reported to Child and Youth Services. Only eight percent reported the abuse to the police. None of the female abusers was ever charged with a crime. For the victims, being threatened, believing it was their fault, being bribed, not knowing that the sexual abuse was wrong, being afraid or having been told that they had imagined it were among the more commonly cited factors that kept them from telling others about the abuse.

Currently available evidence indicates that females rarely disclose when they have been the victims of sexual abuse by another female. They may feel stigmatized because of the homosexual nature of the contact or because of the unusual nature of the female perpetrated abuse. They may fear that female-to-female physical contact will be trivialized or viewed as nonsexual. Female homosexuals may be concerned that their sexual identity may be revealed during disclosure or may wish to protect the homosexual community from censure. They may realistically fear the negative reactions of others. When the perpetrator is a mother, females may have a difficult time discerning that abuse has taken place or may be unwilling to sacrifice the maternal-child bond. In particular, they may also be experiencing other sources of trauma that may render them less able to risk the potentially traumatic disruption of the maternal bond.

Reluctance of Female Sexual Abusers to Acknowledge Having Committed Sexually Abusive Acts

Sexual abusers, when found out, face a number of possible crises at once. Several agencies such as the police, child protective services and the court system descend into their lives, and they may face the public humiliation and distress of their stories being revealed. They may face upheaval as their families fall apart, either because their children are removed from the home or because they themselves are forced to leave or because a partner leaves them. They may face prison or other legal consequences, and have resulting employment or social problems. When offenders abuse in the company of their mates, they may be traumatically separated from their partners, as well. Offenders gain a new status, even among prisoners, as being among the "lowest of the low." For many female sexual abusers, a prior history of trauma has rendered them ill equipped to manage daily affairs, let alone crises such as these.

Not surprisingly, several studies have found that females who sexually molest children are generally reluctant to disclose having committed these acts. One researcher found them even more reluctant than men to disclose. Allen[220] interviewed 65 adult females and 75 adult males involved in substantiated cases of sexual abuse of children. He found the women less likely to acknowledge their offenses. He found the women more likely to have responded to investigations of their offenses with anger towards the informant and investigator and with a sense of having been wrongly accused than was the case for the male offenders. The women were also less likely to report sorrow, guilt, relief or gratitude than the males. Again, it must be noted that pioneering studies such as this are likely to include the more disturbed of the female offenders and it is unclear how well they might generalize to all female sex offenders.

The finding that females are more likely to deny their offenses is not a consistent finding. Matthews[221] reported the opposite finding, based upon her experiences treating 36 female offenders (which might suggest that females are more likely to disclose in the context of a therapeutic relationship than an investigation). Regardless, however, of which of the sexes discloses the more readily, neither gender is believed to readily disclose very often. At times, this denial continues, even after legal consequences have been established.

Davin[222] found that of 76 female sex offenders, incarcerated for crimes of child sexual abuse, 30 denied having committed their crimes during a research interview. Myers[223] noted that of eleven female sexual abusers reported to her in a study of victims, only one had turned herself in. Hislop[224] similarly found that of 13 convicted sex offenders who agreed to take part in federally protected survey research, only four provided information about their sexual activities with children; an additional participant described the activities that had taken place, but maintained that her victim had raped her. Woodring[225] found that among 46 incarcerated female sex offenders against children, six claimed that they had actually been coerced into the sexual activities by their victims. The defense of having been raped by a victim, particularly a male victim, is likely to have more credence when used by a woman than a man. It is not known to what extent this defense has been used to further mask sexual abuse committed by women.

As will be discussed in other chapters, women may have additional reasons to fear disclosure. Very commonly, female sexual abusers are noted to have histories of severe abuse. Some female abusers may associate the experience of a wrongdoing becoming known with terror and brutality. In addition, though the general observation is that females who sexually abuse children are not taken seriously, some have noted that when sexually abusive women are found out, the legal system sometimes responds with a vengeance, beyond what occurs for men. Women may fear that the legal system will respond to what they have done, as something more monstrous than would be the case if they were males.

Societal Views Concerning Women Mask Female Perpetrated Child Sexual Abuse

Neither male nor female victims nor the perpetrators themselves are likely to report female sexual abusers. Additionally, members of society rarely suspect or question that sexual abuse by a female may be taking place. Societal perceptions of women do not include the perception of females as sexual abusers. Many societal views of women preclude their identification as female sexual abusers.

The View of Women as Nonsexual, Nonaggressive Caretakers

Women, and particularly mothers, tend to be viewed in our society as nonsexually aggressive, non-physically aggressive individuals who are, by their nature, protective of children. Often, this is true. However, over generalizing these traits to include all women serves to disguise the abuse of children by female sex offenders.

To consider the possibility that women, including mothers, may be sexual abusers is disquieting. That children are not safe with women has been described as particularly disturbing and threatening.[226] Rosencrans,[227] in explaining why the phenomenon of maternal child sexual abuse is particularly hidden, writes, "This society wants desperately to believe that mothers are inherently good, loving and protective of their children (p. 36)." In a recent magazine article, Feeney[228] summarizes, "to acknowledge that a mother could break the ultimate Oedipal taboo is to affirm that no one can be presumed safe with anyone (p 97)."

It is far more comfortable to deny that women can sexually abuse children.

Stereotypes concerning women's sexuality help to mask sexual abuse by a woman on those occasions when it does occur. Women are often seen as being the passive or submissive recipients of the more sexually aggressive advances of men. Because they may be viewed as responding to[229] or avoiding,[230] rather than initiating sex, and because they are not viewed as capable of intimidating a victim,[231] they are generally not perceived as potential sexual abusers. They are viewed as physically and psychologically incapable of victimizing.[232] Such perceptions decrease the likelihood of children reporting sexual abuse by a woman and of their reports being believed.[233]

Larson and Maison,[234] who published their findings concerning their clinical work and research with women who molested children, stated:

> Socially, we, as a culture, find it particularly disturbing to think that women would sexually abuse children. Our Judeo-Christian heritage places enormous emphasis on women as warm, nurturing mothers. Furthermore, we are, at best, culturally ambivalent about female sexuality. We struggle with the notion of women — particularly mothers — being sexual at all (p. 30).

Many researchers have commented that this cultural perception of women as incapable of committing sexual offenses is contributing to the lack of acknowledgement and research concerning female sexual abusers.[235] Those responsible for protecting children and for making sense of the reports of child sexual abuse by women may have great difficulty doing so. Saradjian and Hanks[236] note that when women sexually abuse children, the unpredictability of the event causes great psychological discomfort that causes individuals to deny or to otherwise rationalize or reinterpret the events.

Some authors have pointed to the fact that women are allowed more intimate contact with children in their daily nurturing activities and that this norm allows for more acts of sexual abuse to go undetected. While some documented acts of sexual abuse by women are certainly aggressive or overtly sexual, some reported activities are disguised as acts of caretaking. Plummer[237] points out that women are not only expected to have a great deal of bodily contact with children, but they are simultaneously viewed as nonsexual, which allows for undetected abuse to occur. The boundary between appropriate and inappropriate touching may be difficult to discern where female caretakers are concerned.[238] Welldon,[239] for example, noted that motherhood is seen as incompatible with perversion to the extent that motherhood is equated with good mental health.

Perhaps because our society views female caretakers as asexual, it more readily tolerates quasi-sexualized behaviors on the part of the mother than on the part of the father. The line distinguishing normal from abusive behaviors may be less clearly drawn for women. Some note, for example, that there is less prohibition regarding partially seductive behaviors on the part of the mother, as opposed to the father.[240]

For example, some authors have documented that mothers in some cultures sometimes stimulate the genitals of infants in order to soothe them, although this practice appears to be under-researched. Goodwin and DiVasto[241] as well as Barry and Johnson[242] have commented that in some cultures it is an acceptable practice for mothers to masturbate their infants. In reviewing the literature, Korbin[243] also noted that in some cultures it is acceptable to fondle, kiss, blow upon or praise the genitals of an infant. Wilkins[244] states

> for centuries mothers have been known to soothe boy babies by stroking and sucking their penises. If such "playful" manipulation of the boy's genitals is common today — and anecdotal evidence suggests that this is the case — the practice is likely to be regarded as a benign expression of a mother's love (p. 1153).

Lawson[245] describes mothering as an "inherently sexual experience" (p. 392). For example, she notes that normal mothering requires the frequent handling of the genitalia for the purposes of hygiene. She states that because mothering is interwoven with sexuality, sexual abuse becomes hard to define. She further asserts that for mothers who do not have knowledge about normal sexual feelings toward their children, the expression of these feelings may become inappropriate.

Because society tolerates a great deal of touching and intimacy between mothers and their children, it may be particularly difficult to recognize when the crossing of the incest barrier has occurred. Rosencrans,[246] as well as other authors, cited examples of daughters whose mothers appeared to become sexually aroused or orgasmic when giving them enemas and of daughters who experienced this as sexually abusive. Similar cases have been described throughout the literature involving cuddling in bed, bathing, spanking, inspecting, changing and so forth. Little has been written about normal sensuality in the mother-child relationship, let alone the point at which the normal sensual behaviors cross the line into abuse.

Role of the Women's Movement in the Masking of Sexual Abuse by Women

Some authors have pointed to the women's movement as a contributor to the under-acknowledgement of the female child molester. Most authors credit feminist ideology with bringing the problems of rape and child sexual abuse into public awareness. However, some authors have pointed out that the women's movement focused almost exclusively on the concerns of women and girls who were exploited by males[247] to the exclusion of focusing on male victims and female offenders. The feminist models for understanding sexual abuse have been described as associating only men as sexually abusive, towards only women.[248]

Some have noted that the feminist theories that serve to explain societal causes of the sexual abuse of females by males do not generalize well to female perpetrators and male victims. For example, the notion that men are socialized to be dominant and aggressive, while women are socialized into a victim's role, contributes to the understanding of sexual abuse. Allen[249] cautioned, however, that when this is accepted as the only explanation for child sexual abuse, it may cloak child sexual abuse by women.

Some authors have also speculated that some feminists may not wish to focus on the problem of the female sex offender, or that some women do not wish to "turn against their own," in acknowledging female sexual abusers. Elliot[250] commented on the concerns of some that focus on the sexual offenses committed by women might distract from the more pervasive problem of sexual abuse committed by men. Mayer[251] similarly speculated that some feminists might be reluctant to acknowledge abusive behavior among females, as the cases may "be publicized disproportionately in order to minimize and justify male offenses (p. 6)."

Forbes[252] directly criticizes focus on female sexual abusers, writing:

> When the overwhelming evidence suggests that it is women and children that are suffering in large numbers from physical and sexual abuse from men, why has a social agenda been constructed that gives such primacy to the topic of "female sexual abusers"? It will make little sense to practitioners working in the field of child protection to redirect attention and resources to the "new problem" of female sexual abusers, when research, analysis and resources in relation to the larger social problem of abuse by men are so inadequate. Whose interests will this shift of emphasis serve? Certainly not women and children. (p. 105).

Macchietto[253] described the related topic of the rape of men by women as being received as "politically incorrect" and described a hostile professional response to his writing about the topic. Kasl[254] reports that women, in general, do not like to acknowledge the possibility that there are female sex offenders. She states that, "As the subordinate group in a patriarchal culture, women do not want to give information to men that will be used against them (p. 261)." She reports that female perpetrators face severe cultural prejudice, which results in termination of parental rights more frequently than for males. She notes reluctance of women to discuss the topic, fearing that males will use the information to be seen as experts on the topic and will neglect to address the cultural factors that differentiate the male and female sex offenders. Curiously, the present author was able to find one of the most comprehensive lists of newspaper clips about female sex offenders in an Internet magazine for fathers.

Several cultural views of women may serve to hide those who sexually abuse children. The stereotype that all women are nonaggressive, nurturing caretakers hides the exceptions and serves to mask child sexual abuse by women. The notion that women are asexual further disguises the female sexual abusers. The popularity of feminist theories in explaining rape has been implicated by some in slowing the understanding of female sexual abusers. Finally, some groups of women may reluctant to expose the female sexual abuser.

Female Sexual Abusers May Not Become Known to Researchers

Female sexual abusers may not be reported by victims, self-revealed or recognized independently by others. When female sexual abusers are reported, or do come to the attention of various authorities, they may not be viewed as having committed serious crimes. As such, they may not enter systems such as the family or criminal courts, protective services or prison systems where they might be studied. They are not subsequently likely to enter mental health treatment at the insistence of these systems and, therefore, are also less likely to be studied from a mental health perspective.

As early as 1944, Apfelberg, Sugar and Pfeffer,[255] who were researching the clinical records of male sex offenders in Bellevue Hospital, mentioned the lack of legal attention paid to female perpetrated sex offenses, stating:

> Cases have been known of women who exposed their genitals but were either not arrested or were charged with intoxication or disorderly contact. We have seen no examples of such charges as impairing the morals of a minor among women although there are instances in which women have seduced minors (p. 768).

Petrovich and Templer[256] similarly remarked that women may have less fear of social retribution for sexual contact with children. Wolfe[257] described the cases of twelve female sex offenders who were referred from the criminal justice system, child protective services and defense attorneys. She observed that of twelve female sex offenders who were seen in outpatient treatment (eleven of whom offended against children) only two were incarcerated, and of these one was incarcerated in a work program. Similarly, Ramsey-Klawsnik[258] remarked that among cases of 83 children who had been sexually abused by a female, there was only one case of a female who was subjected to criminal prosecution. The females were not prosecuted in spite of the fact that the abuse was confirmed through diagnostic evaluation and was often sadistic in nature. In 56% of the cases the abuse included burning, beating, biting or pinching the breasts or genitals of the children or tying them during the sexual assault.

Allen[259] found that, in comparison to men, women child molesters did receive similar consequences. However, only 52% of the 64 females in his sample had charges pressed against them.

In addition to the fact that many female sex offenders are never identified for potential study, there are other problems with researching the female sex offender. Lawson[260] noted that survey research, a commonly used method of study, may be an insufficient manner of gaining information concerning mother-son incest. She reported that in many cases, memories of mother-son incest are repressed and not disclosed outside of the context of long-term therapy. She added that the taboo against the disclosure of mother-son incest is stronger than the taboo against the behavior itself. Similarly, it may be difficult for researchers to gather accurate information about the dynamics of other forms of female perpetrated child sexual abuse. The mental health of both the victim and the perpetrator may require significant denial or distortion of the events.

As a practical matter, Elliott and Peterson[261] noted that mothers, as caretakers, are likely to accompany their children to health care professionals, which may lower the risk of detection. They also add that health care workers may not report abuse because of lack of training, fear of litigation, lack of time or emotional exhaustion.

Briggs and Hawkins[262] also point out that the problem of child sexual abuse was brought to public notice primarily by women and that most child protection programs were written by women, based upon their own perspectives of child sexual abuse. They indicate that more input from men is needed in order to gain a fuller understanding of the special needs of sexually abused boys. Where the understanding of male victimization by females is concerned, the lack of male professionals in the social science fields may somewhat impede the interpretation and practical application of data.

Professionals Are Not Trained to Recognize the Female Sexual Abuser

Presently, if a female is identified as a sex offender, it is likely that she fits the stereotypical profile that those in positions of authority have of a criminal, a female child abuser, a person with mental health problems or a sex offender. When women are identified as sex offenders, it is typically because someone in a position of authority has viewed them as such. Most individuals who have begun to gather information concerning female sex offenders are professionals such as those in the legal system, the child protection system, the prison system or the mental health system. Because of the current lack of information available to them, they must rely on their own perceptions in determining whether or not a given female is a sex offender.

Researchers commonly find that female sex offenders have chaotic upbringings and chaotic or nonexistent relationships with age-appropriate individuals. However, it is possible that these women fit the stereotype of potential offenders. Women from "nice homes," who are pillars of the community, who have created families in which there are no overt problematic behaviors are likely to be overlooked as potential sex offenders. Accusations against them are likely to be perceived as false and these women are likely to slip through the cracks. These high functioning offenders are less likely to be identified for research.

Victims and offenders are unlikely to discuss the crimes of female sexual abusers. Society at large is likely to overlook them. Consequentially, little research is available to guide those who come into professional contact with the female sexual abuser. Those specifically placed in positions to detect, treat and protect those harmed by female sexual abuse, subsequently, are not trained to do so. They may have difficulty identifying victims and helping victims to tell their stories, so the circle of secrecy continues.

The bulk of research and training available for professionals in the area of sexual abuse is based upon the study of male sex offenders. The lack of available research concerning the patterns of offending and profiles of females, and the subsequent reliance upon data related to men, is likely to impede the identification of female sexual abusers. Females may not fit the profiles and patterns of male offenders. Preliminary evidence is mounting to suggest that female sex offenders may differ from males in important ways, including patterns of offenses, psychosocial histories, motivations for offenses and treatment needs.[263] Additionally, female sexuality differs from male sexuality in important ways. Female sexual organs, sexual hormones and brains differ from those of men.

Professionals taking psychological or social histories may not think to ask about potential sexual abuse by a woman, and reports of such abuse may not be taken seriously.[264] Some of the factors that prompt inquiry by professionals when male perpetrated sexual abuse occurs are not present when females are the offenders. For example, when males are sexually victimized, they do not become pregnant.[265] Neither do female victims of female initiated sexual abuse become pregnant. While there have been cases of convicted sexual abusers bearing the offspring of adolescent victims, the adult victimizer may be better able to hide the fact that a victim was involved in a pregnancy. Additionally, some female perpetrated sexual activities (e.g., vaginal or anal penetration with an object, simulated sexual intercourse with females) may be less likely to transmit sexual diseases than is the case when a male vaginally rapes or anally rapes with a penis. Some forms of sexual disease are more readily transmitted from males to females or from males to males during acts of penetration than from females to males or females to females.

Several authors have commented that professionals do not think to inquire about female perpetrated child sexual abuse. Cases of mother-son incest, for example, may be missed because no one thinks to ask about them.[266] Krug[267] commented that professionals are unlikely to connect psychological difficulties with a history of maternal sexual abuse. Professionals, lacking information concerning female sexual abusers, may not believe accounts that they hear even when they are revealed. Welldon[268] remarked, "Incredulity and disbelief are the main reactions encountered, professionals included, by victims when they try to disclose abuse by a woman (p. 40)." Elliot[269] noted that professionals are not trained to recognize the female sexual abuser and described several accounts of adults who were not believed when they disclosed this type of sexual abuse to their therapists.

Saradjian and Hanks[270] commented on the disbelief by professionals and illustrated this point with the case of woman who reported having been sexually abused by her mother. She was initially medicated for this "delusion." When later seeking therapy, she was referred back to psychiatry by a therapist. A later therapist interpreted that it was actually her father that abused her and another told her that she had had false memories implanted by the previous therapists. Myers[271] reported that among the eleven women molested by females as children, whom she had interviewed, one reported that her therapist cried when she reported the abuse, another reported absolute silence on the part of the therapy group to which she disclosed, another reported having to change therapists until she found one that believed her and another reported having been referred out because her therapist had never treated such a case. Another was asked if she had not confused the experience with something else.

Wilkins[272] similarly noted the possible case of mother-son incest involving a seven-year-old child being dismissed as an "impossible fabrication," and added that in such cases doctors must suspend their disbelief. A case of sexual contact between a mother and her inpatient six-year-old son was identified in an early paper;[273] however, responsibility for initiating the sexual contact was placed with the son.

Campbell & Carlson[274] found that even among those highly trained in the area of sexual abuse treatment, few were trained on the topic of female sexual abusers. They surveyed over 1400 conference attendees who had worked with child sexual abuse victims or offenders for an average of 7.7 years, with a yearly average of 62 clients. Fewer than 40% of those working with female offenders had been trained in this area.

The lack of awareness of female sexual abusers may not only impact upon those responsible for treating female sexual abusers, but upon those responsible for protecting the children from them. Freel[275] reported that in four of six cases of female perpetrated child sexual abuse there was evidence of unwillingness to recognize the abuse on the part of the officials and others managing the cases. All four sexually abusive women were given potentially inappropriate access to live with children by the officials managing the cases.

Summary

A variety of factors impede the study of female perpetrated child sexual abuse. At the present time, it is probably safe to assume that the majority of children who are currently being sexually abused by females will not be identified or helped. Should some unusual circumstance cause them to become identified, it is not certain that they will receive mental health treatment that is appropriate to their needs or that they will receive adequate protection from their abusers by those charged with their safety. In part, this will result because their offenders, poorly understood, will not receive adequate mental health treatment.

There are many different reasons why people don't talk about female sex offenders. In mother-child cases the victims face the problem of reporting on the person that is supposed to protect them. The potential loss of the maternal bond is often viewed as more threatening than the abuse.

Males who are abused are reluctant to report the offense. Society's sexual expectations of males can make it hard for them to tell the difference between abuse and a "lucky score." The arousal that males may sometimes experience in an abusive sexual situation can create difficulties in their recognizing that abuse has occurred. Males may also feel that failure to protect themselves is a failure that they would rather not share with others.

Females may tend not to report abuse because acts that are abusive often closely resemble acts that are considered acceptable in our society. They may also be reluctant to reveal their participation in same-sex sexual activities.

Society, as a whole, does not believe that women can be offenders. Stereotypes of women as non-sexual and naturally protective make it hard for cases of abuse to be believed. While the woman's movement has advanced the understanding of male perpetrated sexual abuse, over-extension of models designed to explain such abuse may also hinder the identification of female offenders.

At the heart of the matter is a circular problem: women are not recognized as being possible abusers so reports of female sexual abuse are not believed and the lack of accepted reports leads to the belief that women can't be abusers.

Notes ────────────────────────

[164] Bender & Blau (1937); Chideckel (1935); Wulffen (1934)
[165] Kinsey, Pomeroy & Martin (1948), p. 167
[166] Mathis 1972
[167] Allen (1991)
[168] Saradjian & Hanks (1996)
[169] Craig Allen (1991)
[170] Diane Russell (1983)
[171] James & Nasjleti (1983)
[172] McMullen (1990)
[173] James & Nasjleti (1983)

[174] Faller (1989)
[175] Nasjleti (1980)
[176] Renvoize (1982)
[177] Briggs & Hawkins (1995)
[178] Nasjleti (1980)
[179] Crewdson (1988)
[180] Briggs & Hawkins (1995)
[181] Hindman (1989)
[182] Macchietto (1998)
[183] Sarrel & Masters (1982)
[184] Rentoul & Appleboom (1997)
[185] McMullen (1990)
[186] Briggs & Hawkins (1995)
[187] Rentoul & Appleboom (1997)
[188] Finkelhor (1988)
[189] Froning & Mayman (1990)
[190] Froning & Mayman (1990)
[191] Froning & Mayman (1990)
[192] Mezey & King (1987)
[193] Johnson & Shrier (1987)
[194] Shrier & Johnson (1988)
[195] Risin & Koss (1987)
[196] Barry & Johnson (1958); Renvoize (1982); Rist (1979)
[197] Kempe & Kempe (1984)
[198] Kempe & Kempe (1984)
[199] Rosencrans (1997)
[200] Lawson (1991)
[201] Nasjleti (1980)
[202] Hindman (1989)
[203] de Young (1982)
[204] Kasl (1990)
[205] Rentoul & Appleboom (1997)
[206] Macchietto (1998)
[207] Young (1982)
[208] Sgroi & Sargent (1994)
[209] Hislop (1994)
[210] Rosencrans (1997)
[211] Goodwin & DiVasto (1979)
[212] Mathews (1997)
[213] Myers (1992)
[214] Rosencrans (1997)
[215] Rosencrans (1997)
[216] Mitchell & Morse (1998)
[217] Rosencrans (1997)
[218] Myers (1992)
[219] Mitchell & Morse (1998)
[220] Allen (1991)

[221] Matthews (1994)
[222] Davin (1993)
[223] Myers (1992)
[224] Hislop (1994)
[225] Woodring (1995)
[226] Goldman (1993)
[227] Rosencrans (1997)
[228] Feeney (1994)
[229] Stirling (1994)
[230] Parrot (1998)
[231] Scavo (1989)
[232] Mayer (1992)
[233] Ramsey-Klawsnik (1990)
[234] Larson & Maison (1987)
[235] Banning (1989); Dunbar (1993); Goldman (1993); Lawson (1991); Rosencrans (1997); Turner & Turner (1994)
[236] Saradjian & Hanks (1996)
[237] Plummer (1981)
[238] Plummer (1981); Mayer (1992)
[239] Welldon (1996)
[240] Barry & Johnson (1958)
[241] Goodwin & DiVasto (1979)
[242] Barry & Johnson (1958)
[243] Korbin (1990)
[244] Wilkins (1990)
[245] Lawson (1991)
[246] Rosencrans (1997)
[247] Nielsen (1983)
[248] Finkelhor (1984); Mathews (1997); Paiser (1992)
[249] Allen (1991)
[250] Elliot (1993)
[251] Mayer (1992)
[252] Forbes (1992)
[253] Macchietto (1998)
[254] Kasl (1990)
[255] Apfelberg, Sugar & Pfeffer (1944)
[256] Petrovich & Templer (1984)
[257] Wolfe (1985)
[258] Ramsey-Klawsnik (1990)
[259] Allen (1991)
[260] Lawson (1993)
[261] Elliott & Peterson (1993)
[262] Briggs & Hawkins (1995)
[263] Allen (1991); Dunbar (1993); Hunter et al. (1993); Matthews (1994); Rosencrans (1997)
[264] Rowan et al (1990)
[265] Krug (1989)

[266] Lawson (1991)
[267] Krug (1989)
[268] Welldon (1996)
[269] Elliot (1994)
[270] Saradjian & Hanks (1996)
[271] Myers (1992)
[272] Wilkins (1990)
[273] Bender & Blau (1937)
[274] Campbell & Carlson (1995)
[275] Freel (1995)

4. Rates of Offending by Female Sex Offenders

Throughout the past several decades, documentation of the existence of female child molesters has largely disputed the notion that no women are capable of committing sexual offenses against children. This awareness began with a smattering of case studies that described what were often single cases of women who were known to have been female child molesters. More recently, with the tentative acknowledgment of the existence of female child molesters, researchers have attempted to estimate the numbers of females in the child molester population. Those reporting upon the percentages of females among child molesters have used very different methods to collect information, which makes the studies very difficult to compare. At best, current estimates are preliminary. These difficulties notwithstanding, available evidence suggests that female sex offenders exist in large enough numbers to warrant the attention of individuals in the child protection, legal and mental health fields.

Gathering statistics concerning the percentage of females within the sex offender population is made difficult by several factors. Female child molesters may tend to be identified less frequently than males, which may artificially lower the percentages of females found among groups of child molesters. Researchers also differ in way they define child sexual abuse, the way they define a "case" of child sexual abuse and the way they select groups of sex offenders for study. All of these factors combine to render the currently available studies not directly comparable. They nevertheless serve as documentation that sexual abuse by females is not as rare as was previously believed.

The Problem of Defining Child Sexual Abuse

There is no standard way to define "child sexual abuse" for research purposes. In defining sexual abuse, some researchers consider the nature of the sexual acts that took place. At one extreme, the acts defined as child sexual abuse may include only activities such as intercourse, while at the other, it may also include activities that do not involve physical touch between participants, such as exhibitionism, being made to watch the sexual activities of others, being made to participate in nonsexual contact pornography, threats of sexual harm or the like. Some researchers may examine only those cases of sexual abuse in which local laws have been violated, which are different in different localities.

Other researchers may consider the dynamics of the sexual activities in defining whether sexual abuse has occurred. Some include in their studies only cases in which force has occurred, or threats, or coercion, the definitions of which may vary from study to study. Other researchers may include incidents in which a child or adolescent was ostensibly a willing participant, but under legal age of consent or not legally able to give consent. (Again, legal definitions vary in different localities.) Cases in which one of the participants was in a caretaking role are considered to be indicative of sexual abuse by some researchers, regardless of whether any force or coercion was used. Some researchers may study only incest, which can be defined in different ways, while others consider abuse that occurred between unrelated individuals.

Some investigators will study cases in which the alleged victim's report is the only source of evidence that the sexual abuse has occurred, while others include only those cases in which there is supporting evidence to back up the allegations. Acceptable forms of evidence vary from study to study and may include such things as medical evidence (likely to be available only in some of the cases in which abuse has actually occurred), mental health problems or "substantiation" by a child protective services worker. Some researchers study only those cases in which there has been a conviction or an incarceration.

The ages of the participants are sometimes considered in determining when sexual abuse has occurred. In reviewing cases of child sexual abuse for inclusion in their study, some researchers may include only cases in which sexual contact occurred between individuals with some specified minimum age difference between them, such as five or ten years. Some may include only those cases in which the sexual activities occurred before a child had reached a specific age such as twelve or 16 or 18, before the child had reached the legal age of consent in the child's locality or before the child had reached puberty. Others may specify that for an incident to be counted as child sexual abuse the perpetrator must have reached some minimum age, such as ten, twelve, 16 or 18, or have been post-pubescent.

Researchers create their own definitions of child sexual abuse for the purpose of their own studies. The definitions differ from study to study. Even when different researchers agree that a specific criterion such as age difference, or the use of force, or the relationship between participants, etc. is critical to the definition of child sexual abuse, they may define the criterion differently. In some cases, deciding whether or not to include an individual in a study of female sex offenders becomes a judgment call.

Consider the following example: Eleven-year-old Amy, who is post-pubescent and her twelve-year-old pre-pubescent stepsister have previously been sexually abused and develop sexual behavior problems as a result. They coerce a baby-sitter (age 14), who has no prior sexual experience, into sexual contact with them. They threaten to tell their parents that the baby-sitter has allowed friends to come over while baby-sitting if she refuses.

For the purposes of study, some researchers might rule out one or both of the stepsisters and/or the baby-sitter as child sexual abuse victims because they are too old to be considered children. Some might rule out the eleven and 14 year olds as childhood victims because they are pubescent. Some may rule out the baby-sitter as a victim because she was older than the others or was in a care-taker role or because no actual physical force was used. Some would consider her a victim because she was coerced. Some may consider all of the participants too young to be considered offenders or might consider the age differences to be too close for any to be considered either as offenders or as victims. Some might consider whether any of the participants *experienced* the sexual contacts as abu-sive. Almost certainly, various researchers would differ in terms of how they perceived and classified the events that took place.

Since female sex offenders have been studied only in small numbers, little information is available to assist in determining how child sexual abuse with a female offender should be defined. There is some evidence that in the cases that involve females, the types of sexual contacts that occur can sometimes be differ-ent than is the case with the males. Sexual abuse involving a female can involve her indirect or coerced participation as a co-offender, or may involve activities that appear in the guise of caretaking. Researchers are still learning the types of questions that should be asked in order to discern whether child sexual abuse, particularly by a female, has occurred.

Complicating matters in defining child sexual abuse is the manner by which different researchers have defined a "case" of sexual abuse by a female. Re-searchers mean different things when they report upon a "case" involving female sex offenders. A case might mean, for example: the number of *victims* of female offenders, the number of *female offenders*, the number of *female offender/victim pairings*, the number of actual *acts of sexual contact* involving a female of-fender, or the number of *episodes* of sexual contact involving a female offender. Each of these methods may produce a different number of "cases."

Consider the case of a mother who sexually abuses a ten-year-old daughter on four occasions; the mother's twelve and 18-year-old stepdaughters were par-ticipants on two of the occasions. The mother later abuses a son on one occasion and a female non-family member on two occasions. One criminal sexual act takes place between each offender and victim on each of the episodes in which the abuse took place. Just some of the ways in which these "cases" might be de-scribed and reported in research are

- four cases of victims of female offenders (biological daughter, step-daughter, son, female non-family member)
- two cases of female offenders (mother, older step-daughter)

- thirteen cases of criminal sexual acts
  - mother and daughter x4
  - mother and step-daughter x2
  - older step-daughter and daughter x2
  - older step-daughter and younger step-daughter x2
  - mother and son x1
  - mother and non-family member x2
- five cases of victim/offender pairings
  - mother and step-daughter
  - mother and non-related child
  - mother and son
  - mother and biological daughter
  - older step-daughter and younger step-daughter
- seven episodes of sexual abuse involving a female offender
  - mother and daughter x4 (two with others present)
  - mother and son x1
  - mother and non-family member x2

The Problem of Gathering Information Concerning Female Sex Offenders from Different Sources

Most researchers who study sexually abusive individuals turn to agencies that are responsible for identifying them for legal or mental health interventions. However, few of the agencies that are charged with treating victims and offenders, or with protecting children and society, are trained to recognize the female sex offender. It would be expected then that there would be a greater percentage of women among the sex offenders identified in anonymous surveys of victims in the population at large than, for example, among the sex offenders identified through prison records. Surveys that report on the percentages of females among sex offenders may not be comparable if they involve groups of sex offenders who have been identified by different means.

The percentages of females found among groups of sex offenders depend, in part, upon how the sex offenders have been located. A mother who has offended against two children may be treated in a mental health agency where she is the only female in a therapy group of ten sex offenders. The same mother may be the only female among 100 cases of child sexual abuse that are reviewed for possible prosecution by the district attorney. Her two children may be in a therapy group where they are the only two children among ten to have been molested by a female. The ten children in the therapy group may be from five different families and report having been abuse by a total of 16 offenders.

Depending on how data about this female is gathered, very different information might be reported about the percentage of females in the sex offender population. Various researchers might report that females constitute ten percent of offenders (in the offenders' therapy group); one percent of offenders (in the district attorney's office); or 12.5% of victims' offenders (in the victims' treatment group). It could also be reported that 40% of incestuous families seen in treatment have a female as an offender, or that 20% of victims (in the victims' treatment group) report molestation by a female. Studies that gather information from different sources are not directly comparable. Even when studies gather information from the same types of sources, they are unlikely to be directly comparable because of differences in the fashion in which sexual abuse has been defined and so on.

Researchers generally prefer to investigate groups of people who are similar. If a group of female sex offenders is similar in some way, the results of a study may apply to other groups that are also similar to them. If all of the participants in a study are convicted sex offenders, for example, some conclusions might be drawn from the study that are applicable to other convicted sex offenders but that might not apply to sex offenders who have not been convicted. When a study mixes up groups, it is harder to draw conclusions about how the results might apply to other groups.

Because there are only small numbers of female sex offenders who have been identified by potential researchers, many researchers are willing to study groups of female offenders that contain very different group members. For example, some researchers have reported on the percentage of females in therapy groups for sex offenders that include both convicted and non-convicted offenders.

Studies to date that have reported upon the percentages of females found among populations of sex offenders are not directly comparable. Their primary importance is their ability to confirm that the percentage of sex offenders who are women is significantly above the zero percent often previously assumed.

Studies of Offender Populations

Females Sex Offenders Identified Primarily through Child Protection Agencies

Estimates of the percentages of females among sex offender populations are sometimes based on groups that have come to the attention of authorities. These are typically child protective agencies, although one Canadian study reported upon the number of females among incarcerated sex offenders in Canada. Commonly, studies examining sex offenders who have come to the attention of authorities estimate that females comprise at most five percent of the offenders, although in one study the women were responsible for about twelve percent of all of the abuse. For women to enter these databases, however, someone must report the abuse to an agency and to an individual in the agency who considers the report to be plausible. Unless the child is able to report the abuse independently, he or she must have also reported the abuse to another individual first, who must then have both believed the child and had the willingness and ability to see that the abuse was reported. It is generally believed that females are less likely to be entered into child protective agency records than are males. De Francis[276] for example, found that in cases involving the sexual abuse of males by an adult female, the charge against the female was almost always "impairing the morals of a minor" rather than sexual abuse. Similar statements have been found in more recent literature, as well. (See Table 4.1: Percentages Identified Through Child Protection Agencies.)

Juvenile Female Sex Offenders

Some authors have examined cases in which juveniles engaged in sexual behavior with younger children. The studies below all examined data from the records of social services agencies. Again, to have entered the records of the social services agencies, the offender must have been identified and reported by a child either directly to an agency responsible for protection or to an adult capable of advocating for the child. Some female children may come to the attention of authorities first as victims and then as offenders. The percentages of juvenile offenders who are female, from the limited amount of information available, appear to be somewhat higher than the percentages of adult females found among offender populations.

There may be several reasons for this. First, the female juvenile offenders may be more likely than males to come to the attention of the authorities as victims. It is mandatory in many professions to report the suspected sexual abuse of a child (but not of an adult) so that many younger females may enter counseling where their reactive sexually abusive behaviors are discovered. It is possible that female victims are also more likely to be believed as victims of sexual abuse, as many individuals still find it hard to fathom that males are sexually abused. If the sexually abused males who are victimizing others are not brought into the system as victims, then such groups may contain spuriously large percentages of females. It is also likely that agencies that have the sophistication and training to identify juvenile offenders may also have the training to identify the female offenders. Finally, because of the limited numbers of available studies on the percentages of females among sex offender populations, it may be a somewhat random finding that the percentages of female among the juvenile populations is higher than those among the adults. (See Table 4.2: Percentage Identified Amongst Juvenile Sex Offenders.)

Table 4.1: Percentages Identified Through Child Protection Agencies

Author(s)	Source	Conclusions
De Francis (1969)	250 family interviews with families identified from New York City Child Protective Services records' review	3% of sex offenders against children were female
Finkelhor & Russell (1984)	Reexamining data from two previous studies	Women were the perpetrators in about 5% of the cases of girls, and in 20% of cases of boys
Margolin & Craft (1989)	Reviewed data from 2372 cases of child sexual abuse that had been substantiated by the Iowa Department of Human Services	Female perpetrators had committed 12.5% of the sexual abuse
Kercher & McShane (1985)	Reviewed data from a county Child Protective Services Agency (CPS) (619 cases) and a District's Attorney's Office (495 cases)	Females were found to be perpetrators in about 3% of these cases
Rowan, Langelier & Rowan (1988)	Approximately 600 cases of child molestation located through sex offender evaluations done for the New Hampshire judicial system and Vermont social service agencies and courts	The perpetrator was a woman in only nine (about 1.5%) of the cases
Motiuk & Belcourt (1996)	Review of records of offenders under federal (Canadian) jurisdiction (those serving two years or longer)	Less than 1% of incarcerated Canadian sex offenders were female

Table 4.2 Percentage Identified Amongst Juvenile Sex Offenders

Author(s)	Source	Conclusions
Pierce & Pierce (1987)	37 cases involving juvenile sex offenders found by protective services workers through a review of open protective services records, in seven district offices in Illinois	Approximately 19% of 37 cases involving juvenile sex offenders involved a female offender
U.S. Department of Health, Education and Welfare (1985)	161 individuals aged 19 and younger known by Vermont caseworkers (at the Department of Social Rehabilitation Services and Corrections) to have committed sex offenses	Females constituted 8% of the population
Smith & Israel (1987)	25 families in which there was sibling incest among substantiated cases reported to the Boulder County (Colorado) Sexual Abuse Team within the Department of Social Services	About 20% of the perpetrators were female
Ryan, Miyoshi, Krugman & Fryer (1996)	1000 youth in 30 states followed by the Uniform Data Collection System developed by the National Adolescent Perpetrator Network	2.6% of the juvenile (ages five through twenty-one) offenders were female
Ray & English (1995)	A sample of 650 sexually aggressive children on Washington State public agency caseloads	11% were female

Females Offenders in Mental Health Treatment or Assessment Populations

Other authors have documented the percentages of females among groups of sex offenders who were referred for mental health assessment or treatment. Sources of referral for treatment commonly include the courts, child protection agencies or other mental health agencies. Again it is not commonly found that the females comprise more than five percent of the offender population. For a woman to be sent for treatment or assessment, most commonly hers is a case in which the legal system or a child protection agency has become involved and has found the allegations to be plausible. (See Table 4.3: Percentage Identified Through Mental Health Services.)

Female Offenders in Day Care Populations

Some researchers have focused on sexual abuse by females in day care settings and in sex rings. Perhaps not surprisingly, these researchers commonly find that comparatively large percentages of the offenders in these settings are female. (See Table 4.4: Percentage Identified in Child Care.)

Conclusions Based upon Studies of Offenders

Present estimates, based upon studies of offender populations, primarily those that have come to the attention of authorities, strongly suggest that women constitute the minority of sex offenders. Researchers have not estimated that they comprise more than 20% of the child molester population and most authors have found that females constitute roughly two to four percent of this population. Estimates of the percentages of female child molesters who are among child molesters reported to authorities are not likely to accurately reflect the percentages of females among the child molester population at large, however, since several factors preclude the detection and reporting of the female sex offender.

Most authors are quick to suggest that identifying the percentage of women among reported child molesters is an inadequate means of estimating the total percentage of females among the child molester population at large. Because women are not generally viewed as capable of committing sexual offenses and are likely to be underreported, only more disturbed offenders or those who have committed more blatantly abusive acts may come to the attention of the authorities. Travin, Cullen and Protter,[277] for example, noted that sex crimes by females that were reported involved "bizarre or violent sexually deviant acts," more likely to be taken seriously by authorities.

Table 4.3: Percentage Identified Through Mental Health Services

Author(s)	Source	Conclusions
Faller (1987)	40 sexual perpetrators against children referred to the University of Michigan Interdiscipli-nary Project on Child Abuse and Neglect	14% were women
McCarty (1986)	29 offenders referred to the Dallas Incest Treat-ment Program	Mothers constituted about 4% of the offender popula-tion
Rowan, Langelier & Rowan (1988)	Approximately 600 cases of child molestation lo-cated through sex of-fender evaluations done for the New Hampshire judicial system and Ver-mont social service agen-cies and courts	The perpetrator was a woman in only nine (about 1.5%) of the cases
Travin, Cullen & Protter (1990)	Five female offenders convicted for sexual of-fenses and referred to a sex-offender evaluation and treatment program	The five females who had been convicted for sexual offenses and referred to their sex-offender treat-ment program constituted about 1% of such offenders referred for treatment.
Gomes-Schwartz, Horowitz & Cardareelli (1990)	Perpetrators discovered in a family treatment setting for sexual abuse in a spe-cialty clinic of the New England Medical Center Hospital	About 4% were female

Table 4.4: Percentage Identified in Child Care

Author(s)	Source of Information	Conclusions
Faller (1988)	48 children who were sexually abused in day-care settings	2% were abused by a female and approximately 50% by both a male and a female
Williams & Farrell (1990)	58 alleged perpetrators reported to have sexually abused children in day care	Approximately 38% were female
Finkelhor (1988)	Substantiated sexual abuse occurring nation-wide in 270 day care centers	40% of the abusers were women and 36% of the day care centers studied had female perpetrators. 59% of the 293 boys available for study in these settings were abused by women, as were 59% of the 471 girls
Margolin (1991)	325 case records, for which documentation was sufficient, from founded cases of sexual abuse by non-related child care providers listed in the Iowa Child Abuse Registry	42 of 257 sexual abuse perpetrators (about 16%) were female

Studies of Victim Populations

Female Perpetrators Identified by Victims Receiving Mental Health or Medical Assessment or Treatment

In addition to examining pools of known child molesters, in order to estimate the rates at which women commit sexual offenses, several authors have turned to populations of known child sex abuse victims. Percentages of females among the sex offenders identified by these groups of victims vary greatly. To a large extent these differences are likely to reflect variability in community availability of specialized resources for recognizing and treating sexual abuse in general and the community sensitivity to the possible presence of female sex offenders.

When specialty clinics exist for the evaluation of difficult sexual abuse cases, females may be more likely to appear in agency statistics. However, agencies that exist for the purposes of gathering medical evidence of sexual abuse may be less likely to count females among the offenders identified by patients, as it may be more likely that victims of females are not referred. Females are less likely to leave medical evidence such as sperm or other evidence of anal or vaginal penetration with a penis. The rates, varying here from between about one and 39% of all victims in treatment reporting a female offender, serve primarily to alert those working in child sexual abuse specialty clinics of the need to be aware of female sex offenders. (See Table 4.5: Percentage Identified through Victim's Receiving Treatment.)

Reports of Female Offenders by Other Pools of Victims

The available studies of victims identified among the population at large has found large percentages of individuals who have been molested by females among the population of sexual abuse victims, relative to victims identified in treatment populations. To some extent, the percentages of females in the sex offender population reflected in some of these surveys may be over-inflated; individuals who have a history of sexual abuse by females may be more likely to be interested in responding to a survey on the topic of sexual abuse. However, it is notable that the percentages of females found in these studies is far greater than the percentages of females found among sex offender populations that have been identified through the agencies that are designed to protect children. It is very likely that these agencies are overlooking cases in which females have molested children. (See Table 4.6: Percentage Identified through Other Sources of Victims.)

Female Child Molesters Reported Retrospectively by College Students

Several studies have examined the rates of female sexual perpetration against children by polling college students regarding their history of sexual abuse in childhood. As might be expected, these self-report studies have generally found larger percentages of female perpetrators than are found among those cases of victims identified in treatment populations. Some studies of college students have focused upon female offenders against males only or females only or both genders in combination.

Table 4.5: Percentages Identified Through Victims Receiving Treatment

Author(s)	Source of Information	Conclusions
Faller (1989)	87 boys and 226 girls with validated cases of sexual abuse referred to a program of child sexual abuse specialists from agencies in Michigan, Ohio and Ontario	Of the boys, about 8% had been molested by a female and about 29% had been molested by both a male and a female. Of the girls, about 1% were molested by a female and about 18% by both a male and a female.
Ramsey-Klawsnik (1990)	83 confirmed sexual abuse victims under the age of twelve referred for a mental health evaluation by the Massachusetts Department of Social Services following suspected child sexual abuse	Roughly 23% of the children were abused by females only and approximately 29% were abused by both males and females
Reinhart (1987)	189 males who were sexual abuse victims referred to University of California, Davis Medical Center for child sexual abuse evaluations and a matched control group of 189 female victims	Females were perpetrators about 4% of the time against the males (eight cases) and females were perpetrators against the females in four cases
Cupoli & Sewell (1988)	1059 children aged three months to 16 years receiving a Medical Examiner Sexual Abuse Exam	Female perpetrators accounted for 2% of all episodes of child sexual abuse (or 26 episodes)
Mrazek, Lynch & Bentovim (1987)	Physicians surveyed in the United Kingdom regarding the frequency with which they were seeing cases of sexual abuse	Four natural mothers who were sexual perpetrators comprised about 2% of the sexual abusers reported

Table 4.5: Percentages Identified Through Victims Receiving Treatment, cont.

Author(s)	Source of Information	Conclusions
Kendall-Tackett & Simon (1987)	365 individuals who provided intake interviews upon entering an AMAC (adults molested as children) treatment program in San Jose, California	3% of the offenders reported by adults molested as children were female
Roys & Timms (1995)	400 men seeking mental health treatment in a private practice specializing in the treatment of adult male survivors	Almost 3% had been sexually molested by a primary female caretaker
Ziotnick, Begin, Shea, Pearlstein, Simpson & Costello (1994)	56 women who were admitted to a women's psychiatric treatment unit with a history of severe sexual abuse and physical abuse	Eight (14%) had been sexually abused by their mothers
Farber, Showers, Johnson, Joseph & Oshins (1984)	81 boys and 81 girls (matched for age) who were assessed for sexual abuse by clinicians at a teaching hospital	2% of the children were abused by a female and 6% were abused by both a male and a female
Kasl (1990)	Informally surveyed therapists in the Minneapolis area who work with survivors of childhood sexual abuse	In response to a question concerning the number of their clients who were sexually abused by women, estimates ranged from 10% to 39%

Table 4.6: Percentages Identified Through Other Sources of Victims

Author(s)	Source of Information	Conclusions
Briggs and Hawkins (1995)	Interviews of 194 male subjects who had been sexually abused — identified through the media, men's organizations and the Departments for Correctional Services	28% percent of all respondents reported that they had been used for sex before the age of six by juvenile offenders at least five years older. Among the sub-population of male victims who later became sex offenders themselves, their (juvenile) offenders were equally likely to have been male or female. 42% of convicted sex offenders and 17% of the non-offenders had been sexually abused by adults before the age of six. One third of the subjects who had experienced this abuse were abused by women
Etherington (1997)	25 males responding to an advertisement for male survivors of child sexual abuse	52% were abused by females
Russell (1983)	Random telephone interviews of women in San Francisco. 152 women reported 186 sexually abusive experiences with different perpetrators.	4% of intra-familial perpetrators of child sexual abuse (eight perpetrators) and 4% of extra-familial child sexual abuse (17 perpetrators) were female
Finkelhor et al. (1990)	Nationwide telephone interviews of 1,145 men and 1,481 women	Female offenders who were reported by the respondents accounted for approximately 17% of the sexual abuse against males and approximately 1% of the abuse against females prior to the age of 18
Crewdson (1988)	Over 100 men responding to a newspaper advertisement asking to hear from men who had sexual experiences in childhood	75% reported that their childhood sexual contacts had been with a woman

Table 4.6: Percentages Identified Through Other Sources of Victims, cont.

Author(s)	Source of Information	Conclusions
Cameron, Coburn, Larson, Proctor, Forde & Cameron (1986)	A random survey in which participants were solicited door-to-door to complete a questionnaire	Sexual contact with women when they were under the age of 13 was reported by approximately 6% of the men Fewer than 1% of the women reported sexual contact with an adult woman before the age of 13
Weber, Gearling, Davis & Conlon (1992)	334 sexually active, delinquent males admitted to juvenile detention center completing a health history interview	42% had their first sexual experience with an individual (a female in at least 95% of cases) who was two or more years older

Different criteria used in examining sexual abuse reported in the histories of college students make the studies difficult to compare. However, when male and female college students are considered together, it appears that approximately 13% of the students who have been sexually abused have been abused by a female, suggesting that between approximately one to fifteen percent of college students have experienced sexual abuse in childhood at the hands of a female perpetrator. When males alone are considered, the percentage of victims reporting a female perpetrator is substantially higher (47-60%), with roughly three to sixteen percent of all college men reporting a history of child sexual abuse by a female perpetrator. The percentage of reported female perpetrators against females is smaller, with roughly five to ten percent of perpetrators reported to be female; less than one percent of college women overall report sexual abuse in childhood by a woman. Again, the studies used different definitions of child sexual abuse, and are not directly comparable. (See Table 4.7: Percentage Identified Through Retrospective Reporting of College Students.)

Female College Students Who Acknowledged Being Perpetrators

Perhaps among some of the more surprising findings, are that groups of college students can contain women who anonymously identify themselves as having engaged in sexual activity with a child. At least two studies have documented cases of college women who acknowledge that they had had sexual contact with children significantly younger than they. (See Table 4.8: Female College Students Who Acknowledged Being Perpetrators.)

Table 4.7: Percentage Identified Through Retrospective Reporting of College Students

Author(s)	Source of Information	Conclusions
Landis (1956)	140 college men reporting 215 experiences in childhood with "adult sexual deviates"	Fewer than 1% of these experiences involved interest in or attempted coitus
Landis (1956)	360 college women reporting 531 experiences with "adult sexual deviates"	Of the women, roughly 2% reported a "homosexual approach"
Schultz & Jones (1983)	117 students in West Virginia reporting sexual experiences before age twelve with someone over age 16	13% of offenders were female
Haugaard & Emery (1989)	101 college students reporting sexual experiences before age 17 with an individual more than five years older and at least 16	13% of offenders were female
Fritz, Stoll & Wagner (1981)	Surveyed 952 psychology students at the University of Washington	Of the approximately 5% of males reporting a prepubescent physical contact of an overt sexual nature with a post-adolescent person, about 60% reported the contacts to have been with females Of the roughly 8% of the females reporting childhood molestation, about 10% were molested by a female
Condy, Templer, Brown & Veaco (1987)	Surveyed 359 college men concerning sexual experiences before the age of 16 in which the female was at least five years older than the male and at least 16 years old at the time of contact	Approximately 16% reported a history of such contact. These men had been forced into the activity about 14% of the time, but had forced the woman about 7% of the time
Finkelhor (1979)	530 female and 266 male college students	In 15 cases (about 2%) the students reported involvement with an older woman

Female Sex Offenders

Table 4.7: Retrospective Reporting of College Students, cont.

Author(s)	Source of Information	Conclusions
Risin & Koss (1987)	Surveyed 216 male college students among 32 institutions of higher learning reporting a sexually abusive incident before the age of 14	In 43% of cases the offender was a girl; in 4% of cases both a woman and a girl
Fromuth (1983)	482 college females at Auburn University, 106 of whom reported sexual abuse before the age of 13	5% of the 139 perpetrators of child sexual abuse reported were females

Table 4.8: Female College Students Who Acknowledged Being Perpetrators

Author(s)	Source of Information	Conclusions
Fromuth & Conn (1997)	546 female students at Middle State University	4% acknowledged at least one experience of sexually molesting a younger child (most had been between the ages of ten to fourteen at the time and had molested someone at least five years younger)
Condy, Templer, Brown & Veaco (1987)	638 college women	Less than 1% reported sexual contact with a male child (the study looked only at sexual contacts between the older females and younger males). Females were at least 16 and at least five years older than the males, who were under 16

Sexual Abuse by a Female in the Histories of Sex Offenders

Large numbers of male sex offenders report sexual abuse by a woman in childhood or adolescence. Male sex offenders often report such contact with higher frequency than do other groups of men, with 40-60 percent commonly reporting such contact in recent studies. This raises the possibility that sexual abuse by a female in the histories of sex offenders may play a role in the development of their deviant sexuality. Some argue, however, that it is possible that some sex offenders may report a history of sexual abuse that has actually not occurred.[278] (See Table 4.9.)

Table 4.9: Percentage Identified through Histories of Sex Offenders

Author(s)	Source of Information	Conclusions
Gebhard, Gagnon, Pomeroy & Christenson (1965)	Convicted sex offenders who had had sexual contact before puberty with female who was at least five years older and at least 15	Among those classified as heterosexual offenders vs. children, about 8% had experienced masturbation, mouth-genital or anal contact with an older female, and approximately 4% had experienced coitus Among those convicted sex offenders classified as heterosexual offenders vs. minors, these figures were roughly 14% and 5% respectively Among those classified as heterosexual offenders vs. adults the figures were about 9% and 2% respectively Corresponding figures for homosexual aggressors were against children 11% and 11%; against minors 0% in both categories; and against adults, about 9% and 5%
Allen (1991)	75 males identified by Iowa state social services departments as committing (substantiated) acts of sexual abuse against children and 65 female child molesters located through several midwestern sources, usually child protection agencies	Male child molesters reported that approximately 45% of their sexual abusers in childhood had been female. Female child molesters reported that approximately 7% of their molesters in childhood had been female
Freeman-Longo (1987) (in Allen, 1991)	Rapists that he had worked with	Over 40% of them had been sexually abused by women in childhood

Table 4.9: Percentage Identified through Histories of Sex Offenders, cont.

Author(s)	Source of Information	Conclusions
Gebhard, Gagnon, Pomeroy and Christenson (1965)	Incest offenders	Percentages of offenders having experienced masturbation, oral-genital or anal contact with an older female while pre-pubescent or having had coitus were for the offenders vs. children, about 6% and 4% respectively, for offenders vs. minors, about 6% and 4% respectively, and for offenders vs. adults, 0% in both categories. For homosexual offenders vs. children these figures were 8% and 4% respectively, for offenders vs. minors, about 7% and 4%, and for offenders vs. adults about 4% in both categories
Groth (1979a)	348 convicted rapists and child molesters	44 cases were identified in which these men suffered sexual victimization in childhood at the hands of a female. Sexual trauma between the ages of one to fifteen at the hands of a female adult was noted in the developmental histories of approximately 38% of the rapists reporting such trauma and about 18% of the child molesters who reported the same. Sexual trauma at the hands of a female peer was noted for approximately 24% of the rapists with a history of sexual trauma and for about 5% of the child molesters with the same
Petrovich and Templer (1984)	83 incarcerated rapists	59% had been heterosexually molested in childhood

Table 4.9: Percentage Identified through Histories of Sex Offenders, cont.

Author(s)	Source of Information	Conclusions
Roys & Timms (1995)	500 male sex offenders evaluated for treatment over the course of six years in a private practice offender treatment center	Almost 2% had a history of sexual molestation by a primary female caretaker (mother, stepmother or grandmother) in their childhood years (before the age of 14)
Ryan, Miyoshi, Metzner, Krugman & Fryer (1996)	1,600 juvenile sex offenders from 30 states, followed by the Uniform Data Collection System developed by the National Adolescent Perpetrator Network	22% had been sexually abused by a female
Burgess, Hazelwood, Rokous, Hartman & Burgess (1987)	Interviewed 41 incarcerated serial rapists in twelve different states (each had committed at least ten rapes)	Of the 31 most serious sexual aggressors against these men, approximately 32% were female (only) and 13% were a female and a male

Other Sources of Information on Female Sex Offenders

Sexual Abuse Committed by Female Inmates

One study reported upon the percentages of female inmates who acknowledged having had sexual contact with boys. Among a sample of 172 female inmates surveyed by Condy et al.,[279] approximately eight percent reported having had sexual contact with a male minor; about 62% of these women had had more than one contact and about 46% had had more than one partner. Criteria in this study were that sexual contacts included a female who was at least five years older than the male and at least 16 years old at the time of contact, and in which the male was younger than 16 years of age.

States Providing Sexual Abuse Treatment to Female Sex Offenders

Knopp and Stevenson[280] identified that services to juvenile female sex offenders were available in 43 states and in Washington, DC, although half of the services available were in eight states. In sixty-eight percent of the cases, the services available included treatment.

Services to adult females were available in 45 states and DC, though almost a third of the services were located in five states. In 62% of cases, the services available involved some form of treatment.

Summary

Recent evidence suggests that sexual offenses against children by females are rare in comparison to similar offenses committed by men. However, Allen[281] has commented that while rates at which females commit sexual crimes against children are low when compared with rates at which men commit the same offenses, the actual numbers of children affected by these crimes is substantial. Estimating that about 23% of females are sexually abused in childhood and that an estimated five percent of their offenders are females, Allen used US Census Bureau figures to estimate that 1.5 million females may have been sexually abused by a woman. In a similar fashion, estimating that roughly seven percent of males experience sexual abuse in childhood and that 20% of those abused may have been abused by a female, he estimated that roughly 1.6 million males may have been abused by women. Allen[282] remarked, "Most importantly, it does not really matter to the victims of female sexual abusers that theirs was a low-probability event. What does matter is the possibility that they may experience further stigmatization when professionals disbelieve them (p. 21)."

Differences in methodologies between studies that attempt to estimate the percentages of females among sex offender populations make them difficult to compare. Criteria for defining childhood sexual abuse differ between studies. Sources of information differ between studies. In some, the information was gathered from known or suspected victims, in some from known or suspected perpetrators and in some from various random or highly specific samples of the population at large. Research methods differed between studies and researchers defined "cases" in different ways. Though it difficult to estimate the percentage of females in the child molester population, current studies indicate that, without question, the population of child molesters includes women.

Notes ————————————————————

276 De Francis (1969)
277 Travin, Cullen & Protter (1990)
278 Wakefield & Underwager (1991)
279 Condy et al. (1987)
280 Knopp & Stevenson (1990)
281 Allen (1991)
282 Allen (1991)

5. Effects of Sexual Molestation by a Female on the Child

Impact Specific to Victims of Female Perpetrated Sexual Abuse

Some researchers have commented that when the sexual offender against a child is a woman rather than a man, there may be particular aftereffects for the victim. Welldon[283] reported that desolation and isolation result for the victims of female sex offenses because of the particular silence surrounding these acts. Rosencrans[284] made similar observations, noting that women who were molested by their mothers often experienced a sense of isolation and a sense of being different from other victims of sexual abuse. Some researchers have commented that females who were sexually abused in childhood by both males and females have reported that the abuse by the female was worse because it involved betrayal by one who was counted upon to protect.[285]

Saradjian & Hanks[286] reported that, particularly because sexual abuse by women is under-acknowledged in society, there are several consequences of female perpetrated sexual abuse by a woman. They reported that the confusion between sex and affection is made worse when the offender is a woman. Children may also come to confuse and distort care giving and sex. They reported that children of abuse by female perpetrators may be more likely to feel guilty, shameful, bad and stigmatized when the offender is a woman, and may be more likely to blame themselves for the sexual abuse. The sense of betrayal may also be greater. When the victim is sexually abused by a single female parent or by both parents, Saradjian & Hanks[287] also noted that he or she may develop a particular sense of powerlessness.

Others have also noted that when the perpetrator is a female, it may result in a particular sense of betrayal for the victim. Among the effects of female perpetrated child sexual abuse reported to Myers[288] by eleven women, three women reported a profound sense of betrayal at having been sexually abused by a female, although they had also been abused by men. Mitchell and Morse[289] reported that one of the women who had been victimized reported that sexual abuse by a female is worse than victimization by a man because she perceived that the female offender would know, as opposed to guessing as in the case of the male offender, that she is hurting the victim.

James and Nasjleti[290] similarly stated that sexual abuse victims who are molested by their mothers exhibit more confusion than do other victims. Common problems noted by the authors include both loving and hating the offender, self-loathing and a feeling of having betrayed the offender by telling. They note that in comparison with other children who have been molested, the tendency of a victim to try to view the mother's behavior as acceptable and to view the mother as a good parent is profound.

Some authors have pointed to the problems of role or identity development in the victim when the female offender is a parent or primary caretaker. Saradjian & Hanks[291] cited the difficulty that female victims of women have in establishing a personal identity that is separate from the female offender. Enmeshment with the offender is noted by these authors as a particular problem when that offender is the mother. They cite the case of a woman who underwent large amounts of plastic surgery in order to develop an identity separate from that of the mother who abused her and cite other examples of individuals who desired sex change operations. In some cases, the female offender may have difficulty promoting the daughter's individual identity. When the victim is a daughter, James and Nasjleti[292] state that there may be a lack of recognition of the individuality of the daughter by the offender; the girl may be viewed as an extension of her mother. The mother's sexual acts with the daughter may have a masturbatory quality.

Among females molested by their mothers, Rosencrans[293] similarly noted problems related to the failure of the mother-child bond, a fused identity with the mother, a lack of a sense of boundaries between the mother and the daughter, dependency and mistrust, problems with intimacy, social immaturity or pseudo-maturity and problems with independence. In these cases, the females contended not only with sexual trauma, but also with betrayal by their primary caretaker.

Some authors have reported similar role and identity problems for males molested by their mothers. Kempe and Kempe[294] stated their belief that many forms of (heterosexual) incest involving a male child are often more damaging than incest involving a female child. They postulate that such cases do not allow for individuation and identification with the male parent. James and Nasjleti[295] similarly state that the son who is sexually abused by his mother may find himself in the position of the dominant male in the family in terms of making decisions and meeting the mother's needs. Simultaneously he may be treated as a young child, in that his mother may bathe him, inspect him or have him sleep with her.

Evidence Concerning the Harm to Males from Female Perpetrated Child Sexual Abuse

Emotional Difficulties

A host of emotional difficulties have been described by authors who have treated mental health clients with sexual abuse by a female in their histories. Emotional, behavioral, sexual and relationship difficulties, as well as sexual identity confusion, have been noted by therapists treating survivors of female perpetrated child sexual abuse. It is likely that such cases are biased, in that mental health professionals see only those cases in which problems have developed as a result of sexual abuse, or in which mental health problems may have preceded the sexual abuse. Nonetheless, case studies and studies of victimized individuals who are in treatment serve to point to difficulties that may arise as a result of sexual abuse by a female.

Roys and Timms[296] examined the MMPI profiles of groups of males, focusing particularly on two groups of adult males who had been molested in childhood (before the age of 14) by their primary female caretakers. The two groups consisted of eleven men who were in therapy for sexual abuse and nine men who were in treatment for having sexually offended against others. They found that the arithmetic mean MMPI profile for the eleven non-offending males showed:

> considerable examples of what would be called post-traumatic stress disorder symptoms. The prominent feature of this group is depression with indications of tension, nervousness and anxiety. Insomnia and strong tendencies to worry are suggested. Thoughts or actions of suicide may be present. Complaints of fatigability, chronic tiredness or exhaustion may be stated. A careful examination for psychotic or pre-psychotic conditions should be made. Sexual confusion and/or concerns are also indicated, as well as a sense of passivity (p. 70).

Also discovered by Roys and Timms[297] was that the average profile for nine sex offenders, molested by a primary female caretaker, who were entering treatment showed:

> depression and there is the possibility of suicidal ideation. The elevated Scale 4 (Pd) indicates more impulsivity, anti-social behaviors and thinking as well as family disruptions which may be typical of the sexually offending male. This group, along with elevated depression, has elevated scores on Scales 6, 7 and 8, indicating worry, tension, and fear. This group also shows the low 9 and high 0 Scales which typically indicate personal passivity and a tendency

toward being withdrawn (p. 71-72).

In contrasting these sex offenders who had been molested by female care-takers with other male sex offenders who were either not sexually abused or were sexually abused by males, they concluded that those sex offenders who had been sexually abused by female caretakers were slightly more upset and disturbed.

Males who were not sex offenders but who had been sexually abused by a primary female caretaker were the most upset and disturbed of the groups of males that they studied. (The other groups included non-victimized sex-offenders and non-offenders in therapy; sex-offenders and non-sex offenders who had been sexually victimized by males; and sex-offenders who had been sexually victimized by primary female caretakers.) These individuals often had stronger depression, often with suicidal ideation; problems with sexual identity; and social isolation and passivity.

Because the profiles of the non-offenders who had been sexually abused by females suggested more distress than those of the offenders, the authors postulated that the victims of female sexual abuse who became offenders may have done so as a means of venting their intense distress. They noted that the men in the study who had been sexually abused by a primary female caretaker often entered destructive relationships with women.

Therapists treating male survivors of female perpetrated child sexual abuse have noted a host of emotional, sexual, relationship and behavioral difficulties, as well as sexual identity confusion. Some authors have reported upon cases involving maternal son incest.

In his case study of mother-son incest, Margolis[298] noted that his patient sexually assaulted his mother and was matricidal; he had no close friends as a teen and did not live up to his inferred academic potential. As an adult, he beat his first wife and became suicidal and homicidal when she threatened to leave. His second wife threatened to leave him when he acted irresponsibly while drunk. Masters[299] noted a case of mother-adopted son incest in which the son engaged in homosexual activity, beat a female and killed his mother. Vanderbilt, in her 1992 magazine article, described several cases in which deleterious effects of incest were reported to her. One male, molested by his mother, killed her, stabbed his grandmother and committed suicide.

Wahl[300] described two case studies of males who had sexual contact with their mothers. In both, psychotic symptoms in adulthood appeared to have been exacerbated by sexual contact with their mothers. In the first case, the son also had sexual contact with his older aunt and neighbor and, as a teenager, had observed his mother in the act of coitus. Nightmares, numerous acts of delinquency and sexual contact with his younger brother and other males were a part of his history. As an adult he suffered from social isolation and withdrawal, anxiety and depression, and fear of becoming a homosexual. The second male is also noted to have had sexual relations with his brother. In a case of mother-son incest, Berry[301] attributes the homosexuality of the son to a possible defense against incest and a safeguard against the emergence of psychosis.

Two authors described dissociative symptoms among males who had sexual contact with their mothers. Schoenewolf[302] reported that an individual with multiple personality disorder had been sexually abused in childhood by her mother. Silber[303] described the case of a man who had been sexually abused in childhood by his mother. The man was described as becoming "deeply hypnotic" as a way of coping.

Harper[304] found that of seven boys who were molested by their mothers, behavior problems included aggressive acting out (two cases), sexual acting out (three cases), depressed affect (three cases), cross-dressing (two cases), developmental delay (two cases), emotional disturbance (five cases) and being sexually provocative with the therapist (two cases).

Kempe and Kempe[305] described the case of a 24-year-old concert pianist who engaged in full intercourse with his mother beginning at some point in his childhood or adolescence. He had hysterical paralysis, psychosomatic symptoms, chronic depression, anxiety with phobic elements and signs of schizophrenic behavior. They also described the case of an adolescent who reported sexual abuse by his grandmother; the boy was a heroin abuser who had drug-related legal problems and problems with truancy from school. He had been abandoned by both parents after their divorce.

Bachmann et al.[306] reported upon a case of mother-son incest occurring in the context of a great deal of family violence and pathology and compounded by the fact that the son was sexually molested by his uncle, as well. The son engaged in sexual orgies at the age of 15, had trouble keeping a job, was sentenced to prison for charges including fraud, theft and default. He was committed on 13 occasions to a psychiatric hospital, generally due to suicidal behavior. He was diagnosed as having antisocial personality disorder, borderline personality disorder, an unspecified anxiety disorder and sexual sadism. He was also dependent on prescription drugs.

Raphling et al.[307] noted a case of mother-son incest that occurred in a multi-incestuous family. The son reported having felt depressed and guilty concerning the incident. He later is reported to have forced his wife into abusive sexual relations and to have had sexual relations with his daughters. He also encouraged his son to have sexual relations with his (the son's) sisters and mother.

Crewdson,[308] a newspaper editor and author, reported upon a case of a man who had had incestuous contact with his mother in childhood and adolescence. The sexual contact in one instance involved his maternal aunt. The man wished the contact had never occurred and felt that had it not occurred, he might not have become divorced or have become an alcoholic. He described himself as having sought therapy when he had memories of the sexual contact after his own children had grown up.

Quintano[309] reported upon two cases of males who had histories of enema abuse by their mothers. One suffered from alcohol addiction and was diagnosed with bipolar depression and post-traumatic stress disorder. Additionally, he had a history of compulsive sexual behavior, was homosexual and had sexually abused his siblings. He associated the enemas with anger and punishment. The second man had confusion over his sexual identity. He had been charged with "soliciting for immoral purposes." His sexual concerns included fantasies of raping and of being raped, sadomasochistic fantasies, fetishes and cross-dressing in childhood. He had lower back and hip pain that lessened during therapy for the abuse. His concerns included nightmares, sleep disturbances and medication related depression. His memories of the enemas were associated with intense fear and anger. Schoenewolf[310] also described the case of a man who attributed his masochistic tendencies to the enemas that he received as punishment from his mother in childhood.

Chasnoff et al.[311] noted that two of three infants who were molested by their mothers displayed behavioral abnormalities with excessive sexual acting out in their relationships with other children. They concluded that, while a cause and effect relationship could not be concluded, sexual molestation places children at high risk for behavioral abnormalities.

Two authors have noted early sexual abuse and sexualization by their mothers in the backgrounds of serial killers. For example, a writer discussing the trial of serial killer Arthur J. Shawcross noted the testimony of his psychiatrist that he had been sodomized with a broomstick by his mother, who also required him to have oral sex with her and would beat him afterward.[312] In addition to brutal physical abuse and neglect, Henry Lee Lucas, a rapist and serial killer, is reported to have been forced to watch his mother prostitute herself in their home. The mother also dressed him as a girl in his early school years.[313]

Some cases of males seen in treatment for female perpetrated child sexual abuse have not involved incest. Peluso & Putnam[314] described the case of a 14-year-old boy referred for a medical evaluation and an evaluation for possible hospitalization for severe psychotic depression and suicidal ideation. The boy had had sexual interactions with the mother of the child for whom he baby-sat, and had also been fondled by a babysitter when he was five years of age.

Kasl,[315] citing data gathered by Shirley Carlson, reported that males abused by females tend to internalize shame and guilt and to hold themselves responsible for the sexual contact. They may develop a false sense of power or feelings of being special or in love with the abuser who may also be abusing others. They may also develop feelings of worthlessness or abandonment. Rage, fear and insecurity may develop.

Rosencrans[316] surveyed nine men who had been sexually abused in childhood by their mothers. The men were typically identified for participation in the study after attending presentations on mother-daughter sexual abuse. Among the emotional problems that these men experienced in childhood were depression (56%), anger (22%), hostility (22%) and rage (22%). In adulthood, 78% experienced depression and 89% experienced anxiety. Additionally, in adulthood 89% experienced dependency, 44% experienced anxiety attacks and 67% had self-destructive behaviors. Forty-four percent had made suicide attempts during adulthood and 33% had made suicide attempts during childhood. Sixty-seven percent had drug or alcohol problems both in childhood and in adulthood. Forty-four percent said that the incest was the most damaging experience of their lives.

Among cases involving males who have been sexually abused by females, similar problems have been observed. These have included emotional difficulties and problems of low self-worth, drug and alcohol abuse, violence, dissociation, psychosomatic problems, depression and anxiety, post-traumatic stress, antisocial behaviors and the possible exacerbation of psychosis. Several therapists have also observed concerns more specifically related to sexuality. These have included: problems with relationships and sexual functioning, sexual identity concerns and the propensity to sexually abuse others. Several authors have studied the effects of female perpetrated child sexual abuse on these relationship and sexual concerns in more detail.

Sexual and Relationship Concerns among Males Molested by Females

Several authors have commented, in particular, upon dysfunctions in the areas of relationships and sexuality that have been found to be present in males who have had childhood sexual contact with women. Several authors discussed the effects that female perpetrated child sexual abuse may have on a male with respect to these areas of functioning. Forward and Buck[317] suggested that mother-son incest could lead to isolation, conditioned impotence and fear and resentment of women. Justice and Justice[318] also noted impotence as a possible result of mother-son incest. They also stated that a victim of mother-son incest might become a misogynist, a wife beater, a daughter abuser, a rapist or a murderer. Renvoize[319] suggested that homosexuality, fear of women and an inability to achieve orgasm are all associated with mother-son incest.

Maltz and Holman[320] noted that when sexual abuse occurs with a female offender, the male may fail to separate emotionally from the mother or mother figure. They noted that such contact may impair the male in his ability to establish an emotionally satisfying relationship with a partner and to take the lead in physically intimate activity. He may become uncomfortable around women and may become hostile or abusive towards them. They also noted that it places the male in the difficult position of having to compete with older males instead of experiencing them as role models. They remarked that incest may impair the ability of the male to learn social skills necessary for intimate relationships.

Emotional conflict related to sexuality and to intimate relationships with women has been noted by some authors. Kasl[321] reported that ambivalence and conflict concerning both women and sex may develop among males sexually abused by females. Rinsley[322] commented in the case of a male with borderline personality disorder who was molested by his mother that he could only be sexual if he felt no emotions towards the women with whom he was subsequently involved. Emotional connection with a woman resulted in impotency. Lawson[323] stated that the inability to sustain a long-term monogamous relationship with a female is among the more common symptoms of males who have been molested by their mothers. She reported that a male victim of maternal incest

> cannot maintain sexual intimacy with a female because of the fear of loss of self. Entry into the female body, representing a return to the womb, is so fraught with fear and anxiety of being enveloped and destroyed (which, of course, has already emotionally occurred) that the male must somehow separate his emotional and sexual self (p. 396).

Etherington[324] found that of seven men sexually molested by their mothers, four of the five who had married were divorced.

Maltz and Holman[325] reported that a male survivor of incest with both parents attributed his sexual experiences with other boys and his "enormous amount of masturbation" to the ambiguous nature of the abuse by his parents. He also reported having "old feelings of violation" in situations of sexual vulnerability. Another male survivor was reported by these authors to attribute his difficulties with impotence to his sexual relationship with his mother.

Sexual problems have noted by several authors to occur among males who have been molested by females. Sarrel and Masters[326] attributed the sexual dysfunction seen in some of their clients who had been sexually assaulted by females (either as children or as adults) to their sexual abuse, although ten of the eleven clients had not made this connection. Maltz and Holman[327] described the cases of two men who were molested by their mothers who later experienced impotence and other sexual difficulties. Shrier and Johnson[328] noted sexual dysfunction in 21% of their sample of adolescent males molested by females. Rosencrans[329] surveyed nine men who had been sexually abused in childhood by their mothers. All reported that the abuse had created sexual problems for them both in childhood and in adulthood.

Parenting may be a problem for some males who have been molested by females. Of nine men surveyed by Rosencrans,[330] who had been sexually abused in childhood by their mothers, all said that the sexual abuse by their mothers created problems for them in being parents.

The possibility that males who are sexually abused by women may later sexually abuse others has been raised by several authors.[331] Groth[332] noted that rapists are sexually victimized more by females than by males and suggested that this partially explains their sexual attacks against women. He added that the adult offender's sex crimes may be, in part, a repetition and acting out of the sexual trauma to which he was subjected as a child. High frequencies of molestation by a female have been noted in the histories of incarcerated sex offenders, as previously discussed. Similarly, Burgess et al.[333] found high rates of sexual molestation by females in the histories of serial rapists. They argued that when a female is a sexual aggressor, the boy's thinking changes. He begins to view women as predatory and sexually demanding and "the thinking that females are to be valued and protected becomes confused (288)." Etherington[334] found that of seven men sexually molested by their mothers, two had acted out their abuse, including one who abused his daughter the way that he had been abused. Of nine men surveyed by Rosencrans[335] who had been sexually abused in childhood by their mothers, 33% had sexually molested others in childhood and 44% had molested others in adulthood.

Males who have had early sexual contact with a female may be more prone to revictimization or may be more likely to become promiscuous. Briggs and Hawkins[336] noted that, among boys, early sexualization (before the age of eleven) with an older peer or adult (in many cases a female) led to revictimization for 13% of their sample. Many of the male victims that they sampled were themselves sex offenders, partially as a result of sampling bias. Among delinquent males, Weber et al.[337] found that there was a risk among those who had experienced early sexual intercourse to have a greater number of sexual partners, with related social, psychological and health risks. Krug[338] noted that in 75% of the eight cases of sexualized mother-son relationships, the son had multiple concurrent sex partners in adulthood. Kasl[339] noted that a large percentage of men with sexual addictions have childhood histories of sexual abuse by a female.

Sexual Identity Concerns Among Males Molested by Women

Many researchers and clinicians have observed sexual identity confusion among males who have been molested by females. Several authors and therapists have speculated that men who have been sexually abused by women may later develop sexual identity concerns or may become homosexual as a result of the sexual abuse.[340]

In several small studies authors have found sexual identity concerns, homosexuality or bisexuality among some of the males who were molested by females. Thirty-eight percent of the Krug[341] sample of eight men sexually abused by their mothers were reported to have a sexual identity problem. Johnson and Shrier noted that 28% of the eleven adolescents molested by a female were bisexual, as opposed to eight percent of a control group. Boys who were molested by a female were no more likely to report themselves as homosexual, however, than were unmolested individuals in a control group.[342] Etherington[343] found that of seven men sexually molested by their mothers, one was bisexual and one was asexual. Rosencrans[344] surveyed nine men who had been sexually abused in childhood by their mothers. Eighty-nine percent reported that the sexual abuse had created sexual identity issues. One of the males was homosexual and one of the men was unsure of his sexual identity.

While evidence suggests that some males who have been sexually abused by a female may have sexual identity concerns, one study provided evidence that homosexual males are not more likely to have been sexually abused by a female. Cameron et al.[345] found, for example, that greater percentages of heterosexual men had had sexual advances made to them by an adult female than did bisexual or homosexual men (seven percent versus three percent). They also had greater amounts of actual sexual contact with adult females before the age of 13 (six percent versus three percent). It would appear that while some males who are molested by females may develop sexual identity concerns, sexual molestation by a female is not likely to be a primary cause of homosexuality.

Effects of Female Perpetrated Child Sexual Abuse upon Female Victims

A variety of problems has been identified among females who have been sexually abused by other females. At present, there appear to be a greater number of studies of groups of women who were sexually molested by females in childhood than there are of males. Problems identified among these women have included emotional, behavioral, relationship and sexual problems.

Some authors have also provided summary descriptions of the results of female perpetrated abuse on females or have described case studies. Barry and Johnson[346] reported that in cases of mother-daughter incest, reactions range from no unusual anxiety whatsoever to somatic and neurotic symptoms to psychotic anxiety. Goodwin and DiVasto,[347] in summarizing several cases, reported that mother-daughter incest victims present with symptoms that include encopresis, depression, psychosis and "migraine headaches with homosexual acting out." Phobic and neurotic complaints were noted in a case of granddaughter-grandmother incest. They reported on a case of a young women who had had sexual contact with her mother and who made a self-mutilating suicide attempt during the course of her therapy. Goodwin and DiVasto (1979) also commented based on several case reviews that maternal seductiveness had been implicated in the onset of homosexuality. Holubinskyj & Foley[348] reported upon a case of mother-daughter incest, which began by the time the daughter was a preschooler and continued into her adolescence. The daughter was hyperactive, exhibited bizarre behavior in school, self-mutilated, used drugs and alcohol, ran away from home and was sexually revictimized by others. She was described as having an identity disturbance, depression, sexual confusion and anxiety and a poor self-image. Cooper and Cormier[349] documented the case of a 14-year-old girl who was molested by her mother, who ran away to prevent the abuse. Dolan[350] discussed the results of sexual abuse at the hands of her own mother; a sense of lifetime shame was described as a result of the incest.

Conclusions drawn from studies of larger clinical populations have been similar. The findings are complicated by the fact that several researchers have noted that women who have a history of having been molested by females often tend to have been sexually abused by other offenders as well.[351]

Emotional and Behavioral Problems

Among studies conducted on groups of women with sexual abuse histories with female perpetrators, a number of emotional and behavioral problems have been documented.

Of 93 women surveyed by Rosencrans[352] who were sexually abused by their mothers, 13% reported delinquent behavior in childhood and 23% reported adult stealing. School and achievement problems were also common. A variety of sleep related disturbances were noted among these women. Emotional problems included adult anger (74%) and rage (63%). Eight-five percent experienced adulthood anxiety and 94% experienced adulthood depression. Fifty-seven percent were hypervigilant during adulthood. Seventy-three percent experienced childhood anxiety and childhood phobias were common. Fifteen percent experienced auditory hallucinations during childhood and 18% reported other types of hallucinations.

Swink[353] described at length nine cases of mother-daughter incest that she treated and described the effects of such abuse upon the daughters. Denial, repression and minimization were cited as coping mechanisms used by female victims of maternal incest. Dissociation was utilized by all nine of the survivors and was judged to have been more extreme than in cases of victims of other forms of incest. Two of the daughters had multiple personalities. Flashbacks were described as being as common in maternally incestuously abused women as in other victims of sexual abuse. Rage was also identified as an issue typically faced. The nine women studied all suffered a sense of "existential hopelessness," or a lack of a reason to live. They were described as being disillusioned with religion and subsequently lacking the sense of community provided by organized religions. Stress and depression related concerns were common among these women. Tension, anxiety and an inability to relax were also common difficulties, as were depression, an external locus of control and phobias of things or situations associated with the abuse. Though some guilt was noted in the women who survived incest with their mothers, this was observed to be less than for survivors of sexual abuse in general. Swink[354] identified self-concept difficulties and the sense of having lost their childhoods as common issues faced. Five of nine women were reported to have mild body image distortion and to judge themselves to be less attractive than they actually were.

Among the immediate effects of female perpetrated child sexual abuse reported to Myers[355] by eleven female adults were dissociation, identity and boundary confusion, low self-esteem, acting out behaviors, below capacity school performance, day time enuresis, withdrawal, aggression, frequent crying, hypervigilance, migraines, nightmares and fear of people. One reported that at the time it made her feel close to her abuser. Other symptoms reported by these women included: nightmares (six women), insomnia (six women), depression (ten women), low self-esteem (ten women), body-image issues (ten women), hopelessness (nine women), panic attacks or anxiety (nine women), apathy (nine women), flashbacks (seven women), identity issues (seven women), personal/career goals being affected by abuse (seven women) and memory loss (five cases).

Six of the ten female victims of female perpetrated child sexual abuse interviewed by Paiser[356] reported a negative self-image, six reported difficulty preserving a clear sense of self and seven reported that they felt different from other people. Eight of the participants discussed issues related to experiencing a lack of safety; four stated that they did not feel safe anywhere in the world.

Ogilvie & Daniluk[357] described three cases of females molested in childhood by their mothers. Among the problems noted in these three cases were problems with poor self-esteem and poor self-image and depression. Also noted were shame, stigmatization, self-blame, a sense of betrayal and impaired identity development. There was a tendency for the women to try to be as different as possible from their mothers.

Mitchell and Morse[358] found a variety of mental health problems among 80 women who had been sexually molested by females in childhood. Among these were dissociation, multiple personality disorder, phobias, depression, low self-esteem and intrusive traumatic memories.

Among the emotional and behavioral problems noted among female victims of female perpetrated child sexual abuse are a variety of symptoms related to anxiety, depression and dissociation. Anger or rage is often found. Poor self-image and poor self-esteem are commonly noted. A lack of academic achievement is also commonly found. In some cases, psychotic symptoms or flashbacks occur.

Self-Harm and Compulsive Behaviors

Among a number of women who have been sexually molested in childhood by females, a variety of forms of self-harm and compulsive behaviors have been observed to occur.

Mitchell and Morse[359] found a variety of forms of self-injury among 80 women who had been sexually molested by females in childhood. These included cutting breasts, inner thighs and vaginas; burning skin; injurious masturbation; and ignoring health care needs.

Among the forms of self-harm reported to Myers[360] by eleven female adults who had been molested by females were suicidal thoughts (eleven women), eating disorders (nine women), self-destructive behavior (eight women), suicide attempts (six women) and drug/alcohol abuse (six women).

Paiser[361] reported that five women among ten whom she studied, who had been childhood victims of female perpetrated sexual abuse, had engaged in compulsive or self-abusive behaviors including: eating disorders, drug and alcohol addictions, "workaholism" and the inflicting of pain upon themselves. Four of the ten had experienced suicidal thoughts.

Among the ten female victims of female perpetrated child sexual abuse who were interviewed, Swink[362] found substance abuse in the history of seven of the nine cases of maternal incest described; two of the nine were overeaters. Swink, in addition, found that eight of the nine female victims of maternal incest had considered suicide with a seriousness judged to be greater than that for the average incest survivor. Two of the individuals had engaged in self-abusive behavior. Eight of the nine had been involved in abusive relationships.

Vanderbilt[363] described a female, molested by her grandmother, who was suicidal as an adult and who married an abusive man. Vanderbilt also discussed findings of researchers whom she interviewed, including those of Evert, who discovered that almost two-thirds of the women were too frightened of examinations by dentists or by doctors to avail themselves to treatment. Of 93 women surveyed by Rosencrans[364] who were sexually abused by their mothers, 45% had made suicidal gestures as children, 32% had made suicide attempts in adulthood and 34% reported adult self-mutilation. Sixty-three percent had eating disorders in adulthood and 44% had adult substance abuse problems.

Ogilvie & Daniluk[365] described three cases of females molested in childhood by their mothers. Among the forms of self-harm noted in these three cases were suicidal ideation, self-mutilation and substance abuse. Dolan[366] reported that she had used overeating, using alcohol, becoming a "super-achiever" and overworking as coping mechanisms for her own female perpetrated child sexual abuse; she also indicated that she had used painkillers.

Physical Problems

A number of researchers have begun to identify physical problems reported by female victims of female perpetrated child sexual abuse. Of 93 women who were sexually abused by their mothers surveyed by Rosencrans,[367] a number reported physical problems. Migraine headaches and back pain were common. Cardiopulmonary symptoms, digestive disturbances, reproductive and urinary symptoms, conversion or pseudo-neurological symptoms and surgeries were also common.

Among the effects of female perpetrated child sexual abuse reported to Myers[368] by eleven female adults were physical problems. Six of the eleven women reported physical symptoms that they attributed to the abuse. These included an unspecified problem with reproductive organs, a problem with hip joints locking, frequent yeast infections, migraine headaches, ovarian cysts and irregular menstrual cycles, irregular eating patterns and cancer. Multiple aches and pains were noted by one woman.

Mitchell and Morse[369] similarly noted that among the difficulties reported among 80 females who had been sexually abused by a female were a variety of physical problems.

Swink[370] identified physical stress reactions including headaches, which most of the women experienced, neck tension, a spastic colon, leg weakness and tunnel vision among the problems experienced by nine victims of female perpetrated abuse whom she treated.

Sexual and Relationship Concerns among Females Molested by Females

Several researchers have identified relationship problems among females who have been sexually abused in childhood by a female. Problems which have been observed have included concerns related to parenting or the abuse of children, problems trusting and forming relationships, sexual problems, sexual acting out against others and repeated victimization.

Many female survivors of female perpetrated child sexual abuse report problems in relationships. Problems with both male and female relationships were among the difficulties reported by 80 females who had been sexually abused by a female.[371]

Among relationship problems related to female perpetrated child sexual abuse reported to Myers[372] by eleven female adults were problems with trust, identity, setting boundaries and the need to feel in control. Of 93 women surveyed by Rosencrans[373] who were sexually abused by their mothers, problems included conflicts related to dependency and attachment, problems with intimacy and trust and difficulty forming relationships. Ogilvie & Daniluk[374] described three cases of females molested in childhood by their mothers. Among these women, problems with trust in intimate relations and sexual relations were noted, as was sexual acting out.

Among the ten female victims of female perpetrated child sexual abuse interviewed by Paiser,[375] six similarly reported a sense of "neediness," that for many resulted in being willing to engage in relationships that were not always in their best interests. Seven reported difficulties with intimacy; trust in interpersonal relationships was reported by all ten as an issue of great concern.

Swink[376] identified several concerns related to relationships among the nine women whom she treated who had been molested by their mothers. All nine of the women avoided traditional dependent female roles and strived for equal relationships with their partners. Need for great control and difficulties with assertiveness in important relationships were noted as common difficulties. Lack of trust and intimacy were identified as common issues. Eight of the nine had been involved in abusive relationships.

Many researchers have also found sexual problems among women who were molested by women in childhood. Myers[377] reported that all of eleven women that she interviewed who had been molested in childhood by females reported that the abuse affected their intimate and/or sexual relationships. Four had difficulty being sexual at all; five reported that sexual activity was frequently interrupted by flashbacks. Other emotional difficulties with sex were also described by these women including: feeling incompetent during sex, feeling frightened, feeling too intrusive, difficulties "being present" during sexual activity and difficulty setting boundaries.

Among the problems reported to Myers[378] by eleven female adults who had been sexually molested by females in childhood were sexual dysfunction (eleven women) and body-image issues (ten women). One of the women in her sample reported that because she was abused by both a male and a female, she could be involved sexually with neither gender without sexual dysfunction.

Among the sexual problems identified by 80 female victims of female perpetrated abuse by Mitchell & Morse[379] were dissociation during sex, the numbing of sexual organs, inability to achieve orgasm, the need to have fantasies related to punishment to reach orgasm, pain, flashbacks and, for those with dissociative disorders, the emergence of alters. Related sexual problems included the perception that sex was an obligation and the inability to refuse sex, the lack of masturbation, inability to touch breasts or genitals and sexually acting out with a niece.

Among ten female victims of female perpetrated child sexual abuse interviewed by Paiser,[380] concerns related to sexuality were also discovered. Four reported that the most negatively impacted area of life was their sexuality. Difficulties attributed to sexual abuse included the need to dissociate during sexual encounters, anxiety during sex and disinterest in sex.

Mitchell and Morse[381] found that, among 80 women who had been sexually molested by females in childhood, problems included a lack of interest in sex and the sexualization of all relationships. Swink[382] identified sex-role and sexuality concerns among the nine women that she treated. Three of the women had periods of promiscuity, six had periods of a lack of desire for sex, one suffered vaginismus.

Of 93 women surveyed by Rosencrans[383] who were sexually abused by their mothers, 15% had sexually abused others in childhood and three percent had sexually abused children in adulthood. Approximately 70 percent had been sexually abused by someone else in addition to their mothers; in some cases the abusers included maternal grandmothers. Eighty-two percent reported sexual problems in adulthood. Dolan[384] also discussed the results of sexual abuse at the hands of her mother and attributed her subsequent sexual abuse by other individuals, in part, to the maternal incest.

Parenting Concerns

Concerns about ability to parent have also been discovered among women who were sexually abused by women in childhood. Swink[385] found that five of nine women treated for sexual abuse by their mothers made deliberate decisions not to have children in order to prevent their abusing them. The four who had children had a history of having physically abused them. Among the ten female victims of female perpetrated child sexual abuse interviewed by Paiser,[386] six discussed concerns related to parenting; most discussed their feelings of trepidation where their ability to parent was concerned. Myers[387] also reported that of eleven victims of female perpetrated child sexual abuse (whose average age was 31) only one had a child. Three wanted children but were afraid that they or someone else would abuse them and two reported the inability to stay in a relationship as the reason that they did not have children. Seven of the women often considered whether or not they would decide to have children. Ogilvie & Daniluk[388] described three cases of females molested in childhood by their mothers. There was a tendency for the women to have fears and doubts regarding their own competency to mother. Of 93 women surveyed by Rosencrans[389] who were sexually abused by their mothers, seventy-four percent reported that the sexual abuse created problems for them in parenting. As adults, ten percent had physically abused children.

Sexual Identity Concerns

Among women molested in childhood by women, many report sexual identity confusion. Many also report their sexual identity to be lesbian or bisexual. Mayer[390] reported that when females are molested by women, sexual identity confusion is common and that homophobia and fear of homosexuality is common. Among the issues faced by eleven female adult victims of childhood sexual abuse by a female, Myers[391] reported that sexual orientation issues were of concern to seven women. Of 93 women surveyed by Rosencrans[392] who were sexually abused by their mothers, 36% identified themselves as lesbians and ten percent identified themselves as bisexual. Among 80 females studied by other authors who had been sexually abused by a female only 51% of the sample was certain of being heterosexual; some did not desire sex or had gone through periods of celibacy[393] Myers[394] reported that in a sample of eleven women molested by females as children, four were lesbian, two were bisexual, three were heterosexual and two were unstated. Paiser[395] noted that of the sample of ten females, three were lesbian, three were bisexual and one was undecided. Confusion about sexual identity was common.

Swink[396] identified sexual identity concerns among the nine women whom she treated. She noted that women molested by their mothers struggled with the issue of sexual identity and stated that such women take longer to decide upon a comfortable sexual identity than do members of the population at large.

Cameron et al.,[397] for example, found larger numbers of homosexual or bisexual females reporting both advances by and sexual contact with an adult female before the age of 13. Eight percent of the bisexual or homosexual females, as opposed to 0.4% of heterosexual females, reported such advances and five percent of homosexual females, as opposed to 0.1% of heterosexual females, reported actual sexual contact with an adult female.

While it is possible that female perpetrated child sexual abuse creates sexual identity confusion or a leaning towards homosexuality or bisexuality, this cannot be proven from retrospective research. An alternative explanation may be that homosexual females may be more likely to be molested as children by other females.

One study found that of four lesbians, who had sexual contact with a female relative, 75% described themselves as having been actively homosexual before the incestuous contact,[398] suggesting that in some cases of homosexual incest, the homosexuality preceded the incest. It is not clear in this study, however, who initiated this contact; it is possible that the individuals reporting incest may themselves have been the initiators. None of these females reported the incest as negative.

Effects of Female Perpetrated Sexual Abuse on a Child: Consistency of Findings

Evidence concerning the effects that sexual contact with females has upon children is sometimes contradictory. Within the literature on the subject exist several accounts of children who were greatly disturbed by the molestation, while other accounts do not reveal such negative consequences. Browne and Finkelhor[399] on reviewing the literature concluded that sexual molestation by a woman is less disturbing to a victim than is sexual molestation by a man. Finkelhor,[400] for example, described his study in which adult males recounting their sexual experiences before the age of 16, revealed five experiences with older women, only two of which were considered abusive. There is some evidence that abuse by a female may, in some cases, be less damaging (or less likely to be damaging) than abuse by a male, particularly when the victim of the female is a male. There is also evidence to support that in some cases individuals who report sexual molestation by an older female do not perceive the sexual contact to have been harmful. However, there is also a great deal of evidence that sexual abuse by a female has had very negative effects on many individuals.

Particularly when victims are giving a retrospective account of abuse that occurred in childhood, some studies have found that not all males report having been negatively affected by sexual molestation by an older female. A difficulty in assessing the impact of childhood sexual molestation upon males, however, is the suspicion that males are disinclined to reveal emotional vulnerabilities, particularly those resulting from victimization experiences or in matters concerning their sexuality. Several authors have noted that males are culturally inclined to mask negative reactions to trauma, such as fear, anxiety and depression.

Others have argued that cases of female perpetrated child sexual molestation in which damage is done to the child are over-represented in mental health literature. Sexual molestation cases in which little harm is done may not come to the attention of protective or legal authorities or to the attention of mental health professionals. As such they may be less likely to find their way into available documentation and research. Catanzarite and Combs[401] raised the point that the reporting and interpretation of mother-son incest may be more likely to surface when physical or psychological damage has occurred. They noted two cases of males whose maternal incest was revealed in encounter groups who were neither "mentally ill nor physically or psychologically damaged (p. 1808)." Barry and Johnson[402] also reported that a colleague had seen a case of mother-son incest in which there was no evidence of psychopathology on the part of the son.

Similarly, in Elliot's research[403] a man retrospectively described incidents of sexual contact that he experienced with a woman when he was between the ages of 13-15 that he believes were "probably OK, and there certainly was no lasting harm. (p. 164)." He also had earlier sexual contacts with his aunt and her friend who were his caretakers. As an adult, he continued to engage in some of the unusual sexual practices that he engaged in with the caretakers. He attributed these sexual behaviors to the earlier sexual contacts with his caretakers, but not to the later relationship that he believed to be harmless. He reported mixed feelings as to whether or not the earlier experiences were harmful. He was bisexual and had been married three times. Another man who had ongoing sexual relations with both his mother (from age eight until his mid twenties) and his older sister (from age ten continuing through his retirement years), reported that he felt that he had not been harmed by the sexual contact. He reported that neither he nor his sister had emotional aftereffects, and that both had done well in school and successfully married, although they continued to have sex through adulthood. He reported that the sexual contact seemed quite normal.

Some studies have examined the results of child sexual abuse by a female among groups of individuals who have given retrospective accounts of their abuse. While the studies typically find that harm was done to some of the victims, they often find that not all victims report having been harmed. Research is limited in its ability to capture all forms of harm that may result from sexual abuse and there is a suspicion among many researchers that males may underplay the harm that is done. These limitations in mind, some studies have found that not all individuals report having been harmed by child sexual abuse by a female, although many are.

One researcher found that males in general reported having been less harmed by sexual contact in childhood, although the offenders were typically male. Landis[404] reported that college males, in general, report childhood sexual experiences with adults to have been less distressing, than do females with similar experiences. The adult offenders in his study were generally males. Boys reporting childhood sexual contact with an adult "deviate" were more likely to report that they were "interested" or "surprised but not frightened" than were the girls. They were less likely than girls to report that they were "frightened," "shocked" or "emotionally upset." It is unclear whether such differences result from true differences in emotional response to sexual abuse, responses of the males to societal expectations of emotional austerity or differences in the types of sexual contact experienced.

Fritz et al.[405] found that college males who were molested in childhood, the majority by females, tended to be neutral or even positive about their experiences and were likely to view the experience as initiation. Finkelhor[406] similarly reported that women tended to provoke less fear in the children with whom they had sexual contact than did males, based upon a survey of college students who had had such sexual contacts as children. These students were more likely to have been interested by the experience and to report fewer negative feelings about it in retrospect. The majority of individuals who reported having had these experiences were male. He noted that some of the boy's experiences with older women were viewed as "initiation rites" and were viewed positively. When the experiences reported involved force, however, they were more often than not regarded negatively. He reported that the boys tended to have reacted less negatively than the girls, even when their experiences were similar. It is difficult in this study to piece out whether differences in reactions were due to the boy's socialization regarding sexual contact or to the fact that the sexual contact for the females may have involved the stigma of homosexual contact or possibly due to differences in the types of women who seek out boys as opposed to girls for sexual contact.

Haugaard and Emery[407] reported on 101 college students reporting sexual abuse, 13% of whom were abused by a female. These, however, included seven cases of males abused by females who reported the experience to have been positive. Analyzed together with three women who reported their heterosexual molestation to have been positive, this group reported less pressure to participate, having felt less guilt at the time and less severe types of impact. No differences were found between this group and those who reported that their experiences were not positive, in terms of the amount of guilt currently felt and the amount of impact that the experience had on their lives.

With research that identifies harm to the victims based upon their subjective opinions, a limitation is that behavioral problems may not be identified. Some researchers have identified behavioral problems that appear to be tied to sexual abuse by a female among individuals who report that they were not harmed by the sexual contact.

Condy et al.,[408] for example, noted that the experience of having been sexually engaged by an older female was not experienced negatively among all of her subjects, even among those who themselves were imprisoned for a sexual offense. She surveyed men in college and those in prison for a variety of offenses. The experience of having had sexual contact with an older female before the age of 16 was reported to have been "good" by about 51% and 66% of the college and imprisoned men respectively. It was recorded as "bad" in only 25% and six percent of cases and "mixed" in twelve percent and 25% of cases, again of the college and imprisoned men, respectively.

Notably, however, among the incarcerated men, the experience was reported to have been "good" by about 68% of the rapists reporting such experiences and by 50% of the child molesters. The fact that the imprisoned sex offenders denied that the experience had impacted them, in spite of the fact that they had gone on to commit sexual offenses, may support the notion that some males may in fact be harmed by such contacts, but be less likely to acknowledge the sexual abuse as emotionally damaging. About 43% of the prison men and 37% of the college men felt that the experience had had a good effect on their adult sex life. Notably, about 46% of the rapists and 18% of the child molesters felt that the experience had a positive effect upon their sex lives.

Men were also likely to have experienced the contact as "bad" in cases where the offender forced the sexual activity upon them or in cases where the offender was a mother, an aunt or a sister. More positive reactions were noted in cases in which the female was a friend. If the boy was forced, the effect on his adult sex life and his feelings about the event were unfavorable. Condy[409] also noted a trend for sexual contact at a younger age to be associated with a negative effect on adult sex life, though this trend was not statistically significant.

Another study suggests the possibility that some males, who do not perceive early sexual contact with a female as abusive, may nevertheless develop behavioral problems as a result of the experiences. In a study of male delinquents who reported early sexual initiation with a female, Weber et al.[410] reported that only a few such males identified themselves as having been sexually abused. They noted however, that the behavioral aftereffects that they reported resembled those seen in other sexually abused children.

Similarly, Briggs and Hawkins[411] noted that while several males who had been sexually fondled by their grandmothers before the age of six reported the experiences to be "pleasant and harmless," that the experiences led to an obsession with sexual activity, which in turn led to vulnerability to more violent abuse by males. In addition, all of the men who had been sexually molested by their mothers were among the group of sex offenders studied, rather than other members of the sample of male victims of sexual abuse in childhood.

One study examining the impact of maternal incest on children found that all participants experienced the abuse as harmful. Of 93 women surveyed by Rosencrans[412] who were sexually abused by their mothers, forty-four percent reported that the sexual contact had been the most damaging experience of their lives and that they sometimes feared that they would never be able to recover from it. None reported that the sexual abuse had not been damaging. On a five point Likert scale, ranging from one (no damaging impact) to five (most damaging experience of my life, and I sometimes fear I will never be able to recover from it), all of the women chose a three (damaging, but I am hopeful I will recover fully) or higher. Twenty-seven percent rated themselves at three, and 29% as a four. On the same scale, none of nine sons molested by their mothers responded with either a one or a two, indicating that all felt the experience to have been harmful. Eleven percent indicated that the experience had been the most damaging of their lives, with the remaining individuals equally divided between a three and a four on the scale.

In cases in which researchers examine subjects who have more recently experienced childhood sexual abuse by a female, there is sometimes evidence of more significant harm to the victim. However, children that are identified for study are commonly not a random sample and have often been identified by adults as in need of assistance (and thus entered systems such as mental health, child protective services, the court systems, etc.). Ramsey-Klawsnik[413] reported that, in addition to physical injury and disease, child victims of sexual abuse by a female offender displayed several emotional and behavioral problems. She reported upon cases of confirmed sexual abuse by a female in which the child received a mental health evaluation.

She reported upon the symptoms displayed among 24 children abused by both a female and a male and for 19 children abused by only a female. Difficulties noted were as follows: intense fear reactions (54% both, 58% female only), nightmares and sleep disturbances (21% each category), sexualized behaviors (58% both, 53% female only), regressive behaviors (75% both, 26% female only), hyperactivity (46% both, five percent female only), aggressive behaviors and biting (42% both, 32% female only), disturbed peer interactions (58% both, 21% female only), preoccupation with death (13% both, 32% female only). Males were noted to have displayed more symptomatic behavior than did females.

Shrier and Johnson[414] noted in their sample of eleven adolescent boys reporting a history of molestation by females, that 73% reported the immediate effects of such molestation to have been "strong" or "devastating" on a four-point Likert scale (devastating, strong, some effect, not much effect). These boys were identified during a medical examination unrelated to sexual abuse. At the time of the study, 54% reported that the experience continued to have a strong or devastating effect on their lives. Johnson and Shrier,[415] summarizing their observations of the results of sexual abuse on boys (by either a male or a female perpetrator), concluded that "the vast majority of our study group are functioning well overall and are asymptomatic with the exception of mild to moderate impairments in the areas of sexual identity, sexual functioning, self-esteem, and interpersonal relationships (p 652)." They concluded that "childhood sexual victimization, whether by male or female molesters, is a high risk experience that markedly increases the likelihood of acute and future disturbances in important areas of functioning (p. 652). "

Data concerning the consistency with which a child molested by a female will be negatively affected are inconsistent. Current research does not capture all of the possible effects that sexual abuse may have upon a child. Further, the populations surveyed are not random samples. Some have argued that not all children, and particularly not all male children, will be harmed by such contact. Of course, researchers who find that children are not harmed by sexual contact by a female may not have incorporated all types of "harm" into their studies. Regardless of the consistency with which children are harmed by such sexual contact, several deleterious effects upon many child victims of female perpetrators have been noted. These have included a host of emotional, relationship, and behavioral difficulties, sexual dysfunctions and sexual acting out. Sexual identity concerns have also been noted among individuals who have had sexual contact with females in childhood. It is uncertain what percentage of victims will suffer ill effects from female perpetrated sexual molestation. That many do, however, necessitates that those responsible for the well being of children take steps to understand the dynamics of female perpetrated child sexual abuse.

Summary

While women who have contact of a sexual nature with children are scarcely acknowledged in the literature, in recent years there has been growing evidence that they exist and that they are seriously harming at least some of the children with whom they have contact. Individuals who have been sexually molested in childhood by a female may experience a variety of concerns. These may include emotional-behavioral concerns, concerns related to sexuality and relationships and so forth. In some cases the harm done is particularly severe, and includes a variety of psychiatric disorders, self-harm and harm to others. The extent of the trauma that some female perpetrators of child sexual abuse have inflicted upon victims has been greatly overlooked. While it is possible that not all individuals are severely harmed by early sexual contact with a female, many undoubtedly are.

Notes ——————————————————————————

[283] Welldon (1996)
[284] Rosencrans (1997)
[285] Saradjian & Hanks (1996)
[286] Saradjian & Hanks (1996)
[287] Saradjian & Hanks (1996)
[288] Myers (1992)
[289] Mitchell & Morse (1998)
[290] James & Nasjleti (1983)
[291] Saradjian & Hanks (1996)
[292] James & Nasjleti (1983)
[293] Rosencrans (1997)
[294] Kempe & Kempe (1984)
[295] James & Nasjleti (1983)
[296] Roys & Timms (1995)
[297] Roys & Timms (1995)
[298] Margolis (1984)
[299] Masters (1963)
[300] Wahl (1960)
[301] Berry (1975)
[302] Schoenewolf (1991)
[303] Silber (1979)
[304] Harper (1993)
[305] Kempe & Kempe (1984)
[306] Bachmann et al. (1994)
[307] Raphling et al. (1967)
[308] Crewdson (1988)
[309] Quintano (1992)
[310] Schoenewolf (1991)
[311] Chasnoff et al. (1986)
[312] Bass (1991)

[313] Norris (1991)
[314] Peluso & Putnam (1996)
[315] Kasl (1990)
[316] Rosencrans (1997)
[317] Forward & Buck (1978)
[318] Justice & Justice (1979)
[319] Renvoize (1982)
[320] Maltz & Holman (1987)
[321] Kasl (1990)
[322] Rinsley (1978)
[323] Lawson (1991)
[324] Etherington (1997)
[325] Maltz & Holman (1987)
[326] Sarrel & Masters (1982)
[327] Maltz & Holman (1987)
[328] Shrier & Johnson (1988)
[329] Rosencrans (1997)
[330] Rosencrans (1997)
[331] Hunter (1990); Justice & Justice (1979); Maltz & Holman (1987); Margolis (1984); Nasjleti (1980); Raphling et al. 1967; Rosencrans (1997)
[332] Groth (1979a)
[333] Burgess et al. (1988)
[334] Etherington (1997)
[335] Rosencrans (1997)
[336] Briggs & Hawkins (1995)
[337] Weber et al. (1992)
[338] Krug (1989)
[339] Kasl (1990)
[340] Justice & Justice (1979); Berry (1975); Maltz & Holman (1987); Mathis (1972); Margolis (1984); Masters (1963); Renvoize (1982); Wahl (1960)
[341] Krug (1989)
[342] Johnson & Shrier (1987)
[343] Etherington (1997)
[344] Rosencrans (1997)
[345] Cameron et al. (1986)
[346] Barry & Johnson (1958)
[347] Goodwin & DiVasto (1979)
[348] Holubinskyj & Foley (1986)
[349] Cooper & Cormier (1990)
[350] Dolan (1991)
[351] Myers (1992); Paiser (1992); Rosencrans (1997); Swink (1989)
[352] Rosencrans (1997)
[353] Swink (1989)
[354] Swink (1989)
[355] Myers (1992)
[356] Paiser (1992)
[357] Ogilvie & Daniluk (1995)

[358] Mitchell & Morse (1998)
[359] Mitchell & Morse (1998)
[360] Myers (1992)
[361] Paiser (1992)
[362] Swink (1989)
[363] Vanderbilt (1992)
[364] Rosencrans (1997)
[365] Ogilvie & Daniluk (1995)
[366] Dolan (1991)
[367] Rosencrans (1997)
[368] Myers (1992)
[369] Mitchell & Morse (1998)
[370] Swink (1989)
[371] Mitchell & Morse (1998)
[372] Myers (1992)
[373] Rosencrans (1997)
[374] Ogilvie & Daniluk (1995)
[375] Paiser (1992)
[376] Swink (1989)
[377] Myers (1992)
[378] Myers (1992)
[379] Mitchell & Morse (1998)
[380] Paiser (1992)
[381] Mitchell & Morse (1998)
[382] Swink (1989)
[383] Rosencrans (1997)
[384] Dolan (1991)
[385] Swink (1989)
[386] Paiser (1992)
[387] Myers (1992)
[388] Ogilvie & Daniluk (1995)
[389] Rosencrans (1997)
[390] Mayer (1992)
[391] Myers (1992)
[392] Rosencrans (1997)
[393] Mitchell & Morse (1998)
[394] Myers (1992)
[395] Paiser (1992)
[396] Swink (1989)
[397] Cameron et al. (1986)
[398] Simari & Baskin (1982)
[399] Browne & Finkelhor (1986)
[400] Finkelhor (1984)
[401] Catanzarite & Combs (1980)
[402] Barry & Johnson (1958)
[403] Elliot (1993)
[404] Landis (1956)

[405] Fritz et al. (1981)
[406] Finkelhor (1979)
[407] Haugaard & Emery (1989)
[408] Condy et al. (1987)
[409] Condy (1985)
[410] Weber et al. (1992)
[411] Briggs & Hawkins (1995)
[412] Rosencrans (1997)
[413] Ramsey-Klawsnik (1990)
[414] Shrier & Johnson (1988)
[415] Shrier (1987)

6. Childhood Sexual Victimization Histories of Female Sex Offenders

Commonly found in the histories of female child molesters are backgrounds that include severe trauma. Symptoms stemming from a history of personal trauma have implications for the areas of focus of the treatment for female sex offenders (such as self-esteem, guilt, body image, anxiety, depression and the like). In addition, severe trauma has implications for the ability of the female sex offender to participate in the therapeutic process itself. A history of severe trauma may impact multiple areas of functioning that have direct implications for the ability of the offender to participate in the therapeutic relationship.

Among the more common findings by researchers who have investigated the psychosocial histories of female sex offenders is that many of them have been sexually abused in childhood. The sexual abuse in the backgrounds of female sexual abusers is commonly found to be severe along a variety of parameters. It may begin at a young age, involve many or closely related perpetrators, involve more intrusive acts or violence and may occur with frequency or over a long duration. Not uncommonly additional forms of child abuse are found in the histories of women who become sexual abusers, often in addition to childhood sexual abuse. Other forms of family-of-origin dysfunction are also common, as well as other forms of trauma. Abuse in the female sexual abuser's psychosocial history may be found in her adulthood as well.

As research concerning female sex offenders continues, it is possible that subtypes will emerge that tend to have less abuse and pathology in their backgrounds. Given that women are rarely thought of as potential sex offenders, it is quite possible that those currently being identified are those with gross and apparent pathology in their histories or gross and apparent pathology in their behaviors stemming from pathological histories. These women may be among the easiest cases to consider as potential child molesters. Their social presentation or symptom patterns may more readily lead them to be considered as possible abusers. They may be among those who are more likely to come to the attention of researchers in the mental health, child protection and criminal justice fields.

Others with less pathological histories may exist but be less subject to identification. Mathews, Hunter and Vuz,[416] for example, discovered a small group of outpatient adolescent female offenders with less history of psychosocial trauma, who were motivated to offend primarily by curiosity. Faller[417] also found four cases of adolescent female perpetrators who appeared to gravitate to children because of a lack of appeal or access to peers. It may be the case that a history of psychosocial trauma or resulting pathology gives credence to accusations against female offenders, which presently causes them to be more readily identified. This in mind, however, current evidence suggests that therapists should be cognizant of the possibility that the female sexual abusers who come to their attention may have histories of trauma in their backgrounds. They should take note of the common finding that this trauma often includes sexual abuse.

Sexual Abuse in the Backgrounds of Female Sexual Abusers

From Case Studies

Preliminary reports of single cases of females sexually abusing children and adolescents began to trickle in during the 1970's and 1980's. Authors describing these cases frequently observed that these women had their own childhood sexual abuse histories. Justice and Justice,[418] for example, stated that mother-son incest offenders who are promiscuous come from "backgrounds of early sexual stimulation, loose standards in the family, or beliefs that a male must be serviced with sex for him to feel affection for a woman or even to have any interest in her (p. 149)." Meiselman[419] also noted that a mother that molests her son might have incest experiences of her own. Groth[420] described such a case.

As others began to describe cases of women engaging in sexual contacts with children, it continued to be noted that these women who had sexual contacts with children had themselves been sexually abused. Several case descriptions found female sex offenders to have histories of childhood sexual abuse or of incestuous relationships.[421]

Freel[422] described the cases of six female child molesters. Four were sexually abused as children; in an additional case, a female sexual abuser gave birth to the child of her sister's partner, a man who had been violent with her. Chasnoff et al.[423] also reported upon substance abusing mothers who sexually abused their infants. They found that two of the three mothers, though not sexually abused in childhood, had been raped in adulthood.

From Studies of Treatment and Evaluation Groups

Preliminary studies of groups of female sexual abusers have begun to confirm the impressions of those who have written about case studies. Many now believe that a history of childhood sexual abuse may be common among female sexual abusers. Typically, studies have demonstrated that from almost half to nearly all of female sexual abusers have their own histories of sexual abuse. Faller,[424] for example, found that 48% of her evaluation and treatment sample of 40 women offenders had histories of sexual abuse in childhood. Matthews et al.[425] found that all but one of 16 offenders (94%) who were in an assessment and treatment group had histories of childhood victimization. In another group of 17 mothers in an incest treatment program (for whom the background information was available), 76% had childhood victimization experiences and for another twelve percent there were "strong indications" of prior incest victimizations.[426] Wolfe[427] found that 58% of her sample of twelve female sex offenders (which included one offender against an adult) had been sexually abused in childhood. Larson and Maison[428] noted that of 15 sex offenders treated in a prison setting (with an additional women who experienced intense sexual fantasies towards children), ten (66%) had been sexually abused in childhood. Rowan et al.[429] stated that in three of nine cases of women evaluated for having sexually molested children, the women had been sexually molested in childhood. This lower percentage of approximately 33% may be due to the fact that the data were collected by evaluators, rather than a therapist, or may be due to the somewhat smaller sample.

From Surveys, Interviews and Record Reviews

Some data concerning the numbers of female sexual abusers who were themselves sexually abused in childhood were collected not by the primary therapist or evaluator but by researchers who interviewed or surveyed the offenders or who reviewed their legal or clinical records. These researchers have also found that very large percentages of female sexual abusers have sexual abuse histories.

Fromuth and Conn[430] surveyed college women and found that some had had sexual contact with children, primarily when they (the women) were children or adolescents. These women were between the ages of nine and eighteen at the time of their sexual contact with children who were at least five years younger. This study is notable in that none of the experiences had come to the attention of the police or had been discussed with a counselor by the women; 88% had previously told no one of the experiences. Fromuth and Conn[431] nevertheless found that even in these undetected cases, most of the female offenders had sexual abuse experiences themselves. Importantly, they were more likely to have been sexually abused themselves than were the other (nonoffender) female college students. Seventy-seven percent of the offenders had been sexually abused, while 28% of their non-offending college peers had been sexually abused.

Allen[432] found that 72% of 65 female sex abusers, identified primarily through child protective services records, reported that they had histories of having been sexually abused in childhood. In a later study, Pothast and Allen[433] similarly found that among 38 female sex offenders against children, 76% had been sexually abused as children.

Condy et al.[434] found that among 16 women in prison who acknowledged having sexual contacts with boys or adolescents, 81% had themselves had early sexual contact with an older person. Hislop[435] found that of 43 women surveyed in prisons, drug rehabilitation centers and sexual abuse treatment centers, who acknowledged or who had been convicted of sexual contact with children or adolescents, 75% reported their own histories of childhood sexual abuse. Davin[436] similarly found that 78% of 45 imprisoned female sex offenders who offended with a co-offender and 76% of 29 imprisoned female sex offenders who offended independently were themselves sexually abused in childhood.

Green and Kaplan[437] found that their entire sample of eleven incarcerated female sex offenders against children had been sexually abused in childhood. The sample included not only women who had direct sexual contact with children but also women who were co-offenders or accomplices in sexual crimes against children.

Knopp and Lackey[438] collected data from 44 providers of treatment to female perpetrators of sexual abuse. They found that eleven of the nineteen treatment center respondents reported that 100% of their adult female sex offenders had been sexually abused prior to offending.

Saradjian and Hanks[439] reported that among 14 women who sexually offended against young children, all had been sexually abused. Among ten women who offended against adolescents, all had been sexually abused. Among twelve women who had sexually offended with a male co-offender, 75% had been sexually abused. These authors found that the rates of sexual abuse among female sexual abusers were greater than those found among a non-offending group of women, in which only 36% had been sexually abused. They also found that the offenders were more likely to report that they were abused by the one person in childhood who provided attention or affection.

Sexual Abuse among Child and Adolescent Female Sexual Abusers

In some cases, female adolescents and even female children sexually abuse others. As is the case with adults, many of these young females have been found to have histories of their own sexual abuse. Sometimes the adolescent female's personal sexual abuse history is the reason for her initial referral into therapy.[440] Mayer[441] presented case illustrations of eight adolescent females who were among 17 adolescents initially referred for treatment for having been sexually abused, who revealed that they themselves had committed sexual offenses.

Offending may also be discovered first. Fehrenbach and Monastersky[442] found that 50% of 28 adolescent females in a sex offender treatment program were discovered to have themselves been sexually abused. Jackson[443] estimated that 30-40% of adolescent offenders reported having been sexually abused.

Mathews, Hunter and Vuz[444] studied 67 adolescent female offenders from a combined group of both inpatient and outpatient treatment facilities. Seventy-eight percent (52 of the girls) had been molested.

Johnson[445] noted that 100% of a sample of 13 female children who had sexually molested other children had themselves been victims of sexual abuse. Notably, 85% of their molesters had been family members, and of these offenders (against the sexually abusive female children), 23% were women. Mayer[446] reported on six cases of three- to six-year-old children who acted out sexually against other children and/or animals. All had been severely sexually abused at a very young age.

Knopp and Lackey[447] collected data from 44 treatment providers of treatment to female perpetrators. They found that most data collection sites reported that 100% of female perpetrators that they treated across several age groups had themselves been sexually molested. For female sex offenders below the age of eleven, all data collections sites reported that 100% of these young children had been sexually abused prior to offending. Fourteen of the 16 treatment provider respondents reported that 100% of the offenders between the ages of eleven and seventeen had been sexually abused prior to offending.

In related research, Johansen[448] found that in comparison to non-abused children, sexually abused children could be distinguished by their higher frequency of sexual behaviors. Among 23 three to six year olds, she found several sexual behaviors that distinguished (substantiated and suspected) victims from non-victims. Of twelve sexually abused girls, for example, 13% had imitated sexual intercourse, 18% had tried to view pictures of nude individuals, 18% had talked about sexual activities, 30% had masturbated with their hands, 44% had sat with their crotches exposed and 31% were described as sexually aggressive. These behaviors were occurring one to three times or more per month. Additional sexualized behaviors occurred "frequently" (more than once per month) only among the sexually abused females. These included: touching other people's private parts, putting a mouth on other people's private parts, making sexual sounds, asking others to engage in sexual acts, trying to undress others against their will, asking parents to stop sexual behavior and inserting/trying to insert objects into their own anuses or vaginas.

Sexual Abuse of Female Sexual Abusers Suspected by Their Victims

Some authors have noted that it is common for victims of female sexual abusers to have the belief that the women who sexually abused them were themselves sexually abused as children. Paiser[449] made the observation that among the ten female victims whom she interviewed, there were several cases in which the victims believed that their female sexual abusers had themselves been sexually abused. Myers[450] also made similar comments based upon her interviews with eleven women molested in childhood by an older female. Many of the women in Myers's study believed that the female abuser had experienced other forms of childhood abuse as well. Among 93 women who were sexually abused by their mothers, Rosencrans[451] found that 51% thought that these mothers had themselves been sexually abused.

Childhood Sexual Abuse in the Backgrounds of Female Sexual Abusers is Often Severe

Researchers who have examined the nature of abusive sexual experiences in the childhoods of female sexual abusers have often found very severe abuse. Severity of childhood sexual abuse may be considered in several ways. These often include: the intrusiveness of the sexual acts, the frequency of the abusive events, the length of time throughout which they occurred, whether force was used, the relationship to the perpetrator, the age of the child at the onset of the abuse and the number of perpetrators. Recent studies have begun to examine not only the presence of sexual abuse in the childhoods of female sexual abusers, but the severity of that sexual abuse.

Freel[452] commented that of six female child molesters, half had been severely sexually abused in terms of the type of abuse, the length of the abuse, the "nearness" of the abuser and the number of abusers. Two of the female sexual abusers reported sexual abuse by their own mothers. Larson and Maison[453] noted that of 15 sex offenders treated in a prison setting (with an additional women who experienced intense sexual fantasies towards children), seven of the ten who reported childhood sexual abuse had been sexually abused by their fathers.

Hislop[454] found that when sexual abuse was experienced in the childhood of women who had molested children, it was generally severe in nature. Thirty-two of the 43 women studied or 75% reported a history of sexual contact before the age of 16 that was either forced or that involved a person who was five or more years older (with an average age difference of over 18 years). The average age at which the abuse began was seven and a half years. An estimated average of seven and a half years transpired between the first and the last sexually abusive incidents. Fifty-eight percent of the 43 women had been molested by at least one relative or step-relative. Twenty of the women had more than one person sexually abuse them (ranging from two to seven offenders). In 53 of the 74 cases of female-abuser-as-childhood-victim pairings with an offender (72%), the women described the sexual contact as having occurred against their will. In 65% of the 74 pairings, intercourse occurred. Cases of group sex and of anal sex were noted.

Davin[455] similarly found that 78% of 45 female sex offenders who offended with a co-offender and 76% of 29 female sex offenders who offended independently were themselves sexually abused in childhood. These women were among 76 female sex offenders incarcerated in seven states for crimes of child sexual abuse against minors under the age of 18. Parents (natural, step-, adoptive and foster) accounted for 54% of the abusers reported by independent offenders and 37% of the abusers of women who were co-offenders. For 30% of the 29 independent offenders and eleven percent of the 45 co-offenders, the sexual abuse consisted of several acts of sexual intercourse, beginning under the age of ten. The sexual abuse began at an average age of six and a half years for the independent offenders and seven and a half years for co-offenders.

Among the 22 college women who had sexual contact with younger children, while themselves between the ages of nine through eighteen, Fromuth and Conn[456] found evidence of severe sexual abuse. Six of the women had at least two offenders. The women had been sexually abused by family members in 54% of cases, often by cousins. Among those offenders who had been sexually abused, 59% reported at least one experience that had involved force. Twenty-four percent of abused offenders reported at least one abusive relationship that had involved intercourse or oral-genital contact. Eighty-eight percent of the abused offenders viewed their sexual abuse experiences as having been negative.

Among eleven imprisoned female sex offenders, Green and Kaplan[457] also found evidence of severe childhood sexual abuse. All eleven had been abused by family members. Six (55%) reported sexual intercourse with a father or father surrogate. Five offenders were molested by multiple perpetrators. Two were victimized by females, in addition to being molested by males.

Similar results were obtained by Mathews, Hunter and Vuz,[458] who studied 67 adolescent female offenders from a combined group of both inpatient and outpatient treatment facilities. Seventy-eight percent (52 of the girls) had been molested. Of the 51 girls for whom data were provided, seventy-five percent had been molested by more than one offender. Seventy-three percent of the 51 reported the use of force by a molester. The average number of offenders against these adolescents was 4.5. Data available for the 50 of the 52 offenders who reported their own history of sexual abuse indicated that 64% of these offenders/victims had been victimized at or before the age of five. Fifty-eight percent of the 50 sexually abused adolescent female sexual abusers had experienced vaginal or anal rape as a part of their abuse.

Pothast and Allen[459] found that of 38 women who had molested children, 76% had sexual abuse histories of their own. Those with sexual abuse histories in childhood reported a combined total of 67 people who had molested them in childhood, suggesting that many of these women had been sexually offended against by more than one person. Many of the 67 people were relatives. Seventeen percent were fathers or father figures; three percent were mothers; eight percent were siblings (including half-siblings and step-siblings); 18% were other relatives; 55% were non-relatives. Over half of the cases involved sexual abuse more serious than fondling.

Saradjian and Hanks[460] found particularly severe abuse among the 14 women who had sexually offended against young children. All had been sexually abused and the abuse was often severe, beginning in early childhood and lasting many years. Half of these women had been abused into adulthood by their abusers — four had been sexually assaulted on their wedding day. Among twelve women who had sexually offended with a male co-offender, 75% had been sexually abused. Four of these women had been sexually involved with their fathers in relationships they described as loving.

Cautions Concerning Study Comparisons

A difficulty in comparing studies in which child sexual abuse occurs is that there are no standard definitions of child sexual abuse. Studies tend to use different criteria in determining whom to include for the purpose of study, as a child victim or as a perpetrator against a child. Researchers also selectively decide which sexual activities to include as "sexually abusive."

Sometimes study participants are asked through the use of a checklist whether they have participated in any of a number of sexual activities. A particular problem with this method, where the study of female offenders is concerned, is that data have just begun to be explored concerning the nature of the sexual activities that women have with children. Researchers may not be asking the appropriate questions to assess accurately all of the types of sexual abuse that females perpetrate.

In addition to the problem of defining child sexual abuse, researchers typically study only limited groups, such as prisoners, child or adult victims, incest offenders and so forth. Research results may vary among populations studied, and research findings based upon these populations may not generalize well to those female sex offenders who do not enter criminal justice, child protection or mental health systems. No study is known to currently exist that has randomly questioned the female population at large concerning their sexual activities with children. Ethical considerations would require researchers both to safeguard their research participants and to report perpetrators of child abuse. The problems of distorted self-report in these circumstances would make this a difficult undertaking.

Finally, researchers may differ in their methods of collecting data (review of therapy records, interview, survey, review of legal records, etc.) and in the nature of their relationships with the female offender (therapist, investigator, telephone surveyor, etc.). Either of these may impact upon the information revealed.

For these reasons, the studies of the sexual abuse in the histories of female sex offenders are not directly comparable. They serve, rather, to alert those working with females who have sexually abused children that many of these offenders will have sexual abuse histories of their own. This common history variable may provide insight into the motives and the psychological functioning of the female sexual abuser.

Summary

Current research related to female sex offenders is limited in that the samples of these women who have come to the attention of authorities are small and likely to be biased. Research related to the sexual victimization histories of these women is additionally limited by problems in defining sexual abuse. Nonetheless, the conclusion that women who sexually abuse children often have their own histories of sexual victimization is among the more robust findings in studies of this kind. Women who sexually abuse children are commonly found to have traumatic sexual victimization histories. They are often found to have been first abused at a young age, to have been abused by a closely related individual, to have been abused by multiple perpetrators, to have been abused frequently, to have been abused over a long period of time and/or to have experienced intrusive sexual acts as a part of their abuse.

These histories of sexual abuse have implications for multiple areas of functioning in the offenders' lives. A history of sexual abuse often has implications related to the ability of the victimized individual to participate in interpersonal relationships, including the therapeutic relationship itself. This may be particularly true for offenders who have also experienced other forms of interpersonal trauma, and for women who have not had supportive interpersonal relationships, which might mitigate the impact of childhood sexual trauma.

Notes —————————————————————
[416] Mathews, Hunter & Vuz (1997)
[417] Faller (1995)
[418] Justice & Justice (1979)
[419] Meiselman (1978)
[420] Groth (1979a)
[421] Cooper & Cormier (1990); Cooper et al. 1990; de Young (1982); Freel (1995); Higgs, Canavan & Meyer (1992); Korbin (1986); Marvasti (1986); O'Connor (1987); Sheldrick (1991); Travin et al. (1990)

[422] Freel (1995)
[423] Chasnoff et al. (1986)
[424] Faller (1988)
[425] Matthews et al. (1989)
[426] McCarty (1986)
[427] Wolfe (1985)
[428] Larson & Maison (1987)
[429] Rowan et al. (1990)
[430] Fromuth & Conn (1997)
[431] Fromuth & Conn (1997)
[432] Allen (1991)
[433] Pothast & Allen (1994)
[434] Condy et al. (1987)
[435] Hislop (1999)
[436] Davin (1999)
[437] Green & Kaplan (1994)
[438] Knopp & Lackey (1987)
[439] Saradjian & Hanks (1996)
[440] Scavo (1989)
[441] Mayer (1992)
[442] Fehrenbach & Monastersky (1988)
[443] Jackson (1986)
[444] Mathews, Hunter & Vuz (1997)
[445] Johnson (1989)
[446] Mayer (1992)
[447] Knopp & Lackey (1987)
[448] Johansen (1990)
[449] Paiser (1992)
[450] Myers (1992)
[451] Rosencrans (1997)
[452] Freel (1995)
[453] Larson & Maison (1987)
[454] Hislop (1999)
[455] Davin (1999)
[456] Fromuth & Conn (1997)
[457] Green & Kaplan (1994)
[458] Mathews, Hunter & Vuz (1997)
[459] Pothast & Allen (1994)
[460] Saradjian & Hanks (1996)

7. Nonsexual Abuse and Trauma Histories of Female Sex Offenders

Available research supports the premise that females who sexually molest children often have traumatic psychosocial histories themselves. In addition to sexual abuse, chaos in the family of origin is commonly found among females who molest children, as are other types of abuse or neglect. Often the abuse is uncommonly severe in nature. For many female sex offenders, the abuse and dysfunction in families of origin is recreated in their relationships and subsequent families.

Symptoms stemming from personal histories of trauma have implications for the areas of focus for treatment of the female offender (such as esteem, guilt, depression and anxiety and the like). However, severe trauma has implications for the ability of the female offender to participate in the therapeutic process itself. The female offender in treatment may initially lack the ability to form a trusting relationship with the therapist or to attend and learn in the therapy session. She may lack the coping resources and the self-esteem to actively and accurately address offending and victimization concerns. As will be discussed in later chapters, a severe history of trauma may impact upon multiple areas of functioning that have direct implications concerning the ability of the offender to participate in the therapeutic relationship.

Not uncommonly, female child molesters are found to have histories of trauma in childhood. Though perhaps somewhat less common than sexual abuse, researchers and therapists often find physical abuse, neglect, verbal abuse and abandonment in the families of origin of female child molesters. Other forms of family-of-origin dysfunction are common, as well, such as drug and alcohol abuse in the home, spousal battery and multiple parental partners and spouses. Other forms of trauma and dysfunction have also been documented.

Abuse in the female sex offender's psychosocial history is commonly found in her adulthood as well. She may have love relationships in which she is battered, raped or made to sexually abuse children.

It is possible that as the subject of female sex offenders becomes more fully explored in the research literature, subtypes of female offenders will be increasingly discovered for whom there is not a history of trauma. However, given the common finding of trauma in the background of female sex offenders presently being identified, this in an area that should be explored by the therapist who treats the female sex offender.

Childhood Physical Abuse and Other Forms of (Nonsexual) Childhood Victimization Among Female Sex Offenders

While somewhat less frequently observed than sexual abuse in the childhood backgrounds of female sex abusers of children, physical abuse and severe physical discipline have also been observed with some degree of frequency. Several authors have noted childhood physical abuse, as well as other forms of abuse and trauma in the backgrounds of some of the females who molest children. As with sexual abuse, definitions of child abuse may vary between studies.

From Case Studies

Authors reporting on case studies have noted physical and other forms of child abuse in the backgrounds of female sex offenders. Groth,[461] for example, described the case of a 20-year-old single woman who molested her niece; the woman was described as having been a neglected and abused child. Mayer[462] described the cases of eight adolescent female offenders receiving their own sexual abuse treatment. Of these, two had been physically abused. Mayer also described the case of an adult female perpetrator who had been physically abused in childhood and of a second female sex offender who recounted both physical and sexual abuse at the hands of her mother. Higgs, Canavan and Meyer[463] described the case of an adolescent female offender who feared her father's outbursts and displays of aggression; they also noted the medical neglect of a sibling, resulting in severe hearing loss. Freel[464] found that of six female child molesters found in authority records, four had been removed from their homes and placed "in care." Childhood physical abuse, emotional abuse, neglect, threats of violence or witnessing family violence were noted in five of the six cases, generally in addition to sexual abuse. Holubinskyj & Foley[465] reported on the case of a female molested by a mother who had been interned as an adolescent in a Nazi forced labor camp. de Young[466] noted that two of four incestuous mothers whom she interviewed were from disorganized family backgrounds and that both had been incestuously victimized. The families were characterized by economic deprivation, frequent uprooting of the families and multiple marriages of the mothers.

The Committee on Sexual Offences Against Children and Youth[467] described eight cases of female offenders, highlighting some of the types of problems that may be found in their backgrounds. In the first, the female was brought up by an aunt and uncle who were heavy drinkers. The second entered an early marriage after her parents divorced. The third was raised in several condemned homes until a child protection agency assumed custody due to neglect; her father was described as an alcoholic. The fourth was raised by her single mother who received welfare assistance. No background information is available on the fifth. The sixth was sexually assaulted by her father over a period of years. The seventh did not have background information. The eighth was raised in a family in which relationships were poor and in which her father was an alcoholic. The committee concluded that all had come from unstable family backgrounds and that several had gown up in poverty.

From Treatment Samples

Among the female sex offenders seen in treatment are women who report a childhood physical abuse history. Travin et al.[468] noted a history of childhood physical abuse in three of the five cases of females referred to a sex offender program. They noted that a fourth individual had a history of childhood neglect. Regarding an additional four cases of females who committed sex offenses (two cases were of exhibitionism) but who were not convicted of sexual crimes, they commented that all had a history of severe, repeated physical, sexual or psychological abuse or some combination of these. McCarty[469] reported physical abuse in two of seventeen cases of mothers who offended sexually against their children, for whom such data were available.

From Prison Samples

Histories of childhood physical abuse and other sorts of abuse are also commonly found by researchers who survey such histories among incarcerated female sex offenders. Green and Kaplan[470] reported that of eleven incarcerated female sex offenders, five had mothers or maternal care figures who were physically abusive and six had fathers or father figures who were physically abusive. Some had other family members who were physically abusive as well. The offenders had experienced beatings that were given with hands, fists, sticks, belts, belt buckles, broomsticks and shoes. Additionally, three of the eleven female sex offender's mothers and two of the fathers were neglectful, emotionally unavailable or abandoning.

Larson and Maison[471] reported that of the 16 females treated in a prison setting for sexual offenses against children (15 offenders and one case which involved intense fantasy concerning children without an actual offense), three had been physically abused, seven had been emotionally abused and one woman had been neglected by her parents. Additionally, one woman had experienced parental abandonment in her childhood. They remarked that all of the offenders had been physically and/or sexually and/or emotionally abused in childhood.

Davin[472] reported that among imprisoned female sex offenders, many had histories of childhood physical and psychological abuse. Almost 36% of co-offenders and 20% of independent offenders reported that they were often spanked with objects, usually belts, between the ages of birth to thirteen years. Twenty percent of both co-offenders and independent offenders had been psychologically abused.

Other Samples

Histories of physical and other types of abuse are commonly discovered by researchers who examine the backgrounds of female sex offenders from a variety of settings. Allen[473] reported that among 65 reported female sex offenders against children, located primarily through CPS records, many had experienced abuse by their parents during their adolescent years. He reported that 55% had been slapped in adolescence, 45% were hit with an object, 42% were spanked and 40% were pushed, grabbed or shoved. Twenty-two percent had an object thrown at them or had been kicked, bitten or hit with a fist. Twenty-two percent had been beaten up. Three percent had been burned or scalded by their parents in adolescence, five percent were threatened with a gun or a knife and two percent had experienced a gun or a knife being used on them by their parents.

Hislop[474] found that twelve percent of 43 female sex offenders, the majority of whom were imprisoned, with a minority from treatment settings, reported that they themselves were injured by an adult (as badly as "a cut, a bruise, swollen skin or worse") about one to five times in a typical month while growing up. Seven percent said that this occurred ten to twenty times per month and an additional seven percent noted that the event was frequent. Others also reported that this occurred but with less frequency.

Saradjian and Hanks[475] reported that among female offenders against young children, 64% (nine of fourteen) had been physically abused; only 43% (a total of four) had received proper treatment for the injury. Eight of the women were abused regularly throughout childhood and six were abused by more than one person. Ninety-three percent of these 14 women were disciplined through the use of smacking or hitting. Fifty-four percent had been emotionally abused.

These authors also reported that among female offenders against teenagers, 30% (three of ten) experienced physical abuse and only one of these three received proper treatment for the injuries. Eighty percent of these ten women were smacked or hit as discipline. While some of the abusive incidents were serious, none of the women reported that the abuse was a regular occurrence. Forty-five percent had been emotionally abused.

Among female offenders who first offended after having been coerced by a male, 25% (three of twelve) had been physically abused in childhood; only one of the three received appropriate treatment for injuries. Seventy-five percent of the women in this group had been smacked or hit as discipline. Three of the women reported physical abuse by their mothers. Four reported "discipline" by their fathers that left injuries, although none described this discipline as abuse. Forty-three percent had been emotionally abused.

In a control group also used by the authors, only 14% (five of thirty-six) were physically abused with 80% (four of five) receiving proper treatment. Eighty percent of these were hit or smacked as discipline. Physical abuse defined by these authors included bodily injuries such as bruises, cuts, burns, head injuries, fractures, abdominal injuries and poisoning. They found that the women who had been the most frequently physically abused and who had suffered the most severe emotional abuse as children were more likely to sadistically abuse their victims.

From Child/Adolescent Samples

Physical abuse has also been found in the histories of female children and adolescents who commit sexual offenses. Of Johnson's[476] sample of 13 female children who sexually molested other children, four had been physically abused. Fehrenbach and Monastersky[477] found that 21% of 28 female adolescent sex offenders had been physically abused. Mathews, Hunter and Vuz[478] found that among 67 adolescent female sexual abusers who were enrolled in an inpatient or in an outpatient treatment facility, 39 of the 65 for whom data were reported (60%) had histories of physical abuse.

Family Pathology/Instability in Families-of-Origin of Female Sex Offenders

Various types of pathology and family problems have been found in the families-of-origin of females who have sexual contact with children. Groth[479] was among the first to have noted an unstable family life in the case of a female perpetrator. Masters[480] noted that incest may occur in families where the mother or sister is promiscuous or is involved in prostitution or where the son is involved in the father's wage-earner role. Paiser,[481] in studying female survivors of female perpetrated sexual abuse, noted, "The family in which sexual abuse occurs tends to exhibit certain interactional patterns that do not allow the victimized child to grow, separate and move into relationships with the world at large (p. 31)." Poor relationships between the parents of the offenders, generations of abuse, instability and chaos and drug/alcohol problems have all been noted in the family backgrounds of female sex offenders.

Family Pathology/Instability in Cases of Sibling Incest

In cases of sibling incest, poor parental relationships and/or unstable home environments are often found. Justice and Justice[482] described the home in which sibling incest occurs as one in which the condition of the family is chaotic and in which the parents are passive, preoccupied or sexually loose.

Sexual abuse among siblings identified in CPS or District Attorney (DA) files was found by Kercher and McShane[483] to have occurred most commonly when the child was living with only one natural parent and least commonly when the child was living with both natural parents or with neither natural parent.

Smith and Israel[484] found that among 25 families in which there was sibling incest, females were perpetrators against their siblings in 20% of the cases; all had mothers who were engaging in extramarital affairs. They also noted that among the 25 cases of sibling incest, family pathology, including distant inaccessible parents, a history of multi-generational familial sexual abuse, "seductive" or "puritanical" mothers and family secrets were common.

Family Pathology/Instability in Cases of Child Female Offenders

Johnson[485] noted that six of her sample of thirteen female child perpetrators were living with single mothers. Three lived with relatives because their parents were unfit; one lived with a mother and stepfather, one with a stepmother and father. Only one lived with both biological parents, and in this case, she was being molested by her father.

Johnson[486] also noted that the offenders' mothers had series of unsuccessful relationships with men; all but one had experienced physical abuse from at least one man. These mothers of female child offenders were depressed and dependent and had low self-esteem. All but two of the mothers of the female child offenders had been sexually molested themselves during childhood and the remaining two were reluctant to discuss the issue. None of these women had had positive childhoods themselves. The majority of the child offenders' mothers (at least 54%) had had drug or alcohol problems during their daughters' lifetimes. The author noted that the majority of mothers of offenders had discussed their sexual needs and problems with their daughters and that role reversals frequently occurred in the interest of meeting the mothers' dependency needs.

Of the fathers of the child female offenders in this study, five had molested their daughters, one had molested his daughter with his wife, one had left his family during a period when the mother was molesting his daughter and five had never lived with their daughters for a sustained period of time.

The natural fathers were erratic, abrasive, and verbally, emotionally, and/or physically abusive men. They were unable to hold steady jobs and had been involved in illegal activities at least once in their lives. Each had volatile tempers and was emotionally distant from his family-of-origin, and his daughter and her mother... Most were involved in drug and alcohol abuse.[487]

Physical and sexual abuse histories were noted among members of the extended families as well. In 92% of these families, one or more parents or grandparents had been a victim of physical abuse and in 92%, at least one parent or grandparent had been sexually abused.

Higgs, Canavan and Meyer[488] described the case of a single adolescent female offender. They noted that when this offender was three years of age, her mother was hospitalized with manic-depressive illness. She (the offender) was sent to live with both her maternal and paternal grandparents who were "harsh and rejecting."

Ray and English,[489] in describing a sample of sexually aggressive children that included several females, stated, "These children's birth homes were apt to have experienced domestic violence, abuse, and an inability to handle anger productively. Domestic violence was present frequently, and there were confused parent roles (p. 447)."

Family-of-Origin Pathology/Instability: Adult Female Offenders

Similar family-of-origin instability and pathology is often reported by female adult offenders. Cooper and Cormier[490] reported a case of a mother, incestuously involved with her daughter, who was raised in an extremely impoverished and chaotic environment. Additionally, Holubinskyj & Foley[491] reported upon a case study of a female who was abused by her mother who had lost her own family when she was interned in a Nazi concentration camp.

Allen[492] found evidence of possible unstable relationships among the parents of female sex offenders. Of 65 female offenders, largely identified through child protective services records, the mothers of 55% had only one spouse/partner. Twenty-three percent had two, 17% reported three or more and five percent of the offenders did not know how many spouses/partners their mothers had. Of the fathers of these 65 female sex offenders, 51% had only one spouse or partner, 26% had two partners and eleven percent had three or more. Nine percent of the female offenders did not know how many partners or spouses their fathers had had.

Hislop[493] found evidence of possible drug/alcohol abuse and violence in the families of female offenders. Of 43 offenders, 23% reported that drug or alcohol use was a daily occurrence in their family of origin. Seven percent reported that they saw their mothers injured (with "a cut, a bruise, swollen skin or worse") ten to twenty times in a typical month, with twelve percent indicating that this occurred one to five times per month and an additional seven percent indicating that the event was a frequent occurrence.

McCarty[494] similarly noted multiple caretakers (29%), a traumatic breakup of their parents' marriage (41%) and alcoholic parents (29%) in the family histories of offending mothers. In addition, growing up outside of the family home was noted in the background of one offending mother and having had a mentally ill mother was noted in the background of another.

Similarly, among eleven incarcerated female sex offenders, Green and Kaplan[495] reported that only four had grown up in intact families with both parents; mothers of two of the offenders had been battered by their spouses.

Travin et al.[496] found a lack of parental support in the backgrounds of female sex offenders. They noted that in five cases of females who were referred to a sex offender treatment program, none had been able to receive help from her mother or other adult caregivers when she was physically, sexually or psychologically abused during childhood.

Multi-generational abuse is sometimes found in female sex offenders' family histories. Swink's[497] description of nine women who were molested by their mothers included one mother who was abused by her own father and physically abused by her mother.

Current evidence suggests that female child molesters are often raised in unstable families-of-origin. Larson and Maison[498] hypothesized, after intensive study of female sex offenders, that the families of origin of their sample of female offenders helped them to develop the ability to commit sexual offenses.

Freel[499] noted that among six females who molested children, four had spent parts of their childhood in out-of-home placements, "in care." Among the problems noted in the families of origin of these child molesters were multiple marriages and relationships of the mother, psychosomatic illness of the mother, parental fighting and violence, violence from older siblings and maternal mental health problems

Long-standing relationship problems are often found to be the norm among female sex offenders. Saradjian and Hanks[500] found that none of the female offenders against both very young children or against adolescents remembered having ever been cuddled or physically comforted by any individual who did not also sexually abuse her. While somewhat less pronounced, this was also a theme among women who were coerced into offending by a male co-offender. Each of the female offenders with siblings recalled being the most unloved and most harshly treated of the children. Very few had positive relationships with their siblings. Very few of the offenders, and none of the offenders against very young children, had friendships during childhood.

Available evidence, for the most part, consists of data for offenders who have been processed through child protection or legal avenues or who have come to the attention of mental health professionals. These may not be representative of women who have sexual contact with children that goes undetected.

An exception to the normal way of finding sexual offenders was the sample of college students described by Fromuth and Conn.[501] These authors did not find differences between perpetrators and non-perpetrators on family background measures. The 22 female offenders in their study had never been reported to the police and had never discussed their offending experiences with a counselor. Most had not told anyone about their offenses, which they had perpetrated between the ages of nine and eighteen. The authors did not find differences between college females with and without a history of sexual contact with children in terms of their scores on the Parental Support Scale or the Parental Bonding Instrument.

Husbands and Mates of Female Child Molesters

What literature is available concerning female child sexual molesters suggests that many have difficulties or may experience further trauma in their relationships with spouses or mates. They may have difficulty forming or sustaining love relationships. Sometimes, the women do not have a primary or love relationship with an adult at the time of their involvement with children and are sometimes using a child or an adolescent as a primary partner. Love relationships of the female sex offender are often not stable, and in cases where the female offender has an ongoing mate, the relationship is often tumultuous. In many cases the partner has a drug or alcohol problem or is physically or sexually abusive toward the woman or towards her children. In some cases, women fearing such brutality become sexually involved with their children as a result of having been coerced by their partners.

Case Studies

That female perpetrators have difficulties with their marriages or romantic relationships has been noted in the discussions of several cases of female offenders. Some female perpetrators are reported to be experiencing difficulties or abuse in their primary love or marital relationship[502] or divorce[503] at the time of their perpetrations. Larson and Maison[504] reported that of 16 women treated for concerns related to sexual offending in a prison setting, the women were often victims of physical and sexual abuse within their marriages. Grayson[505] quoted researcher Larson as saying, "For some of these women, sex with a child was the nicest and only non-violent sex they had known (p. 10)."

A variety of problems have been noted between female sex offenders and their mates. Some have mates who are alcoholic.[506] Holubinskyj & Foley[507] reported upon a case of a female offender who was distant from her husband, who was chronically ill. Freel[508] noted the case of a female child molester whose mate committed suicide. Cooper and Cormier[509] reported on an incestuous mother who had six children with different fathers. Freel[510] observed a female child molester who had five children with four partners. Violence towards female child molesters by their male mates was noted in three of six cases.

Some female sex offenders are reported to be living without a mate or with a physically or psychologically absent mate at the time of their offenses[511] and may use an adolescent or male child to fulfill the role of husband or mate. Intrusiveness into the lives of their sons by incestuous mothers has been noted by some authors.[512]

Some authors cite the absence of a spouse as a risk factor for mother-son incest. Masters[513] cited rejection by a marriage partner as a possible contributor to incestuous relations. Bachmann and Bossi[514] described mother-son incest as a symbolic indicator for the mother's longing for the absent partner. Lawson[515] noted that in mother-son incest absence of a mate is a risk factor, as it leaves the mother's emotional and sexual needs unmet and intensifies the mother-child relationship without mitigation. It further leaves the male child unprotected and vulnerable to displays of seduction towards men. Kasl[516] noted that women are socialized to be dependent upon men and to feel incomplete without a man. In the absence of a male partner, they may turn to a son or younger male. James and Nasjleti[517] also noted that a spousal relationship that is emotionally empty or absent is common to women who molest their children and noted that they may place their sons in the husband role and vice versa. Elliot[518] described a case of a male who began incestuous contact with his adopted mother after she was left by her husband and was devastated.

Some female perpetrators commit their offenses with their mates.[519] Some female offenders are reported to be generally promiscuous[520] or to have a history of several marriages.[521] Many authors who have examined cases of female sex offenders against children have found an absence of a positive primary love relationship or a love relationship that is highly dysfunctional.

One study highlights the variety of problems within the primary love relationship that has been found in the histories of female sex offenders. The Committee on Sexual Offences Against Children and Youth[522] reported upon eight female sex offenders. One married twice and committed the sexual acts with her second husband. Another was married twice, the first time at the age of 16. The fourth was married twice, with the first marriage ending in divorce and the second ending with the death of her husband shortly after the wedding. The fifth offended with her partner. The seventh was married twice and offended with her second husband, who had a long criminal record. The eighth was married twice and offended with her second husband. The remaining offenders were juveniles.

The committee concluded that six of the eight had broken marriages and/or several sexual partners.

Reports of Multiple Forms of Pathology Between Female Offenders and their Mates

Several authors have examined groups of female sex offenders and their relationships with their mates or husbands and have commented on several forms of problems in large percentages of these relationships. Many find that some of the women do not have a primary love relationship at the time of their offenses. A healthy love relationship at the time of offending appears to be unusual among the female sex offenders studied to date.

Hislop[523] found that thirty-four percent of 35 women reported that the typical state of their love lives at the time of their offenses was to have had a negative relationship. Eleven percent indicated that is was typical for them to have just ended a relationship and nine percent indicated that it was typical not to have been involved with an adult or same-age love relationship for over a year during their offenses. Only three of the 35 women (nine percent) indicated that they were involved in a good relationship. Others responded to the question idiosyncratically, generally indicating that they were not in a good relationship at the time of their offenses.

Rowan et al.[524] reported that in some cases women sexually abused their victims with a male who was often a mate. In six of nine cases of sexual abuse of children by women, the female had acted in the company of a dominant male. They described one case of a female who assisted a male in raping a 13-year-old girl out of fear that this alcoholic boyfriend would beat her if she refused. Several other authors have also described cases of women who sexually abuse children in the context of having been forced by a male partner.[525] Saradjian & Hanks[526] reported that among women who offended with the man who coerced them, the majority were cohabiting with the man. Most of the women who offended on their own lived alone at the time of their offending.

McCarty[527] reported marital crises, early marriages, multiple marriages and promiscuity among female sex offenders. She noted unstable relationships among mothers who were incest offenders. She noted that 42% of the independent offenders and 56% of the co-offenders had histories of "sexual indiscretions" with men. Two co-offenders and one independent offender had a history of prostitution. de Young[528] noted that two of four incestuous mothers escaped abusive homes by entering early marriages.

Among a sample of convicted female sex offenders against children, motivations cited for the offenses included factors related to chaotic love relationships. O'Connor[529] noted fear of being beaten by a boyfriend, boredom following a broken marriage (complicated by drug and alcohol abuse) and revenge against an unfaithful husband as motives listed by convicted female sex offenders against children. He also noted two cases of female offenders whose husbands were both physically and sexually violent towards them and who were additionally alcohol and/or drug abusers. One case is noted of an offender who was married to a man who beat her and who became a chronically mentally ill patient.

Abandonment, violence and alcohol abuse by some of the men chosen as partners by maternal offenders was described by Swink.[530] She described several cases of females who were molested by their mothers, some of whom gave retrospective information related to their mothers' relationships. Among nine cases of females molested by their mothers were two cases in which the mothers' husbands left the family and four cases in which the husbands were alcoholics. Additionally, one of these mothers had a boyfriend who physically and sexually abused her children; one had a husband who had sexual affairs with men, women and their children's friends; one of the husbands physically and sexually abused the children and had affairs; one of the husbands was physically abusive towards the children; and one of the husbands sexually abused the children.

Marital Status, Number of Mates/Partners

Many researchers examining the relationships of female sex offenders find that their relationships, in addition to containing multiple forms of pathology, are often unstable. Many find that female sex offenders have multiple marriages or multiple sexual relationships. It is apparently rare for a female sex offender to have a single marriage that is stable and healthy.

Allen[531] did not find evidence of stable, monogamous relationships among the majority of female sex offenders. The mean number of spouses or live-in relationships reported by the female offenders in his study was two, with a range from zero to seven. Twenty-six percent had only one sexual partner (not including the victims) during the previous five years, while nine percent had had more than ten partners. The mean number of partners was 3.6.

Harper[532] found that of seven mothers who molested their children, there was a history of serial or de facto relationships in the case of five. She noted that the interpersonal relationships of these offenders tended to be dysfunctional.

Hislop[533] found that offenders often reported large numbers of adult male sexual partners, as well as adult female sexual partners. Often their stated sexual preference was inconsistent with their reported history of actual sexual activities. Only twelve percent reported a single marriage or history of having lived with a single lover; 30% reported two such pairings; two percent reported that they had never been married or lived with a lover. The majority had three or more marriages or "live-ins."

McCarty[534] reported that 85% the women in her sample of maternal incest offenders had married in their teens, with 31% married at age 15 or younger. Co-offending mothers usually were in their second or third marriage. The independently offending mothers were often experiencing a crisis in their marriage at the time of their offenses.

Kercher and McShane[535] found that the majority of female offenders identified through CPS and DA records were unmarried: 37% of the females were single, 26% were separated or divorced, 26% were married and one (three percent) was in a common law marriage. The marital status of the others was unknown.

Wolfe[536] similarly noted that many offenders were unmarried and/or were in dysfunctional relationships. Three of twelve female sex offenders in her sample were divorced, three were single and six were married. Three offenders against children, and one offender against an adult indicated that they committed their offenses in compliance with the desires of a male on whom they depended for survival.

Green and Kaplan[537] reported that many female offenders were unmarried and/or had been in abusive relationships. Six of the eleven had never been married.

Larson and Maison[538] also noted that of 16 women treated in a prison setting (15 for sexual abuse of children or adolescents, one for intense sexual fantasies involving children), two were divorced, three were never married, ten were married and for one there was no information. Eight of the women abused the children in concert with their husbands

While multiple partners and break-ups with partners appear to be problematic among groups of female sex offenders, it is important to recognize that most studies do not compare groups of female sex offenders to other groups of women. Thus, while it is likely that problems with male relationships often exist among female sex offenders, it is not clear whether these problems exceed those of groups of women found in the same populations as the female sex offenders. For example, Saradjian & Hanks[539] reported that the female offenders in their study had fewer adult sexual partners than did a comparison group. They noted, however, that all of the offenders had been extensively physically, sexually and/or emotionally abused in their relationships with their adult partners.

Studies of the Physical Abuse Husbands/Mates Commit on Female Sex Offenders

Several authors have commented specifically on the finding that physical abuse of the female offender by her male partner is not an unusual experience among groups of female sex offenders. Many female sex offenders have suffered from physical abuse at the hands of those whom they have chosen as mates.

Allen[540] found evidence of physical abuse to be common between female sex offenders and their spouses or live-in mates. He reported that fifty-four percent of female offenders had been pushed, shoved or grabbed by their spouse;

23% had been beaten up by the spouse; 15% had been threatened with a gun or knife; 28% had been kicked, bitten or hit with a fist; 28% reported that a spouse had thrown something at them; 18% had been hit with something; five percent had been burned or scalded; and three percent had had a gun or a knife used on them by a spouse or partner. The female offenders had also harmed their spouses. Green and Kaplan[541] reported that many female offenders had been in abusive relationships. Of eleven incarcerated female sex offenders, eight had been physically assaulted by their boyfriends.

Larson and Maison[542] reported that of 16 women treated for concerns related to sexual offending in a prison setting, the women were often victims of physical and sexual abuse within their marriages. As stated earlier, Grayson[543] quoted researcher Larson as saying, "For some of these women, sex with a child was the nicest and only non-violent sex they had known (p. 10). "

Saradjian & Hanks[544] reported that all of the eleven female sex offenders in their study had been extensively physically, sexually and/or emotionally abused in their relationships with their adult partners. They often married or formed relationships in order to escape their families of origin. They found that among offenders against young children, 64% were hospitalized at least once due to their partner's violence. In spite of this, none had ever left a partner; relationships ended when the men left.

Summary

Available data suggest that many female child molesters have great difficulty in their primary love relationships. They are often without a primary love relationship. They may also be emotionally disenfranchised from their current partner or spouse or may have a history of several spouses or partners. At times a crisis in a relationship with a mate may precipitate the sexual offense. In those cases in which a female offender has a primary love relationship, the relationship is often highly dysfunctional. Commonly found among the mates of female sex offenders are men who are physically, sexually or emotionally abusive towards the woman or her children, or men with alcohol or drug problems. The female sex offender may also be abusive towards her partner.

Conclusions such as these, it must be noted, have been based upon findings primarily from populations of offenders who have come to the attention of authorities or mental health practitioners. As such, they may not be representative of all women who offend against children, but whose crimes do not come to the attention of the authorities. It may be the case that women who exist in highly dysfunctional environments are more likely to be investigated when a charge of sexual abuse is made against them. Little is known about the relationships of female sex offenders who escape the attention of authorities.

[461] Groth (1979a)
[462] Mayer (1992)
[463] Higgs, Canavan & Meyer (1992)
[464] Freel (1995)
[465] Holubinskyj & Foley (1986)
[466] de Young (1982)
[467] Committee on Sexual Offences Against Children and Youth (1984)
[468] Travin et al. (1990)
[469] McCarty (1986)
[470] Green & Kaplan (1994)
[471] Larson & Maison (1987)
[472] Davin (1998)
[473] Allen (1991)
[474] Hislop (1998)
[475] Saradjian & Hanks (1996)
[476] Johnson's (1989)
[477] Fehrenbach & Monastersky (1988)
[478] Mathews, Hunter & Vuz (1997)
[479] Groth (1979a)
[480] Masters (1963)
[481] Paiser (1992)
[482] Justice & Justice (1979)
[483] Kercher & McShane (1985)
[484] Smith & Israel (1987)
[485] Johnson (1989)
[486] Johnson (1989)
[487] Johnson (1989), p. 575
[488] Higgs, Canavan & Meyer (1997)
[489] Ray & English (1995)
[490] Cooper & Cormier (1990)
[491] Holubinskyj & Foley (1986)
[492] Allen (1991)
[493] Hislop (1998)
[494] McCarty (1986)
[495] Green & Kaplan (1993)
[496] Travin et al. (1990)
[497] Swink's (1989)
[498] Larson & Maison (1987)
[499] Freel (1995)
[500] Saradjian & Hanks (1996)
[501] Fromuth & Conn (1997)
[502] Bachmann et al., 1994; Groth (1979a); Lukianowicz (1972); Margolis (1984); Marvasti (1986); Travin et al. (1990); Wahl (1960); Weinberg (1955)
[503] Maltz & Holman (1987)
[504] Larson & Maison (1987)
[505] Grayson (1989)
[506] Bachmann et al. (1994); Freel (1995)

[507] Holubinskyj & Foley (1986)
[508] Freel (1995)
[509] Cooper & Cormier (1990)
[510] Freel (1995)
[511] Dolan (1991); Groth (1979a); Hindman (1989); Justice & Justice (1979); Lukianowicz (1972); Margolis (1984); Marvasti (1986); Mayer (1983); Meiselman (1978); Shengold (1980); Swink (1989); Weinberg (1955)
[512] Berendzen & Palmer (1993); Hindman (1989)
[513] Masters (1963)
[514] Bachmann & Bossi (1993)
[515] Lawson (1991)
[516] Kasl (1990)
[517] James & Nasjleti (1983)
[518] Elliot (1993)
[519] Davin (1998); Freel (1995); Larson & Maison (1987); McCarty (1986); Rowan et al. (1990); Wolfe (1985)
[520] Groth 1979a; Lukianowicz (1972); Wahl (1960); Weinberg (1955)
[521] Freel (1995); McCarty (1986); Wahl (1960); Weinberg (1955)
[522] Committee on Sexual Offences Against Children and Youth (1984)
[523] Hislop (1998)
[524] Rowan et al. (1990)
[525] Davin (1998); Faller (1988); Larson & Maison (1987); Matthew, Mathews & Speltz (1989); McCarty (1986); Saradjian & Hanks (1996); Swink (1989); Wolfe (1985)
[526] Saradjian & Hanks (1996)
[527] McCarty (1986)
[528] de Young (1982)
[529] O'Connor (1987)
[530] Swink (1989)
[531] Allen (1991)
[532] Harper (1993)
[533] Hislop (1994)
[534] McCarty (1986)
[535] Kercher & Mc Shane (1985)
[536] Wolfe (1985)
[537] Green & Kaplan (1993)
[538] Larson & Maison (1987)
[539] Saradjian & Hanks (1996)
[540] Allen (1991)
[541] Green & Kaplan (1993)
[542] Larson & Maison (1987)
[543] Grayson (1989)
[544] Saradjian & Hanks (1996)

8. Diagnoses and Co-morbid Problems Common to Female Sex Offenders

Psychological Difficulties of the Female Offender

Several authors have found that women who commit sexual offenses have a variety of psychological disturbances. It is unclear, based on currently available research, whether those offenders are representative of all female sex offenders. It may be the case that women who commit sexual offenses but who do not exhibit gross pathology in other areas of their lives are never identified for research through the common channels. For example, they may elude the criminal justice, child protection or mental health institutions through which most female sex offenders reported upon to date have been identified.

Case studies that appeared in the early literature concerning women who commit sex offenses often described women who had very serious disturbances, or who were psychotic. For example, several of the currently available mother-son incest case studies came to the attention of investigators because the mother or son was involved in psychiatric treatment or had come into trouble with the law.[545] More recent literature, however, has described a more heterogeneous population with respect to psychological functioning. While females who commit sexual offenses against children may demonstrate a wide array of disturbances, those who exhibit overtly psychotic symptoms appear to be in the minority. It is likely that those who were psychotic or severely impaired were among the most likely to become identified as female sex offenders.

A variety of psychological problems are commonly found among populations of female sex offenders, although not all female sex offenders meet diagnostic criteria for a psychiatric diagnosis. Recent studies have begun to estimate the numbers of female sex offenders who carry mental health diagnoses, although this research is severely limited by the fact that those who are the more severely disturbed may also be more likely to be identified as offenders. O'Connor[546] noted that 48% of 25 British women convicted of indecent assault on persons under 16 or of gross indecency with children had a history of a psychiatric diagnosis and treatment. Hislop[547] surveyed female offenders from a variety of sources, the majority of whom were not previously identified as such by authorities. Of the 43 (predominantly incarcerated) female sex offenders providing background data, Hislop[548] found that 21 (49%) had a history of using psychiatric medication. Twenty-two (51%) had a history of having been treated in a psychiatric hospital. Not uncommonly, the women had been both hospitalized and placed on medication at some point in their lives; such was the case for 17 of the 43 women (40%). Only 17 of the women (40%) had neither been hospitalized nor placed on psychiatric medication.

Researchers reporting on female sex offenders who have come to the attention of authorities commonly report a variety of mental health concerns. Various personality disorders are also found among identified female sex offenders. Consistent with the common finding of physical and sexual abuse in their histories, many female sex offenders are found to be suffering from post-traumatic stress or, occasionally, from dissociation. Depression and anxiety disorders appear to be common problems. Numerous authors have commented that many female sex offenders have drug or alcohol problems.

Several authors have also remarked upon the general dysfunction in the lives of female sex offenders. For example many have observed that they may achieve (educationally and vocationally) below their levels of ability, that they are highly dependent upon others, that they have poor social skills and that their life styles are frequently chaotic. Some female sex offenders are observed to be intellectually limited.

Importantly, however, not all female child molesters have such obvious pathology. Paiser[549] noted that some maternal incest offenders were highly esteemed members of their communities and were quite functional. These offenders were described by her subjects, who had been victims. The offenders, therefore, were not necessarily among the pools of disturbed or criminal populations who typically come to the attention of researchers. Similarly, Mitchell & Morse[550] surveyed 80 women who had been sexually molested by females and found situations in which the female offenders were of upper or middle class. Finkelhor, Williams and Burns[551] reported upon cases involving sexual molestation in day care centers, in which cases the women involved were generally employed in the child care industry. Saradjian and Hanks[552] reported on a case of a female sex offender with ties to aristocracy. Among eight adolescent female offenders, Turner and Turner[553] noted that one carried no mental health diagnosis. Very little is known about women who have sexual contact with children, but who do not come to the attention of child protective services, the criminal justice system or mental health services. The women who escape the attention of these systems are likely to be more highly functioning individuals.

A recent study examined female child molesters who were identified in a population of college students. None of the women in the study had been questioned by the police. Fromuth and Conn,[554] the researchers, discovered 22 women who had had previous sexual contact with younger children (at least five years younger) when they themselves were between the ages of nine and eighteen. That they were all college students indicated a degree of psychosocial functioning among these women. The authors did not find differences between these women and their college peers on the Global Severity Index of the Hopkins Symptom Checklist (SCL-90). In at least some cases, women with a history of sexual abusing may not have psychological problems that are readily measurable and may have adequate levels of psychosocial functioning. When female abusers are less overtly disturbed, and perhaps able to demonstrate more conventional functioning and greater intelligence, they may tend to escape detection.

This in mind, it may be useful for the clinician who is evaluating the female offender to be aware of those disorders which have been previously found among female offenders. Several psychiatric diagnoses have been commonly found among identified populations of female child molesters.

Schizophrenia and Psychotic Disorders

Though not so common among female sex offenders as might be expected, given the reports in early case studies, schizophrenia and other psychotic disorders have nonetheless been found among a minority of female sex offenders. Psychotic disorders, such as schizophrenia, involve a loss of touch with reality and may include such symptoms as delusions, hallucinations or disordered behavior and thinking.

Early case studies sometimes included descriptions of sexual offending among women who were schizophrenic. Lukianowicz,[555] for example, noted a case of mother-son incest in which the mother was schizophrenic and also of limited intelligence. Mathis[556] also reported upon a case of mother-son incest in which the mother was both psychotic and moderately mentally retarded; he felt that mothers who had sexual contact with their sons had "an emotional disturbance of psychotic depth (p. 135)," were mentally retarded or had organic brain damage that impaired impulse control and the ability to think clearly.

Caution must be taken in the evaluation of psychosis among female sex offenders, however. Saradjian & Hanks[557] cautioned that some female offenders may be classified as psychotic on the basis of their sexual behavior alone, rather than a proper psychiatric examination. Such was suggested in a case study by Berry[558] of a male whose relationship with his mother had been sexualized but did not include direct sexual contact: "...the extraordinary overt sexual seductiveness of the mother suggests psychotic impairment (p. 154)." Saradjian & Hanks[559] further noted that women may justify their offenses by a claim of mental illness at the time of their offenses.

Where groups of female sex offenders have been studied, psychotic disorders are sometimes found, but not typically among the majority of offenders. O'Connor,[560] for example, noted that of the 19 British women who had committed indecent assaults against children under the age of 16, one carried a diagnosis of schizophrenia. Of six who had committed indecencies with children, one was schizophrenic and one had a schizoaffective disorder; both had been hospitalized for psychiatric treatment.

Others have also noted psychotic disorders among the minority of female sex offenders in their samples. Among groups of female offenders who have been identified as such, preliminary studies have often found somewhere in the neighborhood of one in ten to be psychotic or schizophrenic. It is likely that this approximate ratio will decrease as society becomes increasingly able to recognize the female child molester among groups of women who do not have obvious and severe pathology.

Several researchers have found schizophrenia among a minority of females who have molested children. Rowan et al.[561] commented that among nine cases of females evaluated for sexual offenses against children, one was diagnosed as schizophrenic. Wolfe[562] found that only one of twelve female sex offenders was mentally ill, suffering from schizophrenia. Harper[563] found that of seven mothers who molested their children, two had a schizophrenic illness. Swink[564] described the cases of nine women sexually abused by their mothers; one of these maternal offenders had had a psychotic break. Turner and Turner[565] reported upon eight adolescent females who molested children, one of whom was schizophrenic. Faller[566] found that 48% of the 40 female child molesters in her study had mental difficulties; of these, 18% had suffered at some time from psychosis. In her 1995 report, she indicated that of 72 female child molesters, 23 women (32%) had psychosis or severe depression. In three of the women, delusions appeared to precipitate the sexual abuse.

In a study that specifically examined females with psychiatric difficulties, a small number of women with psychotic disorders were also found to have molested children. In evaluating individuals who were referred because of psychiatric difficulties, Travin et al.[567] discovered four individuals who had acted out sexually against children either with direct sexual contact or with exhibitionism; one was an individual with paranoid schizophrenia and one was an individual with schizoaffective disorder.

Condy et al.[568] are among the only researchers who have reported upon females who had not necessarily come to the attention of authorities for their sexual contacts with young males. They found that prison women who had been sexually involved with boys and adolescents scored higher on the Schizophrenia and Hypomania Scales of the Minnesota Multiphasic Personality Inventory (MMPI) Mini-Mult than did non-involved prison women, but by less than one standard deviation. They concluded that while elevations on these scales are associated with unconventional lifestyles and socially inappropriate behaviors, the bulk of the evidence did not suggest that psychosis is typical among these women. Again this suggests that women who have not been discovered for their offenses may be among the less overtly disturbed of the female child molesters.

For women who are schizophrenic, sexual pathology may be a function of the psychotic disorder. Arieti[569] documented sexual changes that occurred in some female patients who were diagnosed with schizophrenia. He noted that promiscuity and obvious seduction became more common. He commented on the increasing role of sexual symbolism in the delusions and ideas of reference for some patients with schizophrenia. He noted other sexual changes in these women, including the observation that some female patients began to have vaginal orgasms after recovering from psychosis, when they had previously been able to achieve only clitoral orgasms. It is possible that some women who are psychotic molest children as a function of their disorder.

In a similar study, Saba, Salvadorini, Galeone, Pellicano & Rainer[570] described the treatment of four women who were schizophrenic with sexual delusions and erotic aggressiveness; two were homosexual. After a 30-day period of treatment with cyproterone acetate, three of the women showed a reduction in hypersexuality.

Depression and Other Mood Disorders

Mood disorders are commonly observed in case studies of female child molesters. Given the extent of abuse and the number of traumatic life events that are common to this population, the frequent observation of problems with depression is not unexpected.

Depression has been documented in several case studies. Lukianowicz[571] noted a case of mother-son incest in which the mother was depressed and a case of aunt/nephew incest in which the aunt was hypomanic. Depression and violence on the part of the female offender have been noted in a case study by Shengold.[572] Groth[573] similarly noted depression and rage in the case a female perpetrator. Mayer[574] described a case of an adult female offender with a low IQ, as having been diagnosed with depression. Cooper, Swaminath, Baxter and Poulin[575] described a case in which ongoing depression was a problem for a 20-year-old female sex offender, in addition to her other psychiatric problems.

Clinical impressions that female child molesters might often be depressed, based upon case studies, have been supported in research regarding groups of female child molesters. Depression is commonly found among groups of female child molesters. O'Connor[576] noted that of 19 women who had committed indecent assault against children under the age of 16, five carried diagnoses of depression. Swink[577] described the cases of nine women sexually abused by their mothers; one of the mothers saw a psychiatrist for depression and one, who had been in treatment with a psychiatrist, made suicide attempts. Travin et al.[578] noted that in one case (among five) of a woman referred for having sexually molested, the woman was depressed, anxious and dependent. Green and Kaplan[579] reported that among eleven incarcerated female child molesters, seven experienced either a past or current episode of major depression.

Whereas these studies examined diagnoses among women who were known to be child molesters, another study did the reverse. It was discovered that among groups of women with (more severe) psychiatric disorders related to depression (together with other disorders), that some of the women had molested children. In evaluating individuals who were referred for psychiatric difficulties, Travin et al.[580] included observations of four individuals who acted out sexually against children (either with direct sexual contact or with exhibitionism); one was an individual with severe bipolar disorder and one had schizoaffective disorder.

Evidence of depression among female sex abusers has been documented in at least one study using psychological testing. Woodring[581] found evidence of depression, anxiety and vague physical complaints among independently offending, incarcerated female sex offenders, based upon psychological testing.

Depression and anxiety have also been found among populations of female children and adolescents who sexually molest other children. Johnson[582] noted that in her sample of 13 female children who were offenders, all were depressed and anxious. Mathews, Hunter & Vuz[583] found that among 67 adolescent female sex offenders from a combination of an inpatient and an outpatient setting, a mood disturbance "(e.g., depression, anxiety)" was present in over half.

It is possible that the different depressive disorders may relate in different ways to the molestation of children by the women who have the disorders. For example, the manic phases of bipolar disorder have often been associated with hypersexuality. In 1973, in discussing offenders who were made the subject of hospital orders, Walker and McCabe[584] reported upon the case of a 70-year-old manic depressive woman who seduced three boys of age roughly 14. Lawson[585] described the case of a 50-year-old woman with bipolar disorder who ran naked on the beach during a manic episode, shouting obscene remarks to young men along the way, suggesting that they were not "up to the mark" for failing to have intercourse with her. She had other common symptoms of mania, including reckless driving, grandiose behaviors (she had started three books) and so forth.

As with schizophrenia, the manic phase of bipolar disorder may be associated with abnormal sexual functioning for some individuals and may place the female at a higher risk of child molestation in some cases. Delusions, hallucinations or disordered thinking may also contribute to offending among those depressed individuals with psychotic symptoms (as in bipolar disorder, schizoaffective disorder or major depressive episode with psychotic features).

In contrast, those with depression who do not experience manic or psychotic episodes may act out with children by way of meeting a need for connection, temporarily alleviating sadness and the like. For some female child molesters, the depression may be a product of a typically traumatic psychosocial history.

Interestingly, Saradjian and Hanks[586] reported that during the period of time in which female child molesters were offending, problems with depression and anxiety were uncommon among the women who were independently offending either against young children or against adolescents. However, among women who were coerced into offending by a co-offending mate, five of twelve experienced depression, anxiety and suicidal feelings during the period of time that they were offending. It may be the case that depressed women are more easily targeted as co-offenders in child molestation or that offending against a child may serve as a defense against depression for some independent child molesters.

Post-Traumatic Stress Disorder

Post-traumatic stress disorder, by definition, is a reaction to a traumatic event. Symptoms include re-experiencing of the trauma (through nightmares, flashbacks, intrusive memories and so on), increased arousal (outbursts of anger, increased startle response, problems sleeping or concentrating or hypervigilance) and a numbing and general avoiding of stimuli associated with the trauma. Symptoms of post-traumatic stress disorder are commonly found among female sex offenders, consistent with common findings that female sex offenders often have severe abuse histories. Saradjian and Hanks[587] in their study of female offenders noted that several offenders reported flashbacks and painful "body memories" that were related to their histories of abuse. Green and Kaplan[588] reported that among eleven incarcerated female child molesters, eight exhibited post-traumatic stress disorder.

This is a common finding among female adolescent offenders as well. Turner and Turner[589] reported that of eight adolescent female sex offenders, three carried a diagnosis of post-traumatic stress disorder (all of these three were also diagnosed as conduct disordered and one of these was diagnosed, in addition, with borderline personality disorder). Mathews, Hunter & Vuz[590] found that among 67 adolescent female sex offenders from a combination of an inpatient and an outpatient setting, nearly one-half met clinical criteria for a diagnosis of post-traumatic stress disorder.

Given that the majority of female sex offenders appear to have traumatic psychosocial histories, symptoms of post-traumatic stress disorder are likely to occur in a sizable percentage of this population.

Drug and Alcohol Abuse

Several authors have remarked upon the existence of substance abuse in the histories of female sex offenders. With some consistency, researchers have found substance abuse to exist in the backgrounds of many female sex offenders against children. While this may also be a factor that serves to reduce inhibition for the perpetrator during the sexual interactions, one researcher found that among women who abused alcohol and drugs, none offended against children exclusively when she was abusing substances.[591] In this study, none of the women who had had other drug abuse problems, had active substance abuse problems during the period of time that they were abusing children (although some had alcohol abuse problems).

The abuse of alcohol and drugs among maternal incest offenders has been documented in several case studies. Weinberg[592] described a case of mother-son incest in which the mother was an alcoholic, as did Wahl.[593] Maltz and Holman[594] quoted a male survivor of incest with his mother who noted that he began having sex with her after she began drinking heavily and, similarly, Margolis[595] noted a case in which mother-son incest occurred after the mother had been drinking. Bachmann et al.[596] noted a case of mother-son incest in which the mother was addicted to prescription drugs. Sugar[597] described both heavy alcohol use and occasional drug use in the case of a mother who attempted sexual contact with her daughter and described drug abuse in the case of a female who molested her younger female cousin. Goodwin and Divasto[598] also noted a case of mother-daughter incest in which the mother was an alcoholic.

Others have described cases of drug abuse among other female sexual abusers. Kempe and Kempe[599] described the case of a grandmother who had intercourse with her grandson. She was said to be a substance abuser who primarily abused cocaine and alcohol. Higgs, Canavan and Meyer[600] described the case of an adolescent female offender who began abusing drugs and alcohol at about the age of eleven. Chasnoff et al.[601] noted that three of 25 women in a substance abuse program had sexually abused their infants.

Others have researched the frequency of drug and alcohol problems among groups of females who sexually abuse children. These studies have found drug and alcohol abuse to be a particularly common problem among female child molesters. Available evidence, while preliminary, suggests that perhaps one third to one half of the females who sexually molest children may have significant drug or alcohol abuse problems. However, studies to date have primarily involved known female offenders, or offenders who have come to the attention of mental health or correctional agencies. These populations are likely to contain offenders who are among the more disturbed.

This in mind, those who are treating known offenders may wish to screen for substance abuse, given that this is commonly found among known populations of female child molesters. Rowan et al.[602] commented that in three of the nine cases of females evaluated for sexual offenses against children, the woman had a history of drug or alcohol abuse or was using alcohol at the time of the offense. Travin et al.[603] found that five of nine female child molesters had extensive alcohol or substance abuse problems. Harper[604] found that of seven mothers who molested their children, six were addicted to drugs or alcohol. Wolfe[605] found that of twelve female sex offenders, five of were substance abusers. Faller[606] found that of the 40 female child molesters in her study, alcohol was abused in 13 cases, drugs in six cases and both in three cases; in an updated study in 1995, she reported substance abuse in 37 of a new total of 72 females (about 51%). Of 65 female sex offenders in Allen's[607] sample, 17% identified themselves as alcoholics and 26% indicated that they had used drugs. Larson and Maison[608] found that six of the sixteen imprisoned women in treatment for sexual offenses (including one with strong attractions to children who had not actually offended) had chemical dependency problems. Asked how many times in a usual month they preferred to use enough alcohol or drugs so that they experienced a temporary change in behavior, eleven (26%) of Hislop's[609] sample of 43 child molesters reported that they preferred to do so between 25-30 times per month, while another four (nine percent) reported that they preferred to do so 15-20 times per month. Green and Kaplan[610] reported a particularly high rate among eleven incarcerated female child molesters; eight had alcohol or substance abuse problems. O'Connor[611] noted sedative and alcohol abuse in only one of the six cases of convicted British female sex offenders that he reported on. His findings were in contrast to several of the other studies listed here where higher rates were found.

Davin[612] did not find substance abuse among the majority of female offenders, although among co-offenders, about 12.5% used cocaine at least two to three times per week, 20% used marijuana at least once per week and 22.5% drank to intoxication at least once per week. About 20% of co-offenders and 17% of independent offenders were using alcohol at the time of their offenses, while about 30% of co-offenders and 17% of independent offenders were using drugs at the time of the offenses. Psychological testing with the MMPI yielded (MAC-R) scores that were suggestive of substance abuse for the independent offenders but not for the co-offenders.

Adult victims of childhood sexual abuse by women, who tend not to have reported their offenders, also tend to report with some degree of frequency that their offenders had drug or alcohol problems. Swink[613] described the cases of nine women sexually abused by their mothers; five of these mothers were alcoholics or abused drugs. Condy[614] reported that 19% of college men and 20% of prison men who had sexual contact in childhood or adolescence with older females recalled the women as having had drug and alcohol problems.

Problems with drugs and alcohol have also been noted among groups of children who are sexually aggressive. Again, these populations of children have typically been singled out for treatment and may represent the more pathological of the child offenders. Ray and English[615] noted problems with drugs (six cases) and problems with alcohol (five cases) among 34 sexually aggressive female children. Mathews, Hunter and Vuz[616] found that among 67 adolescent female sex offenders, 25% had alcohol or drug abuse problems.

Some authors examined substance abuse history as it related to the type of sexual offending that had taken place. McCarty[617] noted serious drug abuse in 46% of independently offending mothers, in 22% of those who co-offended with a male partner and in 20% of accomplices (who did not have direct sexual contact but who aided another in sexually abusing a child). Matthews[618] reported that 55%, 29% and 33% of female offenders in the subtypes of teacher/lover of adolescent victims, predisposed and co-offending offenders, respectively, had drug/alcohol addiction problems. The adolescent experiences of these offenders included the onset of drug and alcohol abuse for 71%, 29% and 58% of the offenders respectively, in these categories.

Substance abuse is likely to be a problem for a significant number of female child molesters. The substance abuse may represent a means of coping with problems such as depression and anxiety or with more serious mental disturbances. Given that many adult male offenders abuse drugs and alcohol, some women who are abused by family members may inherit a genetic predisposition towards substance abuse. Others may use substances to reduce inhibitions in order to offend or may find that sexual abuse happens when their inhibitions are reduced by substances. Still others may become intoxicated at the direction of a co-offender. The exact relationship of substance abuse to sexual offending when it occurs among females is not yet fully understood.

Eating Disorders

Eating disorders include such problems as obesity, bulimia nervosa (binging and purging) and anorexia nervosa (self-starvation). These disorders are sometimes found in a small but significant minority of female child molesters. Larson and Maison[619] found that six of the sixteen women in treatment for sexual offenses (including one with strong attractions to children who had not actually offended) were more than 40 pounds overweight. Cooper et al.[620] described a case of a female sex offender with multiple diagnoses who was obese.

Vedros[621] noted a case of bulimia among seven teenage sex offenders in residential treatment and noted that all seven had developed weight gain problems. Matthews[622] reported that some female sex offenders starve themselves. Saradjian and Hanks[623] reported that five women in their sample of 36 female offenders were obese, but that none had histories of bulimia or anorexia.

When they occur among female child molesters, eating disorders may represent an attempt at self-nurturing or self-abuse. They may represent an attempt to regulate size, either to gain girth in an attempt to be more powerful or less vulnerable to the sexual interests of others or in an attempt to retain a shape that they believe will bring them sexual attention. For those who have been socialized to behave sexually towards others as a sole means of having social contact, bulimia and self-starvation may be desperate means of attempting to attract this attention. In some cases, starvation or purging may be a means of self-harm. Anorexia nervosa may be a means of attempting to control an environment that is out of control.

Sexual Behavior/Sexual Dysfunction/Paraphilias

While sexual dysfunctions include problems that individuals have with normal sexual functioning, paraphilias have to do with abnormal sexual behaviors. Very little is known about the sexual functioning of the female child molester. However, in the few cases in which sexual problems have been studied, sexual dysfunction or aversion, a lack of sexual boundaries, sexual identity confusion and paraphilias have been found. Some authors have noted atypical sexual fantasies among female sex offenders, although this has not been a consistent finding. The small amount of research available suggests that female offenders may vary greatly in the degree to which they experience sexual problems.

Wolfe[624] reported that five of twelve female sex offenders, all of whom had themselves been sexually abused, had problems related to sexual dysfunction. She reported not finding problems such as peeping and obscene phone calls (examples of paraphilias) among this population.

Mathews, Hunter & Vuz[625] found that among adolescent female sexual offenders with more severe histories of offending, few had sexual involvement with peers; this was noted to be an apparent function of both their young age and of unresolved sexual conflicts stemming from their own sexual victimizations. Some had age-inappropriate sexual interests and arousal. Some appeared to have become sexually aroused by their own victimization experiences.

Davin[626] noted that over a quarter of 30 independent offenders and five percent of 46 co-offenders experienced orgasm while offending.

Hislop[627] found that among 43 women who were either convicted of, or who acknowledged sexual offenses against children, many had a variety of sexual experiences. Many reported sexual contact with large numbers of male partners. Over half also reported a history of sexual contacts with adult women that did not appear to have occurred in the context of childhood abuse, although the results were complicated by the fact that all of the women reporting the sexual contact with women were in prison. Their stated preferences for heterosexual or homosexual relationships often did not match their reported histories of actual sexual behavior. Hislop concluded that some of the women appeared to be "omnisexual," with little ability to establish and/or enforce sexual preferences or boundaries.

A case study provided data that further suggested this possibility as an area for further exploration. Cooper, Swaminath, Baxter and Poulin[628] evaluated a women who had been charged with two counts of sexual assault on two sisters aged four and five; she had inserted objects into their vaginas and performed oral sex on them. The woman had previously been molested by her uncle and had engaged in sexual intercourse with her two brothers; activities with one included sadomasochistic practices. Later the woman had engaged in sexual activities with two family pets and experienced sexual fantasies that included animals. She had violent sexual fantasies concerning children.

As a part of the evaluation by the authors, a vaginal photoplethysmograph was completed, which the authors reported measured vaginal blood flow, vaginal pulse rate, vaginal pulse amplitude and response duration, as sexual arousal measures. These measures were taken as the woman watched pictures of nude adults and children of both genders and as she watched pictures of adult sexual activity, both of heterosexual and homosexual nature. The results of the physiological testing were consistent with her self-report during the testing and indicated that the woman was sexually aroused in response to all of the photos. They concluded that she "showed substantial levels of relatively undifferentiated 'physiological' arousal" which suggested, "polymorphous eroticism, with sadistic, masochistic and pedophiliac elements together with a considerable degree of hostility and aggression (p. 336)."

Cooper et al.[629] also gave this woman psychological tests. They concluded that the results of her MMPI, a commonly used personality inventory, together with the results that she produced on the Derogatis Sexual Functioning Inventory indicated an obsessive preoccupation with sex. Limited sexual knowledge, extreme dissatisfaction with her appearance and negative-conservative attitudes about sex were also noted. Her diagnoses included multiple paraphilias (notably pedophilia), sexual sadism and zoophilia; hypersexuality was also noted.

Having been typically exposed to sexual abuse that is often very severe, in terms of intrusiveness, number of perpetrators, relationship to perpetrators or number of occurrences, it seems likely that many female sex offenders do not develop the ability to develop or enforce sexual preferences and boundaries. For example, promiscuity was described in a case study of a 14-year-old offender by Higgs, Canavan and Meyer.[630]

Mellor, Farid and Craig[631] noted hypersexuality in the case of a woman who had sexually assaulted a man and who was afraid of sexually assaulting young boys. Because of her response to treatment with cyproterone acetate, they postulated that the hypersexuality might be caused by proliferation or hypersensitivity of androgen receptors. In a similar study, Saba, Salvadorini, Galeone, Pellicano & Rainer[632] described the treatment of four women who were schizophrenic with sexual delusions and erotic aggressiveness; after a 30-day treatment with cyproterone acetate, three of the women showed a reduction in hypersexuality. They postulated that a hypersensitive state of the sexual hypothalamic center to androgens was a possible contributor to the hypersexuality.

Some female sex offenders may be specifically aroused by or attracted to children. Fromuth and Conn[633] found that among twenty-two college women who had a history of previous sexual contact with children, 18% expressed a sexual interest in children. This was greater than was the case for women with no history of offending. However, they found no differences between college women with and without a history of offending on measures of Acceptance of Interpersonal Violence, Rape Myth Acceptance or the Adversarial Sexual Beliefs Scale.

Faller[634] noted that some polyincestuous families are also "polymorphous perverse." In such families, there is not only multi-generational incest, but also other paraphilias. The children and adults may be used in pornography and prostitution.

Research has only begun to trickle in concerning the sexual practices and problems of female child molesters. As research continues, it is likely that findings will emerge documenting sexual dysfunction or aversion, confusion regarding sexual identity, hypersexual or omnisexual behavior and other paraphilias.

Dissociative Disorders

Found among descriptions of women who have sexually molested children are cases of women who have symptoms of dissociative disorders, which involve disruptions in the consciousness, memory, identity or perception. Dolan,[635] for example, recalled the mother who had sexual contact with her as being "horribly depressed and trancelike" throughout most of her childhood. Saradjian and Hanks[636] described two atypical perpetrators who had committed their offenses while in a dissociative state. Among five women who were referred after having molested children, Travin et al.[637] described one as suffering from depersonalization disorder (detachment from one's own mental processes or body without loss of reality testing).

In some cases, female child molesters carry a diagnosis of dissociative identity disorder (formerly multiple personality disorder). Individuals with this diagnosis commonly have histories of severe physical and sexual abuse. Paiser[638] noted that one of the ten victims of female perpetrated child sexual abuse revealed that the mother who abused her had a multiple personality disorder. Turner and Turner[639] reported that one member of a group of eight adolescent females seen in therapy for offending carried a diagnosis of multiple personality disorder and that another carried a diagnosis of dissociative disorder, NOS (not otherwise specified).

Personality Disorders/Traits

A variety of inflexible and maladaptive personality traits comprise the ten personality disorders recognized by the DSM-IV. These personality disorders are often found among female child molesters. Borderline personality disorder, avoidant personality disorder and dependent personality disorder are among the most commonly identified in the emerging research. Individuals with borderline personality disorder tend to have unstable relationships, identities and emotions, and also tend to be impulsive. Individuals with avoidant personality disorder are hypersensitive and severely socially inhibited with feelings of inadequacy. Individuals with dependent personality disorder tend to be excessively dependent and submissive; they tend to cling to others and to fear separation.

Green and Kaplan[640] reported that among eleven incarcerated female child molesters, the average number of personality disorders was 3.6. The more common diagnoses were avoidant personality disorder (seven cases), dependent personality disorder (five cases) and borderline personality disorder (five cases). Also found were antisocial personality disorder (four cases), passive-aggressive personality disorder (three cases), obsessive-compulsive personality disorder (two cases), histrionic personality disorder (two cases), narcissistic personality disorder (two cases) and schizoid personality disorder (one case).

Others have also remarked upon female offenders who had personality disorders. Matthew, Mathews & Speltz,[641] have noted the avoidant personality disorder as common among female sex offenders and have also observed borderline personality disorder to be common. O'Connor[642] noted that two among six British women convicted of indecencies with children had personality disorders and that one of the 19 women who had committed indecent assault against children under the age of 16 had an (unspecified) personality disorder. Travin et al.[643] discovered that one of the four individuals who acted out sexually against children had a borderline personality disorder. Cooper et al.[644] included borderline personality disorder among the diagnoses of a female sex offender, along with multiple paraphilias and somatization disorder (hysterical seizures).

Mayer[645] discussed eight adolescent offenders who represented typical cases in a group of 17 female adolescent offenders, all of whom had originally been referred for having been sexually abused. Of these eight cases, one was diagnosed as having a histrionic personality disorder "with dissociative features" Five were diagnosed as either having or developing a borderline personality disorder. Mayer also described the case a female sex offender (who was herself sexually abused by her mother); she was diagnosed as having a borderline personality disorder. Mayer also described a case of an adult female sex offender who carried a diagnosis of borderline personality disorder.

Hislop[646] found evidence for a diagnosis of dependent personality disorder in 16 of 43 cases (37%) of female sex offenders and also noted that many exhibited symptoms of borderline personality disorder.

As additional research emerges, it is possible that other personality disorders will be found to be more common. An overview of the limited available research on this topic raises some questions about the relative absence of antisocial personality disorder among this population. It appears that much of the female sexual offending is driven primarily by trauma, and by disorders related to trauma, rather than by antisocial tendencies in the perpetrators.

Multiple Disorders

Several researchers have described cases in which the female offender is described as meeting criteria for multiple diagnoses. For example, Goodwin and Divasto[647] noted a case of grandmother-granddaughter incest in which the grandmother was described as demented, depressed and hypochondriacal; she also abused barbiturates. Marvasti[648] noted a case in which depression and anxiety existed, as well as drug abuse, and in which the female offender had also been diagnosed with borderline personality disorder. A history of depression and current borderline personality disorder, multiple paraphilias and somatization disorder was noted in the case study by Cooper et al. of a 20-year-old female sex offender.

Mayer[649] discussed eight adolescent offenders who represented typical cases in a group of 17 female adolescent offenders, all of whom had originally been referred for having been sexually abused. Of these eight cases, two had learning disabilities and one was also diagnosed as having attention-deficit disorder. In both cases, the girls were also diagnosed with borderline personality disorder or with a "developing personality disorder." Because of the degree of trauma typically found among female child molesters, the impact upon their functioning may be extreme.

Problems of Limited Intelligence, Learning Problems, School Problems, Attention Deficit/Hyperactivity Problems

Problems related to learning, academic achievement and to the ability to focus and attend have sometimes been observed among female sex offenders. Because of the limited research available, it is unclear to what extent histories of trauma may cause female offenders to be perceived as intellectually slow or as clinically inattentive. Those who are hypervigilant or who have difficulty concentrating as a result of the emotional consequences of severe trauma may be perceived as having intellectual or attention deficits. Their emotional problems may also interfere with their degree of comfort in accompanying an adult into a room for individualized testing, which may impair testing scores. Related difficulties may also impede actual learning, such as occurs in the classroom, giving the impression that the offender's potential is much lower than it is. It is also possible that female offenders who are more obviously intellectually impaired, or who are more impaired in their ability to attend (or to control their impulses, as in some cases of attention-deficit/hyperactivity disorder) are also among those who are the more likely to be discovered.

Several case studies have noted limitations in intelligence among females who sexually molest children. Groth[650] noted limited intelligence in the case of one female offender. Mayer[651] described a case of a depressed adult female offender with "a low IQ." Freel[652] noted one case (of six) in which a female child molester had childhood learning problems and had attended schools for the "educationally sub-normal." In 1973, in discussing offenders who were made the subject of hospital orders, Walker and McCabe[653] reported upon a case of a "young subnormal" woman, who had spent time in a training institution, who married a 17-year-old at the age of 20 and who committed indecent assaults on several young boys and one young girl. A case was also noted of a "severely subnormal girl of 20" who lifted her clothes on a bus, shouted indecencies and made obscene gestures.

Intellectual impairment has also been noted among individuals discovered among groups of female child molesters. Rowan et al.[654] commented that among nine cases of females evaluated for sexual offenses against children, one was mildly retarded and five were of borderline intelligence. Faller[655] found that 48% of the 40 female child molesters in her study had mental difficulties; of these, 33% were mentally retarded or brain damaged. In an updated study in 1995, she reported that of a new total of 72 females, 16 (about 22%) were mentally retarded.

Similar difficulties have been noted among children who sexually molest other children or who are sexually aggressive. Johnson[656] noted academic problems in all 13 of her sample of female child offenders; two had IQs in the mentally retarded range. Ray and English[657] reported that of 34 sexually aggressive female children, seven had problems with hyperactivity. Other problems with school included expulsion (three cases), truancy (fourteen cases) and dropping out (one case). They noted that the intellectual level of their entire sample (which contained a majority of males) was in the normal range.

Additionally, these same problems have been found among populations of female adolescents who molest others. Mayer[658] discussed eight adolescent offenders who represented typical cases in a group of 17 female adolescent offenders, all of whom had originally been referred for having been sexually abused. Of these eight cases, two were learning disabled and one was also diagnosed as having attention-deficit disorder; in both cases, the girls were also diagnosed with borderline personality disorder or with a "developing personality disorder"). Mathews, Hunter and Vuz[659] noted that 23% of 64 adolescent female sexual abusers (for whom data were available, of 67 subjects) combined from inpatient and outpatient facilities had a learning disability; four of the 67 were mildly mentally retarded.

Again, it is not clear whether these individuals may be among the more likely to come to the attention of mental health, criminal justice and protective services agencies for their sexual offending. Further, by no means do all female sex offenders have low IQ's. Larson and Maison[660] found that low IQs were not noted among their prison therapy population, in contrast with other studies. The average IQ was 108, with a range of 92-117 (all average to high average scores). Similarly, Krug[661] reported upon the case of an incestuous mother who had a PhD, and who was on faculty of a prestigious university. Finkelhor and Williams[662] in studying 147 female perpetrators of substantiated sexual abuse in nationwide day care settings reported that many were highly regarded in their communities as "church and civic leaders, intelligent businesswomen, and generally law-abiding citizens (p. 41)." Peluso & Putnam[663] reported upon the case of a 14-year-old male who was molested by a school teacher, and similar cases have been reported in newspapers.

Saradjian and Hanks[664] also reported that many of the female sex offenders about whom they reported were intellectually able, but that the majority had left school at the earliest possible time. They cautioned that while four women were considered to have borderline intelligence, that for three of the women it was clear that such impressions were likely to be due to the effects of repeated trauma and/or poor educational opportunities. They noted that when given relatively abuse-free environments and constructive individual education, the cognitive abilities of these women seemed to improve considerably.

Other Disorders

A variety of other disorders have been described among females who molest children. Because research concerning females who have sexual contact with children is limited, it is unclear whether these disorders are idiosyncratic or whether they may represent significant proportions of the female sex offender population.

McCarty[665] noted that two female sex offenders had brain surgery in their childhoods, resulting in epilepsy. Cooper et al. also described a case in which the offender originally had been diagnosed with epilepsy; however this diagnosis was changed to "hysterical seizures."

Conduct disorders are sometimes noted among adolescent female sex offenders. Mayer[666] discussed eight adolescent offenders; two were diagnosed as conduct disordered. Behavior problems were also noted as common reasons for initial referral into therapy. Turner and Turner[667] identified four cases of conduct disordered adolescent female sex offenders, among eight who were seen in treatment; three of these four individuals also carried a diagnosis of post-traumatic stress disorder.

O'Connor[668] noted that of the 19 British women who had committed indecent assault against children under the age of 16, the diagnoses included one case of a woman for whom the diagnosis was unclear, but she had been taking flupenthixol for three years. Swink[669] described the cases of nine women sexually abused by their mothers; one of the mothers suffered agoraphobia and was under psychiatric care.

Violence

Violent behavior, either towards victims or directed towards others has sometimes been documented among female child molesters. At times, physical abuse accompanies the sexual abuse.[670] Ogilvie & Daniluk[671] described a case that involved skull fractures and broken bones. Cooper et al.[672] noted in their case study that the 20-year-old female offender slapped her victims and was often angry at the time of her offenses. Myers[673] reported that some of the eleven female victims of abuse by an older female reported emotional and physical abuse as well as the sexual abuse. Ramsey-Klawsnik[674] observed that in three fourths of offender-victim pairings, the child was physically as well as sexually abused by the female offender. Of seven men sexually abused by their mothers, Etherington[675] found that four had been physically abused and one emotionally abused by her as well. Faller[676] found that of 72 female offenders against children, 61 had also maltreated their children in other ways. Davin[677] found that of 46 co-offenders about 26% had used physical violence with their spouse and about 16% had used physical violence with their children. Harper[678] found that of seven children sexually molested by their mothers, four were physically abused as well. Mitchell & Morse[679] documented cases of maternal offenders who abused their children through Munchausen-by-Proxy Syndrome, in which an adult makes the child sick or fabricates symptoms in order to get medical attention for the child. Saradjian and Hanks[680] reported that four women whom they studied who targeted young children and two of the women who were coerced into offending had suffocated, strangled or drowned the child to the point of unconsciousness. Two of the women who had sexual contacts with adolescents engaged them in acts of suffocation in order to heighten the sexual excitement of themselves and the adolescent. They also described a case of a woman who sadistically sexually assaulted a teen and left him unconscious, face down in a pond.

Aggressive feelings have also been noted among female child molesters. Many of the female offenders described by Saradjian and Hanks[681] reported feeling aggressive but attempting to "swallow" these feelings; most reported that they were most likely to release these feelings upon a child, rather than any other person. Woodring[682] found evidence of risk to exhibit occasional violent outbursts among independently offending, incarcerated female sex offenders, based upon MMPI-2 testing.

At times, the female sex offenders are abusive towards their mates. Given the frequent finding that many are also abused by their mates, it is unclear the percentage of this violence that is self-defense and the percentage that is another form of perpetration. Allen[683] reported that some of the women had engaged in violent behavior towards their mates. Thirty-eight percent had thrown something at their spouses or partners, 20% had hit them with an object, 16% had kicked, bitten or hit their spouses, eight percent had beaten up a spouse or partner, six percent had threatened their spouse/partner with a knife or gun, two percent had burned or scalded their partners and two percent had used a gun or a knife on their partners.

Other cases of aggression have been noted among case descriptions of female sex offenders. Depression and violence on the part of the female offender has been noted in a case study by Shengold.[684] Holubinskyj & Foley[685] described the case of a female offender who threw a knife at her husband and who shot her daughter's (her victim's) pet dog. Korbin[686] described the case of a female who sexually abused her nephews and who killed her eight-month-old daughter while using PCP. Swink[687] described the cases of nine women sexually abused by their mothers; eight of the mothers were physically abusive and all were described as psychologically abusive and particularly critical.

Among children, physical aggression has been noted to occur along with sexual aggression. Ray and English[688] noted physical fights (21 cases) and temper tantrums (25 cases) among the problems of 34 female children in care who were sexually aggressive.

Harm to Self

Behaviors that are harmful to the self are frequently documented among groups of female sex offenders. Sometimes these behaviors are included in the previously mentioned diagnoses, such as eating disorders or substance abuse disorders. Sometimes they involve direct attempts at self-harm, such as suicide attempts or self-mutilation. Other times the self-harm is less direct, as the case of entering abusive relationships or prostitution. Though at times, running away from an abusive home may be an attempt at self-rescue, for many individuals this is also a behavior that may be self-harmful.

Many authors have noted suicide attempts and self-mutilation among populations of female sex offenders. Turner and Turner[689] noted that self-mutilation and suicidal gestures were common among the eight adolescent female offenders whom they treated. Higgs, Canavan and Meyer[690] described two suicide attempts by an adolescent female offender, who also engaged in self-mutilation. Freel[691] noted suicide or suicidal ideation among three of six female child molesters, as well as in the history of a mother alleged to have herself sexually abused one of the females in this study.

Others have commented upon other forms of self-destructive behavior that occur among this population, in addition to describing the suicide attempts that occur among female child molesters. Saradjian and Hanks[692] reported that during the period of time in which they were not sexually abusing children, many female offenders reported having experienced suicide attempts, self-mutilation and promiscuity. Many also reported suicidal feelings during the period of time in which they were involved in the perpetrations. Mathews, Hunter and Vuz[693] noted suicide attempts among 25% of the adolescent female sex offenders for whom data were available; unprotected sexual encounters were also noted to be common among this population. Ray and English[694] noted suicide attempts among some of the 18 depressed girls among the 34 sexually aggressive girls in their sample; they also reported that the girls had run away in 15 cases.

One author included prostitution as one of the many forms of self-harm that can occur among female child molesters. Matthews[695] noted that female offenders may engage in self-destructive behaviors that not only include things like cutting on themselves, but behaviors such as prostituting themselves or placing themselves in very dangerous situations. McCarty[696] reported that three of seventeen mothers who had offended had been prostitutes. Freel[697] noted a history of prostitution in one of the six cases of female child molesters that he reviewed. Harper[698] found that of seven mothers who molested their children, two were prostitutes. Faller[699] noted prostitution in the histories of some of the female child molesters that she described. Wolfe[700] noted that among twelve female sexual offenders, one was a prostitute and one had participated in a years-long, sadomasochistic lesbian relationship. Several authors have noted that female sex offenders often willingly remain in relationships with abusive male co-offenders.

In an interesting commentary, Welldon[701] remarked that the harm that women do to their babies and children might be perceived as an extension of the harm that they do to themselves, noting that the women often have previous histories of self-abuse or sadomasochistic relationships. Given the perceived lack of boundaries among female sexual offenders, it is indeed likely that some may have difficulty delineating the boundaries between themselves and others, particularly those to whom they have given birth.

Allen[702] found that of 65 female sex offenders the average number of times that the females had run away was 1.8, with 43% of the female offenders reporting that they ran away from home. Given, however, that Allen found large amounts of physical and sexual abuse in the childhood homes of these perpetrators, the running away may have constituted adaptive, rather than antisocial, behavior. Mathews et al[703] reported that 33% of the 51 individuals for whom data were available among 67 adolescent female sexual offenders had histories of runaway behaviors. Again given the amount of abuse reported by participants in this study, runaway behaviors may have been adaptive.

Delinquency/Behavior Problems

Some authors have noted that some female child molesters have behavior problems and problems related to their conduct. However, Allen[704] found only small evidence of juvenile delinquency in the histories of 65 female sex offenders. The average level of thefts during adolescence for the female offenders was 2.6, and the average number of times arrested or appearing in juvenile court was 0.5. Allen[705] also found that 15% of the female offenders had received money for sexual activity and that 80% of these offenders had been paid by two or more people; it is not noted whether this may have occurred in the context of a sexually abusive relationship or during prostitution. Freel[706] noted shoplifting in the history of one of the six cases of female child molesters that he reviewed.

When female sex offenders are discovered in prison settings, they often have histories of conviction for other crimes. However, it is unclear whether these offenders are representative of other female child molesters. For example, Maison and Larson[707] reported that many of the women in their treatment group in prison had been previously convicted for crimes that included prostitution and forgery.

Behavioral problems have been documented among children who offend against other children and who have come to the attention of mental health professionals. Johnson[708] noted other problems in all 13 of her sample of female child offenders; some engaged in stealing, fire setting and running away; all had social problems. Disobedience (28 cases) was noted as problematic among the 34 sexually aggressive female children described by Ray and English.[709] Additional problems noted among these 34 female children included shoplifting (ten cases), property damage (20 cases), stealing (23 cases) and verbal abuse (24 cases). Higgs, Canavan and Meyer[710] also described oppositional behaviors and running away in the behavioral repertoire of a 14-year-old offender with a history of sibling incest. Mathews et al[711] noted "a variety of impulsive delinquent behaviors" including lying among 67 adolescent female sexual offenders.

General Inadequacy of Functioning (Educational, Occupational Problems)

Several authors have remarked upon the general inadequacy in functioning exhibited by large numbers of female sex offenders against children. Evidence for risk of poor work histories was found in the psychological testing of independent female sex offenders by Woodring[712] and several studies have found that female child molesters have difficulty both occupationally and academically. Common problems identified include difficulty independently supporting themselves and failure to complete high school or to meet their academic potential. Often studies find that a number of the female child molesters are supported by public welfare systems. Again, it must be noted that offenders who are functioning less well are probably among the most likely to be identified through child protection, correctional or mental health agencies. Those women who are managing their affairs well and those who are educated are probably the least likely to be perceived as child molesters and the best able to formulate plans and obtain the resources necessary to avoid detection.

Allen[713] noted that 43% of 65 female offenders, primarily identified through child protective services records, reported that they were unemployed. Several of the offenders had no fixed place of residence and moved between several places over the course of weeks. The mean income for the female offenders was $7250, with over 75% earning less than $10,000. He noted, however, that ten percent of the offenders were professionals. Only forty percent of the offenders were high school graduates, with educational levels ranging from the seventh grade to the Masters level. Most of those employed were employed in traditional women's occupations.

Larson and Maison[714] found evidence of both low academic and occupational achievement among a group of female child molesters. In spite of average or above IQs, they found that the average educational attainment among imprisoned female sex offenders was only eleven years, with a range of eight to sixteen years. Twelve years was the mode. Overall, the women held service or factory jobs, with the exception of one woman who was a teacher. They noted that without assistance, the work histories and job skills of most of the women were such that they could not survive.

Others have made similar findings. Davin[715] found that of 76 imprisoned female sex offenders, fewer than half had finished high school. They predominantly held low level and semi-skilled jobs. Wolfe[716] noted the lack of economic self-sufficiency as a common problem among a group of twelve female sex offenders. Only three held jobs at intake. Six of the twelve had not finished high school. Harper[717] found that of seven mothers who molested their children, all came from backgrounds of low socioeconomic status.

Saradjian and Hanks[718] also reported that although intellectually able, many of the female sex offenders about whom they reported were likely to have relatively short employment histories, particularly the women who abused young children. While a nurse, a social worker and a teacher were counted among the offenders that they studied, the authors reported that most of the offenders, regardless of education, performed poorly paid, unskilled work. The women in their study all had substantiated cases known to child protection agencies.

Among eight female sex offenders described by The Committee on Sexual Offenses Against Children and Youth,[719] several had finished only grade ten. One had two years of training at a business school but was unemployed. One worked part-time and offended with a male she met on the job. Another did not work while on probation, although little information was available concerning her previous work and employment history.

Mayer[720] briefly described cases involving adult female offenders. Among them was a case of a female who received Supplemental Security Income, as she was unable to support herself due to her emotional difficulties; another offender received Aid to Families with Dependent Children, as she did not work.

It should be reiterated here that not all of the women who molest children are functioning poorly. Several authors have also reported upon some women who demonstrate adequate or above average levels of educational or occupational functioning. Furthermore, those women who demonstrate obvious pathology or inadequacy of functioning may be among those more likely to be detected and researched. Among 93 women who had been molested by their mothers in childhood, for example, most of whom never identified their mothers as perpetrators while children, many reported their lifestyles with their mothers to have been middle class or upper class.[721]

General Inadequacy of Functioning (Relationship Problems)

Numerous problems in interpersonal relationships have been noted among populations of female child molesters. Though not all female sex offenders have problems in this area, social problems are among the problems most commonly identified in the female child molester population. Many are reported to be socially isolated and to have few sources of adult social support. Others are immature or hostile in their relationships with other people. Many, particularly those who offend with an abusive co-offender, have been noted to choose abusive partners.

Illustrating the problems in interpersonal relationships among female sex offenders are the comments of Saradjian and Hanks.[722] Commenting on interviews with British female child molesters, they remarked, "one of the most overwhelming differences between the women in the groups of offenders and those in the comparison groups is that at the time that they were sexually abusing children, not one woman offender could name a person who was a friend (p. 79-80)." In a similar fashion, Chatham,[723] who surveyed 14 clinicians who had worked with female sex offenders, quoted one as saying, "Perpetrators are usually anti-social, with no female relationships. In other words, they tend to have difficulty in relationships with both sexes (p. 23)."

Problems with interpersonal relationships may be deeply ingrained. Longstanding relationship problems are often found to be the norm among female sex offenders. Saradjian and Hanks[724] found that each of the female offenders who had siblings recalled being the most unloved and most harshly treated of the children. Very few of the female offenders had positive relationships with their siblings. Very few of the offenders and none of the offenders against very young children had friendships during childhood.

Woodring[725] completed psychological testing (MMPI) on incarcerated female sex offenders and found evidence for several interpersonal problems among female sex offenders. He noted that independent female sex offenders may be suspicious of the motives of others; he also noted that they may have poor interpersonal relationships, social maladjustments and difficulties managing their hostility in interpersonal relationships. He also noted interpersonal problems among women who were coerced into offending. Interpersonal sensitivity and a tendency to overreact to criticism were noted among women who co-offended with a partner, in addition to a brooding resentment towards authority.

Davin[726] also completed MMPI-2 testing on incarcerated female sex offenders. She found independent offenders to be "inhibited, self-critical and overly sensitive to rejection. They tend to possess unusual beliefs, may exhibit bizarre actions and are withdrawn and alienating (p. 80)." Evidence of problems with authority, superficiality in relationships and basic distrust was also noted. Among co-offenders, Davin found MMPI-2 evidence indicating that they are "distrustful, submissive, and easily influenced by others (p. 80)."

Those who have treated groups of female sex offenders often remark upon the interpersonal skill deficits of this population. Matthews[727] noted poor social skills among the 36 female sex offender that she has treated over the years. She reported that they tended to be low-status members of their peer groups and to feel as if they belonged nowhere. She added that many would do anything for acceptance. Wolfe[728] noted social isolation as a common problem among a group of twelve female sex offenders; nine were socially isolated. Harper[729] found dysfunctional interpersonal relationships among seven mothers who molested their children.

Two authors wrote about these problems in some detail. Maison and Larson[730] noted that female sex offenders have few relationships. Specifically, the offenders have difficulty negotiating in relationships; when problems come up, often their only perceived alternative is to leave the relationship. Emotional isolation and poor capacity to form relationships were also described by these authors.[731] Additionally, Larson and Maison[732] described the offenders as having dichotomous thinking, with victim or perpetrator roles being primary personality configurations. They also noted a psychosexual immaturity among offenders that often matched the age of the offenders' victims.

These problems may also be common among children who are sexually aggressive. Poor social skills (difficulty with peer relationships) were noted by Ray and English[733] in describing a sample of sexually aggressive children that contained a number of females.

Again, it must be noted that female child molesters with the most overt problems are likely to be over-represented in currently available research. Among those who have not been detected and researched, there may be less pathology and fewer psychosocial problems. A study of women offenders who abused in day care settings found social problems to be somewhat less common than is the case in other populations of female sex offenders. Women working in day care settings have at least the minimal social skills necessary to obtain work and to interact with others in a fashion sufficient to be employed and to be trusted to care for children. Finkelhor and Williams[734] in studying 147 female perpetrators of substantiated sexual abuse in nationwide day care settings reported that only 16% of these women were socially isolated.

Other Co-morbid Problems

A variety of problems in functioning have been observed among female child molesters. Several authors have described personality characteristics that are common to the female child molester population or have described concerns that are common to this group.

Larson and Maison[735] discussed the difficulties seen among 14 imprisoned female sex offenders that they saw in group therapy, together with a woman who turned herself in for the sexual abuse of a male adolescent but who was not charged with a crime and a woman who had intense fantasies about sexual behavior with children but who did not act on her feelings. They found several difficulties including an external locus of control; global shame, rather than behavior-specific guilt; "emotional anesthesia"; and a poor understanding of human sexuality. They observed that women who sexually abuse children are likely to have low self-esteem.

Several rigid defense mechanisms were also noted by these authors, generally as a result of having grown up in dysfunctional or abusive homes. They observed that the women suffered from a sense of "fluid reality," a form of cognitive distortion of reality akin to magical thinking. Blocking memories, dichotomous thinking, minimizing intelligence and behaving dependently were noted as defenses. The authors also noted "fogging" and the distortion of reality by "adding in" pieces.

Woodring[736] completed psychological testing on incarcerated female sex offenders. He found evidence that independent female offenders may feel alienated from the self and the environment. He also found evidence of psychological retreat into fantasy. Evidence of distorted thinking and inflexible problem solving was also found among the coerced co-offenders. Among non-coerced co-offenders, he noted psychological retreat into fantasy, as well as feelings of alienation from the self and the environment.

Other authors have commented on the general lack of control over their lives that these women perceive and upon their tendency to be passive and dependent. Among five women who were referred after having molested children, Travin et al.[737] described problems of passivity, withdrawal, dependency and inadequacy as common. Hislop[738] also noted symptoms of dependency to be common among female child molesters that she surveyed. Saradjian and Hanks[739] similarly noted a perceived lack of control over their destiny and a sense of powerlessness among the female sex offenders who were interviewed. In particular, all of the offenders against young children reported that they did not have, and never had, a sense of power or control over their own lives. There was a trend for the women who were coerced to report even less control over their lives, while the offenders against adolescents reported somewhat more feelings of control than did the other two groups.[740] Pothast and Allen[741] found that, in contrast with a comparison group, 38 female sex offenders against children scored higher on "femininity" on the Short Form Bem Sex-Role Inventory.

Similar problems have been found among populations of adolescent female offenders. Scavo[742] noted that among female adolescent offenders, common difficulties were a poor self-concept, intense anger, feelings of helplessness and social isolation. Turner and Turner[743] noted low self-esteem, self-hatred, poor body image, anger, fear, lack of identity and enmeshment with their mothers as among the problems found in a population of adolescent female offenders. Mathews et al[744] noted internalized negative self-image, impaired capacity for healthy attachments and stunted psychosexual and emotional development among adolescent female offenders.

Among a population of 34 female children, as well as additional male children, with both victimization and sexual aggression histories, Ray and English[745] found problems with nightmares, bed-wetting, behavioral and developmental regression and lack of basic sexual knowledge.

Individuals working with female child molesters should be aware of the numerous types of behavioral, diagnostic, interpersonal and personality problems which may plague individuals in this population.

Diagnostic/Assessment Considerations

Given that research on female sex offenders is in its infancy, the assessment of female sex offenders entering treatment should be as comprehensive as possible.

An intellectual assessment should be completed or, at minimum, a screening should occur for intellectual impairments. While there is no conclusive evidence that most female sex offenders are cognitively impaired, those who are may be among the more likely to be recognized as offenders. Trauma-related emotional distress or inconsistent schooling may have interfered with childhood learning for some offenders. Further, some researchers have noted that female offenders often present as much younger and less intelligent than one would expect given their intelligence quotients. Female offenders may defensively present as incapable in order to have their dependency needs met or may lack the confidence to express their intelligence or may have psychological disorders such as depression that interfere with their ability to function cognitively. Intellectual testing may also reveal abilities that are higher than would be expected given the clinical presentation of the female child molester.

An assessment of intellectual abilities may help the therapist to develop strategies for helping the female sex offender to learn during sessions. Given the numerous emotional and psychological factors that may interfere with learning in the session, verbal and other interventions in therapy should match the offender's capacity as closely as possible. The intellectual presentation of offenders may not be consistent with their actual abilities.

Similarly, while most offenders do not appear to be psychotic, female offenders with psychotic symptoms may be among the more likely to be identified for treatment. Where psychotic symptoms are identified, further assessment will often be warranted because of the history of trauma so commonly found in this population. It is possible that individuals with schizophrenia, mania (particularly given the hypersexuality that may accompany it) and other psychotic disorders may sexually abuse children as a part of the psychotic process. Very little information is currently available, however, concerning women who sexually abuse children as a result of schizophrenia or other psychotic disorders in the absence of trauma histories.

Disorders that resemble schizophrenia or similar psychotic disorders may occur as reactions to trauma. The individual who has had traumatic abusive experiences may experience hallucinations as a symptom of post-traumatic stress disorder, for example. Individuals may have brief psychotic episodes in response to severe stress, such as occurs with trauma. Individuals who have major depressive episodes may experience psychotic symptoms. Individuals experiencing panic or anxiety may also appear psychotic. Individuals who have been severely traumatized and who are hypervigilant may appear paranoid. Trauma victims may also dissociate, which interferes with reality testing. For example, in the case of dissociative identity disorder, a dissociative identity state may be mistaken as a delusion or the communication between identities may be mistaken for auditory hallucinations.[746] Careful differential diagnostic consideration is warranted. Furthermore, diagnosticians must caution against diagnoses of psychosis based upon the presence of sexual offending behavior in and of itself.

Family history is often considered in the diagnosis of schizophrenia and other psychotic disorders. However, it is important to recognize that there is also a correlation between sexual abuse of a daughter and the likelihood that her own mother was also sexually abused. Incest in families is often multi-generational[747] Turner and Turner[748] found that seven of eight mothers of adolescent female offenders had been sexually abused in childhood. Mothers or other family members of female sex offenders who have trauma-based psychotic symptoms may themselves have had trauma-based psychotic symptoms that resembled and were diagnosed as schizophrenia. Beyond the last generation, little was known about sexual abuse and its consequences and the differentiation between schizophrenia and trauma-based psychotic symptoms was unlikely to have been explored by treating clinicians.

Another consideration in evaluating psychotic symptoms that may be reported by a female sex offender is the possibility that she may have been abusing or withdrawing from drugs or alcohol at the time of the symptoms. Several authors have noted that female sex offenders often have substance abuse problems, which may cause psychotic-like symptoms either during use or withdrawal. Substance abuse, dependency and withdrawal disorders should be considered when diagnostically evaluating the female sex offender who reports a history of psychotic symptoms.

Additionally, some authors have described atypical thinking among female sex offenders that may resemble psychosis. Larson and Maison[749] for example, described a "fluid reality" among female sex offenders that resembles magical thinking in children. They describe it as assisting the female offenders to cope. Female sex offenders may defensively distort reality as a means of coping.

Axis I disorders are commonly found among female sex offenders. Commonly identified are depression and anxiety disorders, including post-traumatic stress disorder. Dissociation also occurs at times. A diagnostic evaluation of the female sex offender should consider these disorders. Female sex offenders often have substance abuse problems and consideration of substance abuse problems should be included in a comprehensive evaluation. Eating disorders, while less commonly noted in currently available research, should also be considered. Occasionally, conduct disorders are noted among adolescents, although often co-occurring with trauma-based disorders, such as post-traumatic stress. While common to male sex offenders, antisocial personality disorders are presently thought to be less common among female sex offenders, though documented cases have occurred.

Though less commonly considered in the diagnostic evaluation of female sex offenders presently, evaluation for sexual dysfunction and gender identity disorders is likely to be appropriate, as these are common problems among sexual abuse victims. Little research is available to guide the assessment of sexual and gender identity disorders among female sex offenders. However, sexual dysfunction and gender identity disorders are not uncommon sequelae to childhood sexual abuse or rape.

Sexual dysfunction is unlikely to be among the areas addressed in initial treatment. Given the myriad of problems often seen in the female sex offender and given the possibility of decompensation for female sex offenders, particularly when presented with stimuli that represent the trauma, assessment for sexual dysfunction may be more appropriate after a therapeutic rapport has been established. The need for information concerning sexual functioning must be balanced with the therapist's knowledge of the level of functioning of the offender and her ability to withstand decompensation when personal sexual information is explored.

An assessment of other paraphilias may also be appropriate, although little research is available to guide this assessment. Some women who offend against children may have other paraphilias.

Confusion concerning sexual identity has been identified as an area of potential concern both for female sex offenders and for victims of childhood sexual abuse. This is an additional area for potential evaluation among female sex offenders. Sexual identities of female offenders may warrant exploration; some female sex offenders may be undecided or confused concerning their sexual identities, some may require assistance to be comfortable with their (bisexual, homosexual or heterosexual) identities, some may have a lack of boundaries such that their preferred identity is not enforced.

Female sex offenders should be carefully evaluated for the presence of personality disorders; Green & Kaplan[750] reported that in a sample of eleven female sex offenders evaluated for personality disorders, the offenders met diagnostic criteria for an average of 3.6 personality disorders per subject. Dependency among female sex offenders has been noted by several authors and dependent personality disorder has also been identified as common among female sex offenders. This has been noted to be a particular problem among women who offend with a co-offender. Borderline personality disorder has also been commonly found among female sex offenders in case studies and has been suggested by research. Avoidant personality disorder has also been found to be common.

Green and Kaplan[751] commented on the impulsivity of the female sex offenders. Several authors have described problems among female sex offenders that suggest organic deficits. In some instances, a neuropsychological assessment of the female sex offenders may be appropriate.

Supported by other researchers' descriptions of typically poor functioning, Green & Kaplan[752] also found that the average Global Assessment of Functioning (GAF) score for eleven female sex offenders was 60, indicative of poor overall functioning. Assessment of the female child molester's overall level of functioning, such as a GAF score, should be included in a diagnostic assessment.

In addition to consideration of diagnostic criteria, female sex offenders should be evaluated for their risk of harm to themselves, others and property. While their symptoms in these areas may or may not meet diagnostic criteria for specific diagnoses, they should be noted. Under the category of harm to self, female offenders should be evaluated for previous and current thoughts and behaviors related to:

- self-mutilation/self-harm
- suicide

- drug/alcohol abuse
- running away from home (if a minor)
- willing involvement in abusive relationships, including sexually abusive relationships
- eating disorders (binging/purging/self-starvation)
- prostitution

Consideration should also be given to the possibility that the female sex offender may wish to actively harm others or may have a history of having done so. Additionally, some female offenders may not have the ability to provide for the emotional or physical needs of their children, given their own dependency or other emotional needs. Some may lack the ability to attach to others in their care, given their own severe abuse histories. Areas for assessment include:

- child physical abuse
- verbal/emotional abuse of a child
- neglect/abandonment of a child
- similar abuse of others in their care, for example, elder abuse
- sexual sadism
- homicidal ideation
- aggression towards a mate
- physical or verbal abuse in family or friendship relationships
- physical or sexual harm of animals

The possibility that the offenders may express rage or seek to have dependency needs met through behaviors that harm the properties of others should also be assessed. Such considerations include:

- fire setting
- vandalism or property destruction
- theft

Summary

While research concerning female sex offenders is in its infancy, some areas for evaluation have been identified. Where psychosis is identified, careful evaluation for differential diagnoses is warranted. Drug and alcohol abuse are frequently found among female sex offenders and warrant evaluation. Common areas for Axis I evaluation include depressive and anxiety disorders, dissociation and post-traumatic stress. Personality disorders commonly found are borderline personality disorder, avoidant personality disorder and dependent personality disorder, although others have also been seen among female sex offenders. Intellectual problems and academic problems have been noted, together with the observation that female sex offenders often present as possessing less intelligence than they actually have, perhaps as a means of seeking to have their dependency needs met. Given the impulsivity sometimes found among female sex offenders and the occasional reports of evidence of organic disturbances, neuropsychological assessment may at times be warranted. Female sex offenders should be assessed for problems related to harm against the self, others or property, although they may not always meet diagnostic criteria for related disorders. Female sex offenders have been noted to often lead very dysfunctional lives and may score quite low on the Global Assessment of Functioning or other similar measures.

Notes ————————————————

[545] Margolin (1986)
[546] O'Connor (1987)
[547] Hislop (1999)
[548] Hislop (1998)
[549] Paiser (1992)
[550] Mitchell & Morse (1998)
[551] Finkelhor, Williams & Burns (1988)
[552] Saradjian & Hanks (1996)
[553] Turner & Turner (1994)
[554] Fromuth & Conn (1997)
[555] Lukianowicz (1972)
[556] Mathis (1972)
[557] Saradjian & Hanks (1996)
[558] Berry (1975)
[559] Saradjian & Hanks (1996)
[560] O'Connor (1987)
[561] Rowan et al. (1990)
[562] Wolfe (1985)
[563] Harper (1993)
[564] Swink (1989)
[565] Turner & Turner (1994)
[566] Faller (1987)
[567] Travin et al. (1990)
[568] Condy et al. (1987)
[569] Arieti (1975)
[570] Saba, Salvadorini, Galeone, Pellicano & Rainer (1975)
[571] Lukianowicz (1972)
[572] Shengold (1980)
[573] Groth (1979a)
[574] Mayer (1992)
[575] Cooper, Swaminath, Baxter & Poulin (1990)
[576] O'Connor (1987)
[577] Swink (1989)
[578] Travin et al. (1990)

[579] Green & Kaplan (1994)
[580] Travin et al. (1990)
[581] Woodring (1995)
[582] Johnson (1989)
[583] Mathews, Hunter & Vuz (1997)
[584] Walker & McCabe (1973)
[585] Lawson (1984)
[586] Saradjian & Hanks (1996)
[587] Saradjian & Hanks (1996)
[588] Green & Kaplan (1994)
[589] Turner & Turner (1994)
[590] Mathews, Hunter & Vuz (1997)
[591] Saradjian & Hanks (1995)
[592] Weinberg (1955)
[593] Wahl (1960)
[594] Maltz & Holman (1987)
[595] Margolis (1984)
[596] Bachmann et al. (1994)
[597] Sugar (1983)
[598] Goodwin & Divasto (1979)
[599] Kempe & Kempe (1984)
[600] Higgs, Canavan & Meyer (1997)
[601] Chasnoff et al. (1986)
[602] Rowan et al. (1990)
[603] Travin et al. (1990)
[604] Harper (1993)
[605] Wolfe (1985)
[606] Faller (1987)
[607] Allen's (1991)
[608] Larson & Maison (1987)
[609] Hislop's (1998)
[610] Green & Kaplan (1994)
[611] O'Connor (1987)
[612] Davin (1999)
[613] Swink (1989)
[614] Condy (1985)
[615] Ray & English (1995)
[616] Mathews, Hunter & Vuz (1997)
[617] McCarty (1986)
[618] Matthews (1994)
[619] Larson & Maison (1987)
[620] Cooper et al. (1990)
[621] Vedros (1998)
[622] Matthews (1994)
[623] Saradjian & Hanks (1996)
[624] Wolfe (1985)
[625] Mathews, Hunter & Vuz (1997)

[626] Davin (1999)
[627] Hislop (1999)
[628] Cooper, Swaminath, Baxter & Poulin (1990)
[629] Cooper et al. (1990)
[630] Higgs, Canavan & Meyer (1997)
[631] Mellor, Farid & Craig (1988)
[632] Saba, Salvadorini, Galeone, Pellicano & Rainer (1975)
[633] Fromuth & Conn (1997)
[634] Faller (1995)
[635] Dolan (1991)
[636] Saradjian & Hanks (1996)
[637] Travin et al. (1990)
[638] Paiser (1992)
[639] Turner & Turner (1994)
[640] Green & Kaplan (1994)
[641] Matthew, Mathews & Speltz (1989)
[642] O'Connor (1987)
[643] Travin et al. (1990)
[644] Cooper et al. (1990)
[645] Mayer (1992)
[646] Hislop (1998)
[647] Goodwin & Divasto (1979)
[648] Marvasti (1986)
[649] Mayer (1992)
[650] Groth (1979a)
[651] Mayer (1992)
[652] Freel (1995)
[653] Walker & McCabe (1973)
[654] Rowan et al. (1990)
[655] Faller (1987)
[656] Johnson (1989)
[657] Ray & English (1995)
[658] Mayer (1992)
[659] Mathews, Hunter & Vuz (1997)
[660] Larson & Maison (1987)
[661] Krug (1989)
[662] Finkelhor & Williams (1988)
[663] Peluso & Putnam (1996)
[664] Saradjian & Hanks (1996)
[665] McCarty (1986)
[666] Mayer (1992)
[667] Turner & Turner (1994)
[668] O'Connor (1987)
[669] Swink (1989)
[670] Mitchell & Morse (1998); Ogilvie & Daniluk (1995)
[671] Ogilvie & Daniluk (1995)
[672] Cooper et al. (1990)

[673] Myers (1992)
[674] Ramsey-Klawsnik (1990)
[675] Etherington (1997)
[676] Faller (1995)
[677] Davin (1999)
[678] Harper (1993)
[679] Mitchell & Morse (1998)
[680] Saradjian & Hanks (1996)
[681] Saradjian & Hanks (1996)
[682] Woodring (1995)
[683] Allen (1991)
[684] Shengold (1980)
[685] Holubinskyj & Foley (1986)
[686] Korbin (1986)
[687] Swink (1989)
[688] Ray & English (1995)
[689] Turner & Turner (1994)
[690] Higgs, Canavan & Meyer (1997)
[691] Freel (1995)
[692] Saradjian & Hanks (1995)
[693] Mathews, Hunter & Vuz (1997)
[694] Ray & English (1995)
[695] Matthews (1994)
[696] McCarty (1986)
[697] Freel (1995)
[698] Harper (1993)
[699] Faller (1995)
[700] Wolfe (1985)
[701] Welldon (1996)
[702] Allen (1991)
[703] Mathews et al. (1997)
[704] Allen (1991)
[705] Allen (1991)
[706] Freel (1995)
[707] Maison & Larson (1995)
[708] Johnson (1989)
[709] Ray & English (1995)
[710] Higgs, Canavan & Meyer (1997)
[711] Mathews et al. (1997)
[712] Woodring (1995)
[713] Allen (1991)
[714] Larson & Maison (1987)
[715] Davin (1994)
[716] Wolfe (1985)
[717] Harper (1993)
[718] Saradjian & Hanks (1996)
[719] Committee on Sexual Offenses Against Children and Youth (1984)

[720] Mayer (1992)
[721] Rosencrans (1997)
[722] Saradjian & Hanks (1996)
[723] Chatham (1992)
[724] Saradjian & Hanks (1996)
[725] Woodring (1995)
[726] Davin (1999)
[727] Matthews (1994)
[728] Wolfe (1985)
[729] Harper (1993)
[730] Maison & Larson (1995)
[731] Larson & Maison (1987)
[732] Larson & Maison (1987)
[733] Ray & English (1995)
[734] Finkelhor & Williams (1988)
[735] Larson & Maison (1987)
[736] Woodring (1995)
[737] Travin et al. (1990)
[738] Hislop (1999)
[739] Saradjian & Hanks (1996)
[740] Saradjian & Hanks (1996)
[741] Pothast & Allen (1994)
[742] Scavo (1989)
[743] Turner & Turner (1994)
[744] Mathews et al. (1997)
[745] Ray & English (1995)
[746] DSM-IV (1994)
[747] Cooper & Cormier (1982); Goodwin, McCarthy & Divasto (1981)
[748] Turner & Turner (1994)
[749] Larson & Maison (1987)
[750] Green & Kaplan (1994)
[751] Green & Kaplan (1994)
[752] Green & Kaplan (1994)

9. Handling Client Difficulties with Participation in Therapy

A number of problems stemming from their psychosocial histories may impede the ability of many female sex offenders to participate in the therapeutic relationship. Among these are poor relationship skills, a lack of a sense of safety, poor self-esteem, a poorly consolidated identity, poor learning skills and defenses against anxiety and compensation. It becomes the task of the therapist to manage these problems by attending to the quality of the therapeutic relationship and by using therapeutic techniques that facilitate learning.

Client Difficulties Participating in the Therapeutic Relationship

Poor Relationship Skills

Problems in the relationships of female offenders have been noted by several authors.[753] Individuals who have been abused or traumatized by others may have profound difficulties forming healthy relationships. Difficulties resulting from a history of childhood trauma may not only suggest areas for focus in therapy, but may impair the ability of the individual to engage in the treatment process itself.

Individuals who have experienced trauma directly in their more enduring intimate relationships may lack the ability to form trusting relationships.[754] They may be particularly mistrustful of relationships with authority figures. Severely traumatized female offenders may initially lack the relationship experiences necessary to successfully form a working relationship with the therapist.[755] Some may be generally suspicious, hostile, interpersonally sensitive or resentful of authority.[756]

Female offenders who have grown up in the context of abuse and family dysfunction may have never developed appropriate interpersonal skills. They may have had few opportunities to observe the modeling of appropriate social relationships. Families in which abuse occurs are often isolated; this isolation may be enforced by the abuser in the interest of controlling the family and keeping the abuse secret.[757] Some individuals, aware that their families are unhealthy, curtail their own social relationships, avoiding friendships that would allow family's secrets to be revealed.

Preoccupation with abuse or with dysfunction in the family of origin may interfere with the ability of female sex offenders to learn developmentally appropriate social and relationship skills. Female sex offenders who, as children, were full of rage, hypervigilant, depressed, self-conscious, behaviorally inappropriate and so forth as a result of abuse or family dysfunction, may never have had childhood friends with whom they could develop normal friendship skills. As a result they may have poor social skills and poor relationships as adults.

Larson and Maison[758] have observed that female sex offenders are often emotionally delayed. Children who are traumatized have often spent tremendous energy coping with the trauma at the expense of focus on normal developmental tasks. Turner and Turner[759] observed this in adolescent female sex offenders, "…these young women had been so preoccupied by the task of developing survival and defense mechanisms that they had never experienced the everyday routines of questioning and learning that children ordinarily experience. (p. 48)." Mathews, Hunter and Vuz[760] made similar observations that among adolescent female sexual offenders, "early and repetitive trauma...resulted in stunted emotional and psychosexual development (p. 197)."

Research has commonly found that many female offenders, when they are able to form ties, are overly dependent in their relationships. Many come from dysfunctional and abusive homes where, it may be presumed, their developmentally appropriate dependency needs were not consistently met. Some female sex offenders have been observed to present in a regressed fashion. They relate to others with the underdeveloped skills of a child or adolescent. Larson and Maison[761] observed that for many the developmental age of their social presentation typically matched not only the age that they reported "feeling inside" but also the age of their victims.

Many female sex offenders have concerns regarding power and control in their relationships. Emotional connections may cause them to feel vulnerable to victimization. Rather than relate in a dependent fashion, some female sexual abusers may avoid relating altogether. Mathews et al.[762] noted that among adolescent female sex offenders, "Emotional intimacy is associated with a profound sense of vulnerability and results in various distancing behaviors and projections onto the therapists of the intentions and attributes of previous aggressors (p. 197)." Female child sexual abusers may hesitate to engage in the therapeutic relationship for fear of being exploited.

Among female sex offenders, there may be a tendency to dichotomize relationships into victim/victimizer roles[763] and to defensively choose one of these roles.[764] The offenders may relate to others from the perspective of a helpless victim, or from the stance of a hostile aggressor. The female sexual abuser may attempt to engage the therapist in interactions that resemble victim-victimizer interactions.

Female sexual abusers who are trauma victims may easily perceive either the therapist or themselves as abusive or as powerless. Therapists who exert control or authority over them may be quickly associated with abusers who engender feelings of helplessness, fear, resentment or over compliance in the female offenders. Those who do not take control and "rescue" them may quickly be viewed as ineffectual or powerless.[765] Saradjian and Hanks[766] noted that the power imbalance in the therapeutic relationship is exacerbated by the fact that offenders often have therapy forced upon them. They caution that if the power imbalance is not well managed, the feelings of powerlessness engendered in the female child molester may be a trigger for molestation of a child.

Female sex offenders are not likely to easily and consistently engage in the therapeutic relationship. Their difficulties in forming relationships may render them, at times, difficult or unpleasant to work with in the therapeutic setting and the therapist should have appropriate resources available to manage the potential stress created by working with such clients.

Lack of a Sense of Safety

Multiply traumatized individuals may not only lack a sense of trust but may also lack a basic sense of safety. Some chronic abuse victims remain in a nearly constant anxious state of hyper-arousal. Several researchers have found evidence, based upon the results of MMPI research, that some female sex offenders are hypervigilant, mistrustful, suspicious or paranoid.[767] For hypervigilant individuals who have been previously abused, idiosyncratic elements of the environment may serve as conscious or unconscious warning signs of potential harm or as reminders of harm previously done.

The female sex offender who has been sexually abused by a family member does not necessarily enter therapy with the presupposition that the therapist, for whom there are fewer societal taboos, will not attempt exploitive sexual relations with her. Idiosyncratic elements of the therapy experience may suggest or even insist upon this possibility. Details of the therapy room or the therapist, for example, may raise the anxiety of such a client. The female child abuser may notice that the room contains a couch, that there is a strange man's voice outside the door, that the therapist is between herself and the exit, that the therapist has asked her several questions of a sexual nature, that there are books about sexual response on the shelves, that the therapist seems annoyed or is breathing in a way that suggests the early stages of arousal and so forth. A lack of a sense of safety may interfere with the ability of the female sex offender to attend to the therapeutic conversation.

Lack of Self-Esteem and Identity

Female sex offenders have commonly been observed to lack a positive sense of esteem and a cohesive sense of identity. Identity confusion among independent offenders has also been noted on MMPI-2 testing.[768] Addressing victimization and offending experiences may be experienced by female sex offenders as very threatening to their sense of selves. Female sex offenders often have diagnoses that place them at risk for decompensation to lower levels of functioning under stress. Under stress their sense of identity, often fragile, may become diffuse, and their sense of self-esteem, often poor, may be shattered.

Even in periods of relative stability, female sex offenders may lack a cohesive sense of identity. For those with borderline personality disorder, the sense of identity may be markedly and persistently unstable. Those with eating disorders may have distorted body images, as may those who are victims of trauma. For those with dissociative disorders, the sense of self may not be consistently integrated; the offender may disengage herself from her surroundings. Individuals with psychotic symptoms may experience a distorted sense of themselves. Offenders with depressive disorders may experience themselves as globally and unalterably "bad." Many female sex offenders have experienced themselves in altered states, such as dissociation, drug/alcohol intoxication or psychosis. Additionally, most female sex offenders have been both victims and victimizers. Integrating and making sense of these varied experiences of self may be a difficult task.

In some cases, making sense of a diffuse or nonintegrated sense of identity may be made particularly difficult by problems with memory. Some trauma victims repress or block memories so that they are not easily accessed. Aspects of self that are not recalled are not easily integrated into a cohesive sense of self.

Some offenders may have been abused very early in childhood or in adolescence when the developmental tasks of forming a sense of autonomy or identity were particularly salient. Preoccupation with trauma-related concerns may have interfered with these normal developmental tasks and with the building blocks for a stable sense of identity. Many female sex offenders are observed as regressed or delayed in their social presentation.[769]

Female child molesters' lack of identity cohesion may extend to their sexual identity. They may lack a consistent sense of sexual identity. They may also participate in sexual activities outside of their preferred sexual orientation.[770] They may lack the sense that they can choose and enforce their sexual identity.

Additionally, female sex offenders' sense of reality and sense of self may be continually in flux. Some traumatized female sex offenders may have learned to quickly adapt their beliefs and sense of self to situations, as necessary for survival. As children many had to believe that their own abuse never happened or that they loved their offenders in order to carry on their daily lives and have their survival needs met by the offender. The ability to distort their beliefs and their sense of who they are has been observed by several authors with respect to female sex offenders. Offenders may lack the ability to hold opposing views on the same topic. They may surrender a defense on one day and return to it the next.

Therapists working with female sex offenders commonly note that they tend to possess a low self-esteem.[771] Lack of confidence, poor self-image and negative evaluation of one's self and accomplishments are common to victims of trauma.[772] Female offenders with trauma histories may, in fact, actually lack some of the skills that others possess, which may further impact upon their self-esteem. Carlson,[773] for example, noted that preoccupation with self-protection during or following trauma interferes with the activities that would allow the development of cognitive and social skills. Female sex offenders may realistically assess themselves as having cognitive or social skills deficits.

Threats to an already low sense of self-esteem may interfere with the female sex offender's ability to initially acknowledge her crimes. Female sex offenders who acknowledge their offenses have often been observed to experience a global sense of shame, rather than a behavior-specific sense of guilt.[774] Discussing difficult and traumatic life events is likely to be highly threatening to the self-esteem and identity of the female sex offender.

Defenses against Anxiety and Decompensation

Female sex offenders may use a variety of defenses to protect themselves from admitting to their crimes or the impact of their crimes upon the victims. The defenses may protect them from decompensation, a global sense of shame, identity diffusion, anxiety/depression or other forms of distress, which may sometimes be manifested in problematic behavior. In addition to sexual offending, some female sex offenders are at risk for aggression towards others, such as their mates or the children in their care. Some may harm themselves through self-mutilation, suicidal behaviors, drugs/alcohol, eating, disordered behavior or other behaviors. Some may also commit other illegal acts, such as stealing or fire setting. It is important that maladaptive defense mechanisms be replaced with appropriate coping strategies before material is addressed that is likely to trigger the emotions that may precede these high-risk behaviors. For female offenders who are at risk for decompensation, defenses should not be challenged until effective coping strategies have been addressed.

The defenses of female child molesters may include denial or repression,[775] complete "blocking" of memories[776] or minimization.[777] They may include various excuses or distortions of their behavior commonly heard among male sex offenders, such as providing sex education or responding to the sexual desires of the child.[778] The rationalizations may include being in love with the child.[779]

Females may sometimes have defenses that are distinct from those seen in male offenders. Some may hold the view that they did not have options aside from dependently responding to the requests or demands of a co-offender.[780] de Young[781] remarked that among sexually abused female offenders, one had rationalized her offense by stating that boys are "born knowing more about sex than girls are (p. 68)"; another reported that her own offenses had been loving, while her own abuse had been violent. The defense that boys are less likely to be harmed by sexual contact may be supported by society. Given the severity of many female offenders' abuse, their point of reference may indeed help to support the defense that they were less harmful to their victims than were their own victimizers.

Some female sex offenders have poor coping skills for managing their emotional problems and limited problem solving abilities.[782] They may defensively bend reality in order to cope, as in the "fluid reality" resembling the magical thinking of children described by Larson and Maison[783] or the denial and minimization commonly described by other authors. Some may retreat into fantasy or distort reality by way of coping with distress.[784] Premature exploration of their trauma or offending may spur the use of these defensive distortions or may trigger decompensation.

The defenses of the female offenders may include not only distorted beliefs but also defensive maneuvering in the therapy session. Female sex offenders have been observed to distract the therapist from the topic at hand, to divorce themselves from the process by "fading into the woodwork" and to engage in a defensive lack of comprehension.[785]

Larson and Maison[786] reported that the defenses against having committed the crimes were so strong for some women that "acknowledgement, when it does come, does so in bits and pieces, fading in and out...they do not even remember from week to week whether or not they have acknowledged their involvement, literally believing one week that they did not do it, and the next week they did (p. 30)."

Appropriately pacing therapy is an important task of the therapist. Premature disclosure of intimate, horrifying, humiliating, overwhelming life events outside of the context of a safe environment in which trust has been firmly established in the therapeutic relationship may overwhelm the severely traumatized individual. Appropriate coping mechanisms must also be in place. Furthermore, allowing the client to prematurely disclose highly personal information before a strong rapport has been established creates a model for relationship that does not include the establishment of appropriate boundaries and trust building. Establishing these relationship dynamics as normal may be counter-therapeutic to the offender who is at risk for multiple victimizations. The early work of therapy with female child molesters is a balancing act between gathering enough information necessary to establish safety, particularly for victims, and building the framework for a trusting relationship by appropriately respecting the client's defenses.

Where strong defenses are occurring, it may be indicative that the offender does not yet have the coping strategies for managing the truth and that increased work is necessary in areas such as establishing safety and trust, building identity and self-esteem or developing adaptive defenses or coping resources. Frustration with a client who is not surrendering maladaptive defenses may be an indicator that more attention to these early tasks of therapy is needed.

Poor Learning Skills

A variety of cognitive and emotional difficulties may interfere with the ability of the female sex offender to attend to information received in therapy sessions. Some female sex offenders have been observed to have lower IQs and may have difficulty grasping complex information. Others have been observed to lack academic achievement and learning skills in spite of their normal abilities.[787] Among independent offenders, MMPI-2 testing has documented difficulties with thinking and concentration.[788] Female sex offenders who have been exposed to trauma in their childhoods have often been distracted from the development of normal learning and processing skills. They may not easily attend to information or integrate it with their previous learning.

Those female sex offenders with a particularly tenuous sense of identity, who do not consistently hold the same beliefs or self-concepts from one day to the next, may be inconsistent in their processing and integrating of information from therapy sessions. Some offenders may demonstrate a defensive lack of comprehension described as "thoughtlessness" by Larson and Maison;[789] they may not understand information in a defensive attempt to be taken care of. Emotional disorders such as depression, anxiety, post-traumatic stress and dissociation, which are common diagnoses to female sex offenders, all have the capacity to impede concentration, attention and learning skills. Female child molesters who are hypervigilant may attend to information related to their safety, rather than information related to their treatment. The ability of female child molesters to attend to and process material presented in session may be inconsistent or tenuous.

Common diagnoses among female child molesters are similar to those commonly found among abuse victims and among sexual abuse victims in particular. Poor reality testing during periods of stress is common with some of the more common diagnoses seen among female sex offenders. Individuals with post-traumatic stress disorder may experience symptoms that resemble psychosis in which the traumatic events are re-experienced. With borderline personality disorder, decompensation may include periods of psychotic-like symptoms. In the more severe forms of dissociation the individual may take on other "personalities," in which the sense of self becomes profoundly distorted and the sense of reality becomes impaired and without integration. Individuals with major depressive disorders may also experience psychotic features. Female sex offenders may begin therapy with poor skills for reality testing, which may impede learning.

Therapeutic Stance of the Therapist

With the potential problems of the female sexual abuser in participating in the therapeutic relationship, it becomes the task of the therapist to attend to the therapeutic relationship itself prior to beginning the more in-depth tasks of therapy. The therapist must be able to form an appropriate working relationship with the client, be able to model appropriate behaviors and be able to facilitate learning in the sessions.

The Therapeutic Relationship: Unconditional Positive Regard/Nurturing

Unconditional positive regard has been identified as crucial in the development of the therapeutic relationship with female sex offenders.[790] In describing the development of a therapeutic alliance with trauma victims in general, Herman[791] advocates "persuasion rather than coercion, ideas rather than force, mutuality rather than authoritarian control (p. 136)."

Offenders may tend to distance themselves from the therapeutic relationship or from group therapy members since, given their traumatic histories, getting close with another human being spells danger.[792] Larson and Maison[793] comment that without the ability to attach, female offenders are particularly vulnerable to returning to victim or offender roles. They suggest that the therapist take the role of an "emotional mother" for a period of time.

Mathews, Matthews & Speltz[794] also use the metaphor of "parenting" in working with female offenders. They describe the female sex offenders in their program as follows:

> In regard to their emotional development the women were almost like children. One of the tasks of the group was to re-parent these women in order to help them develop sound emotional responses. They were dependent, fearful, nonassertive, intimidated by authority, and rebellious. They lacked confidence and self-esteem (p. 93).

Female sex offenders may seek to have their dependency needs met as a primary function of therapy. While meeting the dependency needs of the abused client is not a primary goal of therapy, meeting some of the dependency needs in the early stages of therapy may reduce the anxiety of the severely traumatized offender. Providing nurturing or the opportunity to have nurturing experiences may be an important part of the early stage of therapy. The therapist may choose to meet some of these needs by adopting a nurturing stance or by facilitating opportunities to have nurturing experiences. Saradjian and Hanks,[795] for example, advocate for social support networks to be put in place before therapy begins.

Larson and Maison,[796] as well as Turner and Turner,[797] point to the necessity of teaching normal social interactions and of nurturing when working with female sex offenders. Larson and Maison,[798] for example, encouraged the women in their prison group to meet with a leader (who was not a therapist) for social activities; they noted that the women opted, among other activities, to have cakes for one another's birthdays. Some of the women had never had birthday celebrations as children.

With severely traumatized individuals, initially meeting some of the dependency needs in highly concrete, circumscribed and defined ways, for which there are clearly set parameters, may be appropriate. Providing nurturing in concrete forms, such as a cup of tea, a small snack or a greeting card on special occasions, may be appropriate for this population. Such gestures may also assist in the establishment of trust and rapport in this highly mistrustful population.

Maison and Larson[799] caution that in working with the female offender, the therapist must expect to be repeatedly rebuffed. Because of their need to control and to avoid emotional pain, they "ferociously resist emotional connections (p. 154)." Nevertheless, many researchers believe that the relationship between the female sex offender and the therapist may be one of the crucial variables in the success of the therapy.[800]

Therapist Self-Awareness

Severely victimized individuals are often extremely sensitive to the changes in moods of others and may easily perceive when they are being thought of in a negative light. They may be acutely aware of the body language, voice, facial expressions and so forth in others.[801] Some female sex offenders come from families in which sexual meanings are perceived in everyday exchanges;[802] they may perceive sexual intent or meaning on the part of the therapist.[803]

Work with offenders who have been victims is ripe with the potential for counter transference. Therapists should expect to feel themselves being pulled to engage in the role of a victim or victimizer. They may experience sexual overtones or sexualized "testing" from the female offender. Mathews, Hunter and Vuz[804] pointed to the importance of an understanding of transference and counter transference concerns on the part of the therapist working with female sex offenders. Therapists should be aware of their own moods and sexuality during sessions. The therapist should ideally have a trusted supervisor or peer, with whom she can debrief and process the content of the sessions. Saradjian & Hanks[805] point to the importance of the therapist having appropriate supervision, as well as appropriate support distinct from supervision, which focuses on the feelings engendered in the therapist by work with the female offenders.

Matching the Developmental Abilities of the Client

The therapist should be mindful that the female sex offender, given the likelihood of severe victimization, might have developmental delays in socialization. In developing a rapport, it may serve the therapist well to observe the level of social development of the female sex offender.

In developing rapport, it is necessary to incorporate tasks that match the individual's level of development. Many offenders may not be capable of consistently acting in the social role of an adult who is in partnership with another adult. While it should not be the goal to treat the client like a child, finding ways, particularly in the early stage of therapy, to join with the client in an effective manner may require creativity and attention to potential delays in social abilities.

In some cases, integrating some of the items commonly used for play therapy or for work with teenagers may prove useful in rapport development and also in assisting the offender to master developmental tasks missed during childhood, adolescence and young adulthood. In later stages of therapy, of course, as the client's social skills increase, these interactions should be phased out and replaced with other, more adult forms of interaction.

Establishing Trust and Teaching Trust

Female sex offenders may require education concerning the process of trust building and of gradually increasing disclosure as trust is developed. Many may require assistance to recognize signs that an individual such as their therapist is trustworthy. Therapy should assist the offender to appropriately establish the boundaries and set the limits in therapy necessary to develop a sense of trust in the therapist.

Female sex offenders may lack basic information concerning the means by which people develop trust. Discussion concerning signs that someone is or is not trustworthy may be appropriate early in therapy. The therapist may wish to emphasize that individuals often proceed slowly with self-disclosure, "testing the waters" with minimally important or only slightly important or emotionally laden information, as a process of trust building, before increasing self-disclosure to include more distressing or personal information. They may wish to review techniques for communicating that trust has been broken. Larson and Maison[806] noted that offenders in their treatment group often devised tests to determine whether the therapists were trustworthy, at times with the help of the therapists, and that this contributed to trust formation. Welldon[807] recommended that steps be taken to assure the women that the counselor will take proper care and that nothing "awful" will take place.

Consistency and Predictability

Offenders who have been severely victimized have reason for exquisite sensitivity to subtle issues related to exploitation, abandonment, rejection and the like. Many have grown up in homes that lacked predictability.[808] Many severely abused individuals develop a hypervigilance or an early warning system to protect them from potential dangers. To prevent triggering such fears, the therapy environment should be consistent and predictable. Many severely abused individuals develop a hypervigilance or an early warning system to protect them from potential dangers. To prevent triggering such fears the therapy environment should be consistent and predictable.

The context in which therapy occurs should be as consistent as possible. It should provide external support and structure while the offender slowly gains internal organization and stability. The location, room, room set up, time for therapy and so forth should remain as consistent as possible. The routine in the therapy session should also remain as consistent as possible. Turner and Turner,[809] for example, enhanced the self-containment and safety of the group with a beginning and closing ritual created by the group members.

Therapy sessions should be scheduled insofar as possible, during times that are not likely to be cancelled. Advanced warning and explanation may be necessary prior to normal disruptions in treatment for holidays and the like. The severely traumatized individual may require time to process such events, with reassurances from the therapist to prevent the development of mistrust. The therapist should be predictable and follow through on promises. Minor alterations in a promise may confirm for a hypervigilant offender that the therapist is not worthy of trust or that she may be actively exploitive.

Creating a Context

Outside of a firmly established therapeutic context, exploration of victimization and offending concerns may be experienced as an intrusive, overwhelming, humiliating, sexually exploitive series of events, in which the client is pushed by the therapist to relive demeaning and overwhelming occurrences. Because exploration of trauma and offending may be viewed as exploitive, intrusive or abusive by the female offender, its purpose should be thoroughly explained to the severely traumatized offender. Because psychological diagnoses that are common to the offender may interfere with the processing and retention of information, the purpose for and process of therapy should probably be explained several times. A simple to understand and often repeated rationale and explanation of what treatment will entail should be presented to the client prior to beginning active treatment. This also holds true for specific techniques. Outside of a clearly understood context and informed consent to participate in therapy, questions concerning abuse may cause the abused offenders to feel revictimized, having yet another sexual and humiliating experience forced upon them when they have no ability to control or stop it.

The limits of confidentiality should similarly be reviewed several times with the offender. Any limitations to confidentiality, such as required reports to courts, probation officers, lawyers and so forth should be discussed in detail with the client. Limitations common to the practice of psychotherapy, such as disclosure of risk to harm of self or others or the reporting of victims should be discussed with the offender several times. Larson and Maison[810] reported on an incident in which a group of female sex offenders in treatment felt profoundly betrayed by a highly clinically appropriate, safety-related breach in confidentiality concerning one of the group members, in a group in which that particular limitation of confidentiality had been previously reviewed.

Saradjian and Hanks[811] recommend establishing a contract with the offender that clearly states what the therapist and client can expect from treatment. They further recommend that this contract include the forewarning that therapy can be painful, so that painful feelings are not experienced by the offender as failure on the part of the client, therapist or therapy process itself.

Respecting Defenses

The co-morbid problems, psychological diagnoses, psychosocial histories and available psychological testing point to the potential danger of decompensation among female offenders when exploration of victimization and offending is not carefully balanced against the strength of their coping resources. Experiences of therapists working with female child molesters confirm this concern. In working with female offenders it is important to be alert for diagnoses, psychosocial histories, co-morbid problems or psychological testing results that suggest that the individual is readily prone to decompensation. Exploration of traumatic aspects of psychosocial history must be carefully balanced with the female sex offender's history of ability to manage stress. Premature intrusion into the personal trauma of the individual, particularly if it is insistent or if it occurs contrary to the wishes of the offender, recreates the dynamics of abuse.

Female sex offenders may require help to pace the disclosure of their histories of victimizing and offending. Severely victimized individuals may become flooded in therapy and have difficulty both self-monitoring their rate of disclosure and self-regulating their anxiety. Memories of abuse or offending may be perceived as overwhelming. Under circumstances in which there is not a firmly established sense of trust in the therapeutic relationship, individuals who have come to experience the world as solely comprised of victims and victimizers may experience revictimization when this occurs. They may experience the therapist who has encouraged such disclosure as abusive.

Female offenders may utilize simplistic but tenacious defenses. Before these defenses are replaced with healthier coping mechanisms, breaking too rapidly through the defenses may result in impaired functioning for the client. Strong emotion can often be a precursor for several behaviors in which harm is directed towards the self, others or property, including the sexually offending behaviors themselves. Larson and Maison[812] caution, based upon their experiences in treating incest victims that, "If unlocked too quickly, one sometimes sees flooding and decompensation (p. 22)." Regarding the female offenders, they similarly commented, "We believe that a great deal of therapy to shore up their ego strength is needed before they are able and/or willing to unblock (p. 22)." They note that with female sex offenders, direct confrontation provokes either a victim or a perpetrator response, both of which are undesirable.

Turner and Turner[813] issued similar cautions for working with adolescent female sex offenders. They stated, "The plan of our treatment is not to immediately delve into the sexual abuse history but to help the client develop the coping mechanisms that will allow her to become aware of the effects of her history on her present behavior (p. 50)." They further state that, "Treatment must give the client the coping strategies to deal with the emotions that will be triggered when repression is released (p. 47)." Matthews, Mathews and Speltz[814] also make very similar comments, based upon the results of personality testing of female offenders:

> Attacking the weak ego that these women show on the MMPI would probably push them into decompensation, stripping them of the few resources for change that they have (p. 100).

Some have suggested specific techniques for distancing the client from the emotional aspects of her personal history, while still allowing her to process these events. Larson and Maison[815] advocate the use of such techniques as paradox, metaphor, story telling and reframing, for example. Turner and Turner[816] describe techniques such as creating a "news interview" about the group, doing skits with pseudonyms, role-playing and using masks to express feelings. When offenders do not have a fully integrated view of themselves, it may also be useful to acknowledge that "a part of" the offender believes the defense to be true while another part does not. Verbalizations such as "a part of you wants to believe that children are not hurt by sexual abuse" or "some days you think that the abuse happened, but on days like today, you prefer to believe that it did not" may be useful. They not only assist to identify that the offender can hold more than one view on a topic but also set the groundwork for later exploration of factors that cause the views to be different.

Therapists can also use their expert status to normalize the defense and to plant the seed and the expectation that the denial (or another defense) will change, without directly challenging the defense itself. For example, "Some people have a hard time knowing what their victims felt because it is just too hard to think about. Eventually, they get stronger in therapy and they can cope with thinking more about it."

Each of these techniques allows for processing of emotionally laden material without premature discussion of the traumatic elements of an individual's personal history.

Female offenders are not consistently prosecuted, imprisoned or mandated to treatment through the courts and they may continue to retain custody of or have unsupervised access to their children.[817] In cases in which female sex offenders continue to have access to victims, it is particularly important that treatment not increase the emotions often found to precede sexual offending without first assisting the offenders to develop the wherewithal to manage these emotions. Evidence of ability to manage an exploration of trauma and offending may be gleaned from the history of harm to self, others and property; psychiatric diagnosis; psychological testing; mental status; the extent of personal trauma; and available support resources.

Not all female sex offenders carry the diagnoses or have the psychosocial histories that suggest concern related to the potential for decompensation, and some female sex offenders have been observed to readily surrender their defenses in a supportive environment in which they are provided with unconditional positive regard. The concerns about assisting the offender with early therapeutic tasks will vary among clients. Research concerning female sex offenders is in its infancy. As more becomes known about female offenders, perhaps less severely impaired female offenders, who require less time to address the skills necessary to participate in the therapeutic relationship, will be identified for treatment.

Role Modeling

Assertive Communicator

Initially lacking the role models or immediate experiences upon which to build a context for the therapeutic relationship, victims and offenders may adopt patterns of interaction that are familiar to them. Female sex offenders may initially take a passive role in their treatment or a defiant, controlling role. An assertive stance on the part of the therapist allows the offender to participate in a relationship in which the tasks of the relationship are accomplished without aggression or passivity. Establishing assertive communication patterns in the therapy session also allows a context in which the female sex offender may experience and interact with an authority figure who is not abusive or exploitive. It allows the offender to observe effective communication. The therapist may also assist the offender to develop assertiveness skills and encourage her to take an assertive role in her treatment.

Based upon common findings that the severity of trauma tends to be far greater among female sex offenders than among male sex offenders, Mathews, Hunter and Vuz[818] have questioned whether techniques used for male sex offenders, which are commonly highly confrontational, are adequate or sufficient for female offenders. Some authors who have worked with female offenders have recommended against heavy use of confrontation. Larson and Maison[819] note the importance of avoiding confrontation. When distorted information is presented by a female sex offender, the therapist should gently express confusion. Therapists should also reinforce adaptive interactions as they occur.

Larson and Maison[820] describe the technique of reinforcing appropriate behaviors rather than confronting inappropriate behaviors. This technique also has utility in that it facilitates learning. In facilitating the development of a new behavior, frequent reinforcement for successive approximations has been known as a successful technique since the early days of the behavioral psychologists. Female child molesters should be frequently reinforced for using communication skills that approximate appropriately assertive adult interactions.

In some cases, the therapist may have to be creative in order to identify and reinforce skills that represent the best the female offender is initially capable of, while still providing adequate feedback to move therapy forward. For example, "While I don't like that you are yelling at me, I do appreciate that you have made it very clear that one of your goals is to have your children returned." or "Let's talk about what would need to happen for that to occur." or "I am very glad that you are putting your feelings into words. It is clear to me that you are the type of person who is able to find the words to express yourself. Not everyone knows how to do that." or "I really like that you are able to let me know when you disagree with me. When you shake your head like that, I don't understand all of the reasons why you disagree, but I will try to help you to find the words to express yourself. Letting me know that you disagree is the first step and I want you to know that I appreciate that you are beginning to communicate what is on your mind."

In the early stage of therapy, this technique can also be useful in order to help the offender identify and reinforce those strengths that will facilitate her communication in therapy. For example, "You know some people aren't brave enough to even think about their victims or their offending this soon. I wonder what gave you the courage to even admit that it happened." or "When we were talking about things that you could do after our meetings to relax, you came up with four things right off of the bat. It's clear to me that when you put your mind to it, you are able to find solutions to problems. How did you get to be good at this?"

Maison and Larson[821] recommended that female offenders be encouraged to recognize and to make choices in the interest of expanding upon their locus of control. In the prison setting, this included decisions related to whether or not to attend a meal or make a phone call, as well as more difficult life decisions. They pointed out that abuse victims who become perpetrators are likely to assume no responsibility for things that happen in their lives.

Establishing Boundaries

Sexual abuse, both in the form of victimization and perpetration, involves a violation of boundaries. Normal respect for the separateness of individual personal space, feelings, needs, role expectations and so forth are disregarded. Disregard of the tangible and intangible elements that separate people from one another is inherent in experiences of sexual abuse. "These women are very likely to challenge the personal boundaries of the therapist (p. 216)."[822] Care must be taken to firmly establish boundaries in session. This includes physical boundaries, such as allowing ample body space, and mutually established boundaries concerning touch. Idiosyncratic forms of touch may be associated with sexualization and exploitation for abused individuals. Until the clients have developed skills in asserting their preferences with authority figures, therapists run the risk of sexualizing and subtly victimizing their clients with otherwise socially appropriate touching. Role expectations, expectations regarding physical proximity and so forth may have to be assertively described to the client.

Additionally, therapists should be clear about their boundaries concerning the therapeutic relationship. Many female offenders have never experienced an appropriate relationship or the establishment of appropriate parameters in a relationship. The therapist should be clear and firm concerning appropriate limits such as telephone contacts, visits outside of regular times and the like.

Therapy Techniques for Facilitating Learning in the Early Stages of Therapy

Holding the Attention of the Female Sex Offender

Female sex offenders often carry diagnoses such as anxiety or mood disorders that impede their ability to concentrate and pay attention in the session. Many can be expected to have difficulty attending to and processing information. Attention to factors that facilitate learning in the classroom may be useful for clients with difficulties in attending to and retaining information from sessions. For example, the therapist may opt to provide multi-modal learning experiences. Rather than using an exchange of verbalizations as the exclusive medium for information presentation in session, the therapist may opt to provide visual handouts or to have the client write down information, draw or work with art materials. She may provide a video or provide the opportunity for experiential learning such as role-playing. Turner and Turner,[823] for example, include dance therapy in their treatment of adolescent female sex offenders.

For individuals who have particular difficulty paying attention or remaining focused, the therapist may wish to optimize learning by attending to the level of attention of the client. When individuals are too bored or under-stimulated, less learning takes place. Similarly, when individuals are emotionally flooded, they may "tune out" or become overwhelmed and have similar difficulties processing information. Monitoring the female sex offender's ability to attend to and process information, as a function of the level of emotional stimulation during the therapy session, is important. Therapists should monitor the emotional content of the sessions. Other stimulation, such as the brightness of visual materials, the voice level of the therapist and the amount of information covered, should be monitored as well. Stimulation should be adjusted in keeping with the abilities of the client to attend to, focus upon, process and retain the information presented.

Some clients may be easily distracted or be hypervigilant for danger and may require redirection in order to remain focused on the topics at hand. Clients may require similar redirection when they appear to be drifting away from important topics that are within their capacity either to discuss or to assertively refuse to discuss until they are better prepared with coping responses. They may also require redirection away from the topic at hand when they are becoming emotionally overwhelmed by premature disclosure.

Repetition and Reinforcement

Repetition is useful in facilitating learning. For clients who have lower intelligence or for clients who have difficulty learning because of emotional interference repetition may be necessary to facilitate learning. The therapist may repeat or have the client repeat back information in sessions. The therapist may overlap information between sessions or between types of session, for example, by processing group material in individual sessions. She may further reinforce learning by requiring homework assignments or by reviewing previous sessions at the start of each new session. She may arrange for sessions to build upon on one another. For example, if a first session focuses on self-esteem and a second focuses on assertive "I-messages," a third might focus on I-messages related to self-esteem or on the relationship between assertiveness and self-esteem.

Reinforcement facilitates learning. In the acquisition of a new skill, individuals learn more rapidly with frequent reinforcement and by having successive approximations reinforced. The therapist should recognize and verbally reinforce the approximation of and attainment of therapeutic goals such as speaking up in session, asserting an opinion, verbalizing statements related to a positive self-esteem and the like.

The therapist should not only reinforce the client's behaviors verbally but should also provide reinforcing responses to appropriate client interactions in session. Attending to, respecting, appropriately responding to and demonstrating an interest in the client who is attempting to interact appropriately may all be reinforcing to the client. More formal behavior charts that allow for other types of reinforcement for specific target behaviors might also be considered.

Summary

Given the common finding that many female child sexual abusers have themselves been sexually abused, and often traumatized in other ways, it can be expected that many will have difficulty participating in the therapeutic relationship. Poor relationship skills, a lack of a sense of safety, poor self-esteem and a poorly consolidated identity, tenacious defenses and poor learning skills are all likely to interfere with the ability of many female sex offenders to participate in the therapeutic relationship. It falls to the therapist to assist in creating a relationship in which trust and safety are emphasized and in which appropriate relationship skills are modeled. Attention to factors that augment learning in the session is appropriate, given the multitude of problems that the female sex offenders may have that have the potential to interfere with learning in the session.

Notes ────────────────────────────
[753] Chatham (1992); Davin (1999); Larson & Maison (1987); Saradjian & Hanks (1996); Wolfe (1985); Woodring (1995)
[754] Herman (1997)
[755] Larson & Maison (1987)
[756] Woodring (1995)
[757] Herman (1997)
[758] Larson & Maison (1987)
[759] Turner & Turner (1994)
[760] Mathews, Hunter & Vuz (1997)
[761] Larson & Maison (1987)
[762] Mathews et al. (1997)
[763] Larson & Maison (1987); Turner & Turner (1994)
[764] Green & Kaplan (1994); Larson & Maison (1987)
[765] Herman (1997)
[766] Saradjian & Hanks (1996)
[767] Davin (1999); Hudson (1995); Mathews, Matthews & Speltz (1989); Woodring (1995)
[768] Davin (1999)
[769] Larson & Maison (1985); Mathews, Matthews & Speltz (1989)
[770] Hislop (1998)
[771] Larson & Maison (1987); Matthews (1994); Saradjian & Hanks (1996); Turner & Turner (1994)

[772] Carlson (1997)
[773] Carlson (1997)
[774] Larson & Maison (1987); Matthews (1994); Turner & Turner (1994)
[775] Woodring (1995)
[776] Larson & Maison (1987)
[777] Wolfe (1985)
[778] Wolfe (1985)
[779] Larson & Maison; Matthews (1994); Wolfe (1985)
[780] Wolfe (1985)
[781] de Young (1982)
[782] Woodring (1995)
[783] Larson & Maison (1987)
[784] Woodring (1995)
[785] Larson & Maison (1987)
[786] Larson & Maison (1987)
[787] Larson & Maison (1989); Saradjian & Hanks (1996)
[788] Davin (1999)
[789] Larson & Maison (1987)
[790] Turner & Turner (1994); Matthews, Mathews & Speltz (1989); & Larson & Maison (1987)
[791] Herman (1997)
[792] Larson & Maison (1987)
[793] Larson & Maison (1987)
[794] Mathews, Matthews & Speltz (1989)
[795] Saradjian & Hanks (1996)
[796] Larson & Maison (1987)
[797] Turner, & Turner (1994)
[798] Larson & Maison (1987)
[799] Maison & Larson (1995)
[800] Maison & Larson (1995); Saradjian & Hanks (1996)
[801] Herman (1997)
[802] Matthews (1994)
[803] Saradjian & Hanks (1996)
[804] Mathews, Hunter & Vuz (1997)
[805] Saradjian & Hanks (1996)
[806] Larson & Maison (1987)
[807] Welldon (1996)
[808] Maison & Larson (1995)
[809] Turner & Turner (1994)
[810] Larson & Maison (1987)
[811] Saradjian & Hanks (1996)
[812] Larson & Maison (1987)
[813] Turner & Turner (1994)
[814] Matthews, Mathews & Speltz (1989)
[815] Larson & Maison (1987)
[816] Turner & Turner (1994)

[817] Allen (1991); Faller (1995); Freel (1995); Larson & Maison (1987); Mathews, Matthews & Speltz (1989)
[818] Mathews, Hunter & Vuz (1997)
[819] Larson & Maison (1987)
[820] Larson & Maison (1987)
[821] Maison & Larson (1995)
[822] Saradjian & Hanks (1996)
[823] Turner & Turner (1994)

10. The Early Tasks of Therapy

The ultimate purpose of offender therapy is for the female to comprehensively understand her personal patterns and precursors to abusing others, to have a repertoire of alternatives for managing those patterns and precursors and to become practiced at effectively self-monitoring and implementing those alternatives. This requires a comprehensive exploration of the psychosocial history of the offender with a focus on cycles of her offending and, in many cases, on the ways in which her personal victimization may have contributed to offending. Female sex offenders, however, commonly have severely traumatic psychosocial histories, as well as diagnoses that predispose them to decompensate under stress, such as might occur during an exploration of a traumatic personal history. Among the primary tasks for the therapist in the early stage of therapy is assisting the female sex offender to develop the coping skills that are necessary to actively address the problem of sexual offending without defensively distorting reality, relying on denial/minimization or decompensating.

Difficulties resulting from a history of trauma may impair the ability of the individual to engage in the therapeutic relationship necessary for the treatment process. Prior to addressing traumatic areas such as victimization and offending, the therapist should assist the client to develop the sense of safety in the process and the coping resources necessary for this work. Early work in treatment for many more severely victimized offenders should focus on increasing a sense of safety and trust, developing coping resources, improving self-esteem and consolidating identity. In the early stages of therapy with a female sex offender who has been severely victimized, pacing should also be a primary concern.

Clients who require the greatest time and attention to such early tasks of therapy may include those who have experienced severe trauma histories. For example, those who have trauma histories involving multiple forms of trauma, multiple perpetrators, earlier onset of trauma, longer duration or greater frequency of trauma and closer relationships with the perpetrators may require more assistance in these areas. Several of these variables may be related to more serious harm to the victim in cases of child sexual abuse.[824] Clients with severe victimizing histories, fewer coping strategies or support systems and histories of poor reality testing or of harm towards the self, others or property may also require extra time and attention to the early tasks of therapy.

In order to develop the coping skills necessary to accomplish this, the offender must develop a basic sense of trust in the therapist. She must be in an environment that allows her to learn, in spite of her emotional distress and preoccupation with managing or avoiding the unspeakable facts of her life. She must have a sense of identity and of self-esteem that is able to withstand the humiliation and distress of an exploration and scrutiny of the details of the most horrifying, painful and degrading aspects of her life. She must find the means to trust an individual who wants to talk to her about her most shameful behaviors and those secret things which, when revealed, may produce panic, rage, shame and despair. In the context of a life in which she is likely to have been terrorized and sexually exploited by close members of her social network and family, she must develop trust in a stranger.

This is a tall order.

Establishing Safety

Helping the offender to establish safety in her life is the overriding purpose of offender treatment and should be emphasized early in the treatment process by way of laying the groundwork for therapy. Establishing a sense of safety for the traumatized individual is a key component of the early stage of therapy, from the perspective of a variety of authors who have treated trauma victims.[825] Areas of safety to be established include victim safety, as well as the personal and emotional safety of the offender, both in sessions and in general.

A primary task of the initial stage of therapy is to ensure the safety of the victims. If the offender is not in prison or in residential treatment, this may involve consultation with other collaborating agencies such as foster care, probation, police and so on. While a comprehensive review of the details of the cycles of offending may not be possible during the first stage of therapy, the therapist should obtain adequate information to promote the safety of the victims, such as their names and locations. Collaboration with the agencies should be done with the full knowledge of the offender. Saradjian and Hanks[826] recommend that the offenders not have access to children directly after sessions to minimize the likelihood that emotions resulting from therapy will result in further offenses.

Establishing the safety of the offender from individuals who may be physically, sexually or emotionally abusing her is a key consideration early in treatment. Few changes in mental health status are to be expected from individuals who are being actively victimized. Because female sex offenders may have abusive male co-offenders, initial education concerning legal options, community shelter options and other forms of safety planning may be necessary. The therapist should also consider that the female sex offender in treatment may be experiencing physical, sexual or emotional abuse from members of her family of origin, or in other relationships, and may require safety plans for managing these relationships. Abusive relationships begun in the female sex offender's childhood sometimes continue into adulthood.

Because some victims of abuse often do not feel safe anywhere, the therapist may wish to devote some time, initially, to actively improving the victimized offender's sense of personal safety. A focus on practical safety skills is also important since individuals with histories of incestuous victimization are at elevated risk for subsequent revictimization.[827] Female sex offenders may require assistance for maximizing their level of safety in the community. Practical education concerning self-protection in various community situations may assist the offender to develop and experience a preliminary sense of safety.

Some female sex offenders may require assistance in reality testing their safety plans. Some severely victimized offenders have learned to disregard their lack of a sense of safety during the period of their own abuse. Alternately, some may be continually hypervigilant and wary. The therapist may wish to encourage the female sex offender to begin to actively identify and reality test those things that make her feel safe and unsafe. Learning to identify and to reality test cues for safety and for lack of safety may be useful to the female offender who may be both overly fearful and at risk for entering high risk or dangerous situations in order to have her emotional needs met.

Safety rituals, which combine practical safety behaviors with relaxation exercises, may be useful for highly fearful or anxious individuals. Safety rituals might include practical activities such as locking doors/windows or establishing a comfortable body space. They might include surrounding oneself with safe items — favorite blanket, favorite activities, comfort food (if the individual does not have an eating disorder) and the like. They may involve guided imagery exercises or other relaxation exercises or self-statements related to safety. As the relationship begins, the therapist and client might collaborate on rules for a safe environment in session and upon rules for therapy.

Early in therapy, plans should be developed for managing unsafe behaviors related to harm to self, others or property. Patterns that lead up to these behaviors should be identified and alternative plans developed. Alternative plans for safety might include getting to a safe place (including a psychiatric hospital in some cases), not being alone, taking steps to reduce the risk of acting on high risk plans (for example, dowsing matches for fire-setters, avoiding bars for alcoholics, getting rid of weapons for aggressors towards self/others, etc), calling upon a resource such as a crisis hot-line, religious leader or friend. Techniques for stress reduction can also be incorporated into safety plans. Severe symptoms that make the client feel unsafe, such as flashbacks and dissociation, may require similar interventions.

To establish a safe environment in group therapy, the therapist may wish to use similar techniques. Additionally, she may initially wish to orchestrate the flow of verbiage so that it initially flows primarily between herself and the group members, rather than initially encouraging exchanges between clients. Female sex offenders often have poor social skills. Among other female sex offenders they may be highly anxious, given the fact that they are, in one sense, sexual victims among child molesters and, in another, child molesters among victims. Because female sex offenders often enter treatment with poorly developed social skills, encouraging unstructured verbal exchanges between offenders during the stressful onset of treatment may set the stage for exploitive interactions. The therapist may also wish to take more responsibility for structuring the physical aspects of group therapy, in addition to structuring the process of the group. For example, she may wish to set up the chairs for group meetings to ensure adequate body space and boundaries between clients and so forth. In the interest of safety, group rules should be established early.

Improving Self-Esteem

A negative self-esteem and an overriding sense of shame concerning victimization and offending have been identified as reasons that female offenders avoid active exploration of offending and victimization issues. Exploration of traumatic material may also be threatening to the offender's tenuous sense of self. Not only should safety be explored in the preliminary stages of therapy, the therapist should also spend time identifying ways to improve the self-esteem and consolidate the identity of the offender.

Recognition and exploration of the strengths of the offender may assist in this regard and may also provide the therapist with insight concerning the ego strengths that might be drawn upon in order to facilitate therapy. Female sex offenders may be unaware of their positive attributes.

It has been noted by many researchers and clinicians that female offenders often do not achieve to their educational and occupational potential. Many offenders hold low wage jobs or have difficulty managing day-to-day affairs. A component in early work concerning the consolidation of the identity of the female offender and the improvement of self-esteem might include an examination of the life skills of the offender. Female offenders may not recognize their potential to achieve. Some may have been distracted by an abusive or neglectful home life during their school years or may have had inadequate attendance at school because of family chaos. For some offenders, intelligence testing, as well as vocational testing, may be appropriate during the early stages of therapy. Vocational development and planning may be an important component in not only improving self-esteem and identity but also in establishing a sense of safety, given that economic independence may be a necessary step in allowing the individual to live separately from abusive individuals.

Larson and Maison[828] recommend that treatment for female sex offenders include an emphasis on life skills development. Lloyd[829] described a case of a female sex offender in which occupational therapy was a component of a comprehensive hospital program. The author reported that the occupational therapist was involved in the client's budgeting group and vocational counseling/job placement group, in addition to being involved in more traditional offender therapy. Similarly, other members of the treatment team provided leisure counseling and education training, in addition to more traditional forms of therapy and psycho-education. Interventions such as these may also increase external daily structure for the individual who is struggling to reorganize her internal structure.

In some cases these independent strivings may threaten the offender who longs to be taken care of.[830] The therapist should be alert for, and should help the female offender to address, attempts to sabotage progress in such areas as educational or vocational progress.

An exploration of the offender's perceptions of gender and cultural identity may be useful in beginning to explore her self-esteem and identity. Female sex offenders often tend to have a more severe sexual abuse history than do male offenders. They often come from homes in which they witnessed violence against women. Many female offenders come from homes or have created homes in which the female is powerless or submissive. They may tend to view their gender role as one having less power, control and prestige than the male role. This view may be reinforced by society. Work aimed at increasing the self-esteem of the offender may include work related to gender identity. Exploration of female role models, female gender roles or of the positive aspects of being female may serve the offender in increasing her self-esteem.

Offenders are often abused in their families-of-origin by offenders of similar cultural backgrounds. Work in improving their self-esteem may include exploration of their cultural identity and discovery of the positive aspects of their cultural community. While most current studies have observed the majority of female offenders to be Caucasian, an exploration of the positive aspects of cultural identity may be particularly important for female offenders from minority populations that have experienced cultural oppression.

Education concerning the effect of abuse on self-esteem and how self-esteem may be artificially lowered by abuse may also be useful. While in-depth exploration of the dynamics of her own abuse may be premature in the early stage of therapy, education concerning the impact of abuse on self-esteem may be useful to the offender. The offender might be taught, for example, that because the negative impact of abuse can be all encompassing, many abused individuals do not attend to their positive qualities or have the opportunity to recognize and develop them.

Assisting the female sex offender to learn to be able to accept responsibility without a global sense of shame is an important early task of therapy. Some therapists who have worked with female sex offenders note the importance of the offenders being able to accept guilt ("I am guilty of the offense. I engaged in the offenses.") without shame ("Therefore, I am globally a bad person.").[831] Discussion of the fact that an individual may have done horrible things and still retain good qualities may be an important component to raising the self-esteem of the offender. To this end, Saradjian and Hanks[832] note that it is useful to state to the female child molester that all behavior is explainable if not excusable.

This is likely to be a difficult task for female sex offenders who have been severely abused; many may anticipate terror and physical or emotional pain subsequent to admissions of wrongdoing. However, without the sense of self-worth necessary to address material about which they feel guilty, limited processing of important clinical material will occur. Maison and Larson[833] reported that when shameful material is left unprocessed, the individual is left to wonder if she could still be loved were the hidden material made known. A shaming stance on the part of the therapist is likely to be ineffective. Maison and Larson[834] note that being shamed by others concerning their lives is simply "more of the same" for the female sex offenders.

Consolidating Identity

Maison and Larson[835] note that before the offenders are able to address the shame of offending, they must have a cohesive sense of self. Many female offenders do not have a stable sense of identity. Exploration into the self-concept of the offender may be useful at the onset of treatment. The therapist may wish to begin assisting the client in identifying descriptors of herself. She may assist the client to identify current defenses and coping strategies by assisting the client to identify those circumstances in which her self-perception and beliefs change, and whether these changes are temporary or permanent and partial or complete. For offenders who do not have strong verbal or social skills, projects such as drawings or collages that focus on self-concept may be useful in this process.

Some therapists have used body image work to assist traumatized individuals to gain a sense of identity. For example, some have traced the bodies of the clients on paper, to assist in improving body image and to be used as a concrete visual aid for facilitating discussion of body image and identity. A variation of this technique that is less intrusive for individuals who may be sensitive to having their anatomy traced by hand is shadow tracing in which a silhouette is created and traced.

Some offenders have been observed to change their sense of reality and beliefs periodically in order to manage their surroundings. Larson and Maison[836] present techniques for managing this fluid reality. Rather than confront the discrepancies in the views of the offenders, which may cause decompensation, they bring the conflicting views to the attention of the offender and express confusion. Identifying discrepancies in self-perceptions, beliefs and other aspects of identity, and assisting the offender to integrate them, may be useful in aiding the offender to develop a more consistent sense of self.

Turner and Turner[837] point out that prior to developing empathy for others, an offender must have empathy for herself. In order for this to occur, the offender must be able to identify herself as a person worthy of at least minimal amounts of compassion. With a history, commonly of their own trauma, offenders often have difficulty doing this. They must develop both a cohesive sense of self and least a tentative sense that that self has worth before they can develop empathy for themselves and, eventually, capacity to empathize with victims.

Teaching Coping Skills

Many female sex offenders, in addition to being overwhelmed with histories of abuse and the dysfunction of their lives, come from families in which they were not taught or modeled appropriate emotional self-regulation strategies. They may be both more distressed and more lacking in coping resources than are most individuals. Emotions may serve as triggers for memories or for similar emotions that were experienced in the context of life-threatening abuse and may spur "fight or flight" responses. Minor annoyances may trigger rage; small discomforts may trigger panic; small disappointments may be experienced as major betrayals and so forth.

Among female sex offenders who have learned to modulate their emotions are those individuals who have learned to do so through the tenacious use of denial, minimization and repression. Some authors have found that female sex offenders who use simplistic defensive denial demonstrate less overall pathology on psychological testing.[838] The use of defenses such as denial and repression may be in place to prevent decompensation on the part of the female offender. Prior to breaking through these defenses, it may be necessary to develop more adaptive coping strategies. Early attention to the development of coping mechanisms for managing emotions stimulated by work in therapy may be useful in assisting the female sex offender to benefit from the process. Several techniques for managing emotions include relaxation techniques, cognitive techniques, behavioral techniques and so forth.

The techniques of Rational Emotive Therapy[839] or of Cognitive Therapy[840] may have utility in the early stages of treatment. Both espouse the idea that when an event happens, the cognitive appraisal, self-statement or belief of the individual about the event has impact on the consequences of the individual's emotional reaction to that event. The techniques of recognizing, reevaluating and changing the beliefs or attitudes that exacerbate anxiety, depression, dissociation and other forms of decompensation can be taught in the early stages of therapy to assist the client to self-regulate her emotions.

Female sex offenders may also require assistance in order to learn to assertively express their needs when they need help to cope with a problem or to get their needs met. Female offenders are likely to have difficulty communicating their needs in ways that are neither passive nor aggressive. For many the perception of people as falling into the dichotomy of either being victims or offenders may be deeply ingrained. In order to participate as a vulnerable partner in the early stages of the therapeutic relationship, female sex offenders may benefit from assertiveness training.

Assertiveness training, for example, that focuses on "I-messages;" the difference between aggressive, passive-aggressive, passive, and assertive communication; negotiation; "win-win" outcomes; assertive body language; and active listening skills may be necessary to assist the female offender to assert herself. Teaching communication skills may be necessary in order to assist the offender in providing feedback concerning the pacing of therapy, her safety needs in session and so forth.

Because many female sex offenders were placed in situations of abuse, where childhood attempts to cope were futile, many may have learned a sense of helplessness. As such, they may have difficulty setting goals. This difficulty may be compounded by the effects of post-traumatic stress or depression, which can interfere with the ability to imagine a future. Further, the female sex offender may be motivated by dependency needs to avoid independent goal setting and achievement. Female sex offenders may require help to envision the future, to set realistic goals, to break those goals down into manageable steps and to begin to put forth effort toward those steps.

Behavioral techniques and cognitive behavioral techniques, such as the use of self-reinforcement and covert reinforcement, may assist with goal setting. Similarly, behavioral charts, classical conditioning techniques, the management of environmental stimuli and reinforcers may also be taught as means of facilitating goal attainment in the interest of improving self-esteem.

Relaxation Techniques

Early in therapy, severely victimized offenders should be helped to develop emotional self-regulation skills. Many standard relaxation exercises may be useful. Many, however, may need to be tailored to the specific needs of traumatized individuals. For example, progressive muscle relaxation, commonly involves flexing and then relaxing muscles in a progressive sequence, under the direction of a therapist, in order to assist the individual to gain control over the sensations of physical tension and relaxation. For victims of sexual abuse, responding to the directives of an authority figure to perform physical acts may have associations with abuse. Focus on certain muscle groups, for example, tensing and releasing the thighs or buttocks may be similarly sexualized for victims of sexual abuse. Closing the eyes, as is commonly done in progressive muscle relaxation, or assuming a prone position[841] may produce feelings of vulnerability among sexual abuse victims. Modifications, such as mutually choosing muscle group (hands, forearms, shoulders, etc.) that may facilitate relaxation without being threatening, acquiring a tape for home use after session or modifying the position or allowing the eyes to remain open may be appropriate modifications to this technique for female sex offenders.

The technique of guided imagery, which generally involves the therapist guiding the client to picture a tranquil scene with sensory involvement to promote relaxation, may also be useful to assist the offender to deal with negative emotional responses. It should similarly be completed only with some advanced planning. The therapist, for example, would want to be clear that the client had never been sexually abused on a beach or in the woods, prior to using these common images for relaxation purposes. The caveat regarding closing the eyes and reclining would apply to this relaxation technique as well.

Deep breathing exercises may also be useful for promoting relaxation. However, such exercises may mimic sounds heard during sexual arousal or aggression and serve as a trigger to unpleasant memories or flashbacks. These may similarly need to be modified. With all relaxation exercises, there exists a risk for clients who dissociate. For some, the relaxation state produced by various exercises may trigger memories of dissociative episodes that occurred during abuse. Again, modifications may be warranted for such individuals.

Helping the client to discover idiosyncratic means of self-soothing may also be useful. Techniques such as taking a hot bath (if this is not associated with abuse), drinking warm tea, using comfort items such as blankets or comfort foods (if the client does not have an eating disorder), reading and the like can also be explored with the client. Some clients have items that make them feel safe or relaxed, such as recorded music, a poster or a teddy bear. Such objects might be incorporated into the session.

Self-Monitoring and Self-Reflection Skills

Victims of abuse may lack skills in self-monitoring their emotions. Many have been taught to disregard or to tune out their emotional responses during years of abuse and may lack emotional self-awareness. Their emotional responses may be diffuse and they may have difficulty differentiating both types of emotions and degrees of emotions. Disappointment may feel like life-threatening abandonment, which in turn may feel like rage. Conversely, abuse may feel like a normal part of daily living. Learning to label emotions and to rate their severity may prove useful for the female sex offender early in treatment. Initially, the offender might begin by differentiating between good and bad days, and gradually begin to further differentiate the emotions in terms of type and severity. Daily rating sheets, journaling exercises or the like may assist the female sex offender to self-monitor her emotions.

The female sex offender is also likely to lack abilities for actively addressing her own history of victimization and offending. While the goal later in therapy is for the offender to develop a comprehensive understanding of her psychosocial history and her cycle of offending, the offender may lack the resources to do so in the early stages of therapy. This process might be started gradually. For example, rather than initially exploring details of her psychosocial trauma, the offender might begin by charting the "good" and "bad" years of her life or by rating each year of her life on a scale of one to ten.

Summary

Available research indicates that a history of trauma is common among female sexual abusers. Particularly when this history is severe, many female sex offenders may initially lack the ability to focus on an intensive exploration of victimization and offending issues without decompensation or without an increase in maladaptive defenses. Indicators that a female sexual abuser may have particular difficulty in addressing trauma and offending issues may include a history of more severe abuse or abusing; a history of harm to self, others or property; psychiatric diagnoses, psychological testing or a mental status exam that suggest this possibility; and a lack of available coping resources or support networks.

Devoting particular attention to the quality and nature of the therapeutic relationship is important during the early stages of therapy. Additionally, the therapist should spend time with the client building the skills necessary to participate in a comprehensive exploration of psychosocial trauma and its relationship to offending, and to her specific patterns of and alternatives to the sexual offending. This initial focus should include helping the offender to improve practical safety skills and a sense of safety, develop self-esteem and identity cohesion, develop coping and communication skills and learn to accurately self-reflect and self-monitor.

While a focus on such coping skills does not entirely preclude an exploration of offending and victimization concerns, focus on the latter should occur in proportion to the coping resources of the female sexual abuser. The ratio of focus on coping skills to the focus on victimization and offending should initially favor the former. The length of time that this is necessary will vary between clients, depending upon the abilities that they bring with them to therapy.

Ultimately, it will be the task of the therapist and the offender to identify precursors to sexual offending specific to the individual offender, including concerns related to personal victimization where appropriate. As these precursors are discovered, alternatives and skills necessary to practice these alternatives must be identified and developed. Focus on coping resources early in therapy may lay the groundwork for the later identification of healthy alternatives to the precursors to sexual offending. Additionally, focus on such areas as increasing safety, improving self-esteem and identity and improving coping resources and self-reflection skills may begin to lower the risk of offending. While the risk will be much lower once the offender has identified her own personal precursors to offending and has mastered alternatives, this intensive focus may not initially be possible. A focus on victimization and offending should occur at a pace that allows such a focus to move the female sexual abuser forward in treatment rather than backwards.

Notes ————————————————————

[824] Browne & Finkelhor (1986)
[825] Herman (1997)
[826] Saradjian & Hanks (1996)
[827] Russell (1986)
[828] Larson & Maison (1987)
[829] Lloyd (1987)
[830] Larson & Maison (1987)
[831] Larson & Maison (1987); Matthews (1994); Turner &Turner (1994)
[832] Saradjian & Hanks (1996)
[833] Maison & Larson (1995)
[834] Maison & Larson (1995)
[835] Maison & Larson (1995)
[836] Larson & Maison (1987)
[837] Turner & Turner (1994)
[838] Condy (1985); Woodring (1995)
[839] Ellis & Harper (1975)
[840] Beck (1976); Beck & Emery (1985)
[841] Zaidi & Gutierrez-Kovner (1995)

11. Exploring Victimization and Patterns of Offending

Ultimately it must be the task of the female sex offender in treatment, with the help of her therapist, to identify the precursors to her own offending and to identify, develop and practice alternatives to these precursors. This process and its results will undoubtedly be unique to each female sex offender. Because of the lack of research currently available to guide this process, therapy with the female sex offender must be tailored to the individual. Undoubtedly, the precursors to offending in some females will overlap with those that have been identified as precursors for the male sex offender population. It is not the purpose of this book to review the literature on male sex offenders; however, familiarity with this literature is likely to be of use to therapists as they tailor treatment plans to meet the needs of female sex offenders.

Methods for treating female sex offenders currently lack empirical validation. What follows is a starting point for their development. Key factors in the treatment of female sex offenders include the identification of the precursors to abusing for the female child molester. Some of these precursors have begun to be identified in the research on female sex offenders. Because of the likelihood that consequences of trauma serve as precursors to offending among female offenders, an exploration of these trauma-related contributors is likely to be an important component of treatment for the female sex offender. A history of trauma not only suggests areas of exploration in terms of the precursors to offending but has implications for the modification of the therapeutic relationship and the pacing of therapy.

When female child molesters have histories of their own trauma and victimization, these histories should be explored with the goal of understanding how they impacted upon offending. The ultimate goal for the offender is to understand the precursors to offending (including those which may have developed as a result of trauma) and to develop and practice alternatives to these precursors.

Gradual Approach to More Personal, Specific and Emotional Concerns

Female sex offenders are likely to vary in their ability to tolerate a direct exploration of the more emotionally distressing aspects of their psychosocial histories. Some may readily decompensate with direct confrontation concerning their histories of abuse and of abusing. This is likely to be of greater concern among those whose psychosocial histories suggest greater amounts of pathology with fewer buffers and among those whose diagnoses or psychological testing results suggest it as a possibility.

Therapists who have worked with female sex offenders, and those who have worked with trauma victims in general, have tended to recommend that the process of exploring trauma be appropriately balanced against the coping resources of the individual client. Coping resources, including a strong therapeutic rapport, should be established prior to beginning an exploration of trauma and offending. As therapy moves towards an exploration of trauma and offending, it should progress along a continuum from material that is explored from a general, broadly based, cognitive perspective to material that is explored from a more personal, detailed and emotional perspective. The exploration of more traumatic or distressing material should begin in a "one step removed" fashion (as shown in Table 11-1) and progress to a more direct, intensive and personal exploration. In some cases, it may be appropriate to initially include didactic instruction concerning topics related to victimization and offending as a component of therapy.

This progression may minimize the need for the defensive maneuvering so often described on the part of the female sex offender and to also minimize the likelihood of regression in functioning. It also allows the client to experience a relationship that is non-exploitive and that follows the typical progression in normal human relationships from lesser to greater amounts of personal self-disclosure. For female sex offenders, who commonly are found to lack interpersonal skills, appropriate boundaries and trust in others, the facilitation of a relationship that appropriately respects defenses is likely to be an important component of treatment.

There are at least three continuums along which therapists can begin to address issues related to victimization and offending without promoting decompensation and defensive maneuvering on the part of the client. These continuums are

- the progression from the exploration of such material from a global perspective to exploration from the personal perspective of an individual offender
- the progression from the exploration of more general facts to an exploration of the specific details of an individual client's history
- the progression from the exploration of facts or cognitions to the exploration of the offender's emotions

These continuums can also be useful in beginning to explore defenses. For example, the offender who denies committing an offense might be asked, "I don't know exactly what happened in your case. However, many offenders who actually committed their offenses also deny them. What are your thoughts or

Table 11-1: Examples of "One Step Removed" Verbal Interventions

Global Perspective	Personal Perspective
• <u>Most people</u> don't want to be advantage of. • <u>Many victims</u> of abuse have problems later in life because of their abuse.	• <u>You</u> don't want to be taken advantage of. • <u>You (or your victims)</u> could have problems because of the abuse.
General Facts	**Specific Details**
• Most people don't want to be <u>taken advantage</u> of. • Many victims of abuse <u>have problems</u> later in life because of their <u>abuse</u>.	• Most people don't want to <u>find out that pornographic pictures of themselves have been sold</u>. • Many people have <u>nightmares, periods of depression or flashbacks</u> because of <u>rape</u>
Cognitive	**Emotional**
• • Most people <u>don't want</u> to be taken advantage of. • Many victims of abuse still <u>have some thoughts</u> about their abuse later in life.	• • Most people <u>feel exploited and hurt</u> when they are taken advantage of. • Many victims of abuse <u>are distressed about</u> their abuse later in life.
Global/General/Cognitive	**Personal/Specific/Emotional**
• Most people don't want to be taken advantage of. • Many victims of abuse still have some thoughts about their abuse later in life.	• You felt exploited and hurt when you found out that pornographic pictures of you had been sold. • You (or your victims) are still experiencing distress, in the form of nightmares, periods of depression and flashbacks, because of the rape.

guesses concerning why they do this?" This intervention respects the defense of the fragile individual while allowing her to proceed in the cognitive, rather than emotional, realm to begin to understand why the defense is in place. It is also a verbalization that allows the offender to explore her thoughts on why "offenders" commit offenses in a global sense, which she may be able to tolerate before she is able to explore or even acknowledge her own specific reasons for offending. The reasons that she identifies, of course, will be useful projections for the therapist to note for later work in therapy.

The therapist might also make this intervention less personal and more general in order to allow the client even more personal distance for exploring the defense, for example: "Sometimes when people don't like talking about something, they deny that it happened. What are some reasons that you think that this might occur?" When a fragile offender is not yet ready to give up a defense, she may still be able to explore the reason for its existence, if it is addressed from a general, global and cognitive perspective. When she has sufficient alternative coping resources in place, she may be able to further explore her defenses from a more personal, specific and emotional perspective.

Therapists may initially help clients to address traumatic material from a bit of an emotional and personal distance and ease into the more difficult topics for the clients without ignoring important issues. Therapists can begin to help the client develop a perspective for understanding the abuse and a vocabulary for discussing it without initially overwhelming the client. As the therapist begins to use verbalizations in the form of interpretations, reframes or active listening (depending on her/his orientation), moves can be made along each continuum as it become evident that the client is able to tolerate the progression.

A client may spontaneously move from one step of the continuum to the next. In some cases, this will occur because the seed has been planted that allows this to take place. Often, it will be a sign that the client has adequate coping resources, has mastered the more general concepts and is beginning to apply them to herself. However, at times it will occur for reasons that are not helpful to the progress of therapy. The client may be decompensating, may be trying to meet the perceived expectations of the therapist, may be attempting to arouse or intimidate the therapist, may be blurting out information before the therapist has a grasp of the client's coping resources and so forth. In these cases, it is the responsibility of the therapist to slow down the response and ensure that the client has the means of coping with the material presented.

These continuums can allow therapy to progress with resistant or fragile clients. Those who become defensive or who appear to be doing more poorly because of premature interventions can be "stepped back" to verbal interventions that are more readily tolerated. In some cases this may consist of a focus on educational material related to offending or victimization, to be discussed from a personal and more emotional perspective at a later date. Those who are particularly resistant can be "stepped back" to the still earlier tasks of therapy which focus on such areas as trust in the therapist, developing a sense of safety, assertiveness (perhaps concerning the pacing of therapy), developing and practicing coping resources and so forth.

With clients who require more time in therapy, however, alternative means for addressing the safety of potential victims must be taken. Steps that might be taken in the interest of victims' protection will vary with the means available to the therapist. These might include recommending against increasing levels of visitation with victims, recommending against reunification with victims and recommending against release from residential care. These potential contingencies should be discussed with the client at the start of therapy and reviewed as necessary during treatment, in order to minimize their impact on the therapeutic relationship. Ideally, those who are unable to participate in therapy at the earliest stage of treatment should be placed in a setting that allows them and their potential victims optimal safety, such as a residential care facility or a prison setting.

Exploring Victimization and Its Relationship to Offending

Most researchers and clinicians who have worked with female sex offenders have commented upon the extensive personal victimization histories that are common to many of these clients. Most have stated that an exploration of this personal trauma history is an important part of treatment. A few have suggested that, to some extent, the exploration of the personal victimization should precede an exploration of offending because it is unlikely that female sex offenders will feel empathy towards their victims while unresolved issues related to personal victimization (commonly strong defenses or a poor sense of self-worth) do not allow them to feel empathy for themselves.

A crucial component in the exploration of a personal history of victimization for female sex offenders is to make sense of the specific relationship between their victimizations and their offending. While a variety of factors not related to victimization may serve as precursors to offending, the fact that so many female child molesters have been traumatized and, in particular, sexually abused, indicates that this will be an appropriate area for clinical exploration for many female sex offenders.

Personal victimization should not be explored with the female child molester until an excellent rapport has been developed and it has been established that the client has adequate coping resources for managing such an exploration. Otherwise, the process is likely to resemble revictimization and may elevate the risk for regression or decompensation. In the absence of a supportive relationship in which assistance is available for coping, intrusion into personal trauma may elicit aftereffects that place the offender at elevated risk for re-offending or for engaging in other harmful behaviors.

While the potential discovery that an individual offender has been victimized herself may provide valuable clues in understanding her subsequent sexual molestation of children, it does not explain her actions. It remains for each offender to explore, with her therapist when appropriate, the idiosyncratic ways in which her personal history of trauma may relate to her offending.

The consequences of personal victimization and the precursors to offending are likely to be as varied as the offenders themselves. Nevertheless, some of the common aftereffects of child sexual abuse, in particular, and other forms of abuse, in general, may serve as precursors to the victimization of others. The following connections between victimization and offending may be worth exploring with female offenders.

Lack of a Sense of Appropriate Boundaries

Many female sex offenders have been sexually abused. Sexual abuse is a boundary violation. It represents a violation of both the tangible and intangible lines that separate human beings from one another. Freely chosen, the sexual merging of two individuals creates a sense of connection. The diffusion of boundaries serves to increase intimacy. In the absence of a maturely made choice to participate in such a union, however, this diffusion of self may create a sense of confusion and violation. Early sexual violation may leave victims without the sense that people are separate individuals with discrete physical and emotional boundaries and the basic right to enforce these distinctions.

Victims of sexual abuse, particularly in the absence of healthier, alternative experiences, are left with the fundamental knowledge that some people are not allowed to enforce sexual boundaries. The earlier the victimization, the greater the risk that this knowledge will become a cornerstone for the child's worldview. The more often and consistently this message is relayed to the child, particularly in the absence of contradictory information, the more likely it is to be incorporated into the child's fundamental knowledge concerning relationships. Females who have been repeatedly sexually abused may lack the firm sense that other people are separate individuals who have distinct boundaries that they have the right to reinforce.

Particularly in cases where a female has been sexually abused from a young age, with great frequency or duration, by multiple offenders or in the context of a background that does not provide support for alternative perceptions, there is a risk that she may lack an appreciation and respect for the sense of the boundaries that separate individuals. A lack of basic recognition and respect of the boundaries of the self and others is likely to be a factor that contributes to the victimization of children by severely sexually abused women.

A lack of the perception of the boundaries between people and of the rights of individuals to enforce these boundaries may also elevate the risk for the continued sexual victimization directed towards the female who becomes an offender. Some female offenders have been victimized by more than one individual. In some cases, they have also chosen individuals who victimize them as mates. When female offenders offend with an abusive co-offender, the lack of a sense of individuality and the ability to reinforce personal boundaries may help to create the dynamic that allows the relationship with the co-offender to exist.

A cycle may be put in motion whereby the initial sexual intrusion against the female creates a perception that she is not a separate individual who is free to reinforce her sexual boundaries. Without the unquestioned assumption that she has boundaries that separate her physical and emotional self from others, it may not occur to her to avoid or to attempt to prevent subsequent intrusions across these boundaries. She may become an easier target for offenders, which may ultimately result in her becoming involved with an abusive co-offender. With each victimization, she may be less likely to preserve the perception that she has boundaries that are potentially self-protected.

By extension, the notion that all people have sexual boundaries that they may protect may be lost. Without this fundamental concept, she may become increasingly likely to sexually intrude upon others, without a sense that she has violated widely held principles concerning appropriate behavior or the sense that she has violated an individual.

Female sexual abusers may have difficulty in recognizing that children have needs and emotions that are distinct from her own. They may easily become enmeshed with their victims. Indeed, a common difficulty of the female victims of female abusers is the lack of a sense of an identity that is separate from that of the abuser.

Other forms of abuse can also make the boundaries of offenders with others more diffuse. As with sexual abuse, physical abuse is an intrusion into the boundaries of another. It may also facilitate a worldview in the victim that this type of boundary violation is acceptable. It may create difficulties in the female offender in recognizing that she and others have physical and emotional boundaries that should be respected.

When the female has a history of neglect or of unmet physical and emotional needs, another type of boundary violation may occur. Her unmet needs for caretaking may cause her to ignore or to violate the role boundaries between adults and children and, in some cases, between mother and child. Rather than appropriately caring for and protecting children, she may use them to meet her own needs. To the extent that her sexual motivation is for contact comfort, reassurance, nurturing and the like, this factor may contribute to her offending. Her history of abuse, neglect or other trauma may lead to unmet emotional needs, which she may seek to have filled by a child.

Relationship Skills

In some cases a history of abuse or trauma will contribute to a female's offending by impacting upon her relationship skills. Damage suffered as a victim of abuse may interfere with personality development, which may impact upon the relationship skills of the offender. Furthermore, abusive relationships in childhood may serve as deeply ingrained models for understanding and engaging in human interactions, which may further elevate the victim's risk for becoming an offender. Both the poor capacity for interacting with others and a limited understanding of the patterns of interactions in healthy relationships may contribute to the likelihood that a female victim will become an offender.

In some cases, females who were raised in environments of victimization were also raised in environments of social isolation. This social isolation may interfere with the normal development of social skills. Their own offenders may have consciously restricted their activities in the interest of maintaining secrecy surrounding the abuse or as a result of a general jealousy or possessiveness. In some cases the pathology of the abusive home life may have further contributed to social isolation by dissuading visitors. Psychopathology of the victim resulting from the abuse may also contribute to social isolation. The potential behavioral problems of chronic victims may dissuade others from forming friendships with them.

In some cases, female sex offenders have abusive relationships with husbands or mates, who similarly prohibit outside friendships. In these cases, the sexual relationships that offenders have with children may represent attempts to bridge feelings of isolation, such as abandonment, sadness and rejection. Some female offenders begin offending following a separation from a male partner.

In some cases, individuals have a normal period of development and are subsequently traumatized for a long period of time. An individual who is traumatized beyond the age of eleven, as an example, may spend a good deal of time in the following years concentrating on avoiding danger, managing the emotional consequences of abuse and protecting herself as best as she can. Concerns related to the development of normal adolescent social skills such as forming peer groups, learning fundamental dating skills, managing peer pressure, coming to terms with conformity versus individuality, beginning to break away from the family, beginning to develop work skills and so forth may be lost to the individual. She may find that as she grows older, she may have more in common with eleven-year olds than with older individuals, whose social approaches befuddle her. This may help to explain why some offenders are attracted to children who are the same age as they were themselves when they were first abused.

Poor social skills may increase the likelihood of offending by limiting the ability of the women to form social and sexual relationships with stable individuals who are not co-offenders or children. Healthy friendships may lessen the likelihood of offending by serving as coping resources when problems arise that might otherwise serve as precursors to abuse. Female sex offenders, however, often lack friends to whom they might turn when feeling angry, isolated, powerless or financially dependent upon a co-offender. Their lack of social skills may impede their development of social support systems that might otherwise serve as a buffer against offending. A lack of appropriate friendships might also exacerbate these and similar precursors. Without friends, for example, the female child molesters may feel even more isolated, more powerless, more distressed and so forth and these feelings may lead to an offense.

In cases in which females have been abused by a caretaker, social skills may sometimes be particularly impaired. Many female offenders had abusers who, as caretakers, were in positions to have shaped their primary understandings of social relationships. Sexual abuse, by its very nature, involves an inappropriate and exploitive relationship. The sexual abuse in these cases was not only an infliction of trauma but also a failure of caretaking. These women not only had greater trauma but also were provided with fewer resources for mastering the trauma in the form of proper caretaking and comfort. In many cases they were also denied a primary example upon which to model appropriate social skills.

Paradoxically, sexual abuse and other forms of interpersonal trauma may not only result in poor social skills but may also increase the need for social comfort and relating. Some female sex offenders may not only lack an understanding of how to appropriately have their social needs met, they may also have exorbitant, trauma-induced relationship needs. Female sexual abusers who have been raised in homes in which there was a lack of social training which led to a hunger for social contact may be prone to sexually abusing children. The sexual abuse of children or the relationship with an abusive co-offender may represent a poorly conceived and desperate attempt to meet social needs.

Emotional Release

Trauma such as sexual abuse may result in a variety of negative emotions for the victim. Anger, depression and anxiety have all been found among some of the female sexual offenders who were abused as children. Forcing a child, in turn, to be available for sexual contact may serve as an outlet for these emotions. A child may be a target for rage or an outlet for vengeance. In some cases, the abuse of a male child may represent symbolic revenge upon males who have abused the female abuser. When perpetrated upon a female child with whom the offender identifies in some way, it may represent an expression of self-hatred or of gender-hatred. Sexual activity with an available child may also reduce or distract from depression, anxiety or similar emotions, or may serve as a source of emotional comfort for the offender.

Emotional distress can interfere with the ability to think and to direct behavior. For some offenders, sexual activity directed towards children may be a poorly directed response to emotional distress. The offenses may be impulsive, emotionally directed behaviors.

In some cases, emotions such as anger and depression may be conditioned with sexual arousal. These emotions may be sexualized because of repeated pairings with arousal during childhood abuse. For these abusers, sadistic sex or sex that involves emotions such as rage and exploitation may be sexually gratifying.

Some sex offenders offend against others in patterns that begin with negative emotions. Because so many of the female sexual abusers have been sexually abused themselves, it is likely that many had this pattern modeled for them in childhood. This pattern of coping with difficult emotions by sexually assaulting others may have been a primary coping response modeled for them in childhood. Some female offenders are likely to have been taught a deficient repertoire of coping strategies. Chronically victimized individuals, particularly those who were abused in their own families, may have had fewer opportunities to witness appropriate responses to distress during childhood.

Chronically abused individuals may also develop coping responses that contribute to the likelihood of sexual abusing others. In response to chronic emotional distress, they may develop defensive coping responses such as detachment, denial, dissociation and the like. Such defenses, once learned, may serve to reduce the abuser's emotional response to the child's distress or discomfort during her abuse of a child.

Struggle for Identity and Belonging

The trauma histories of female sexual abusers can create problems that impede their sense of a stable identity. Trauma may impede the development of the child before the child's identity is fully established. She may become distracted with managing her traumatic circumstances rather than consolidating her sense of self. Offenders who lack a cohesive sense of self may seek to confirm themselves through sexual relations with others. Through sexual merging with another, they may gain a sense of personal and social identity. Through social and sexual relationships they may incorporate the identity of others into their own. For these offenders, sexual contact with a victim or with a co-offender may represent a desperate struggle for a sense of self. Some may offend in an unhealthy attempt to gain a sense of identity.[842]

A female sexual abuser may also attempt to identify with the person who abused her or with the role of the aggressor in an attempt to abandon her sense of being a victim. Particularly for abusers who have been exposed primarily to victimizers and victims, such as those raised in multi-incestuous families, few alternative roles may be perceived to exist.

Some female offenders may have learned to dichotomize individuals into the roles of abusers or victims and tend to opt for the former. Saradjian and Hanks[843] reported that the targeting, grooming and silencing of victims by female sexual abusers was often similar in method to those used by their own childhood victimizers. Similarly, the abusive acts in some cases were similar to those that had been perpetrated upon them by their own offenders. Female offenders may take on the identity of an abusive person in an attempt to surrender the role of victim, particularly when no other alternative roles are perceived.

Alternately, some of the female abusers have been exposed to a childhood in which the females (or children) are primarily victims and the males are primarily victimizers. In the case of the female co-offender who is forced into the sexual abuse of children by an abusive male co-offender, her identity as a victim may be consistent with her role in the relationship.

In some cases, she may identify with her female victim or view the victim as an extension of herself. This may particularly be the case if the victim is the biological child. If the offender views the victim as an extension of herself, she may view the sexual contact as deserved punishment or degradation.

Distorted Sense of Normalcy

Sexual abuse in the family creates a distorted sense of normalcy. Those who grow up in sexually abusive homes experience sexual abuse as their reality. The sense of normalcy in non-abusive homes must be experienced elsewhere or imagined.

Families are largely responsible for shaping the values of and the sense of normalcy in children. For many families, participating in religious ceremonies, visiting extended family, participating in chores, taking part in educational activities, resolving conflict and so forth are all a part of the daily activities that are learned as a part of family life. Incestuously abused children, similarly, experience sex and secrecy as a part of the everyday activities of children. They are immersed in environments that present as reality the idea that children are supposed to meet the sexual needs of adults. This reality may be carried into their adult lives.

For example, Saradjian and Hanks[844] found that, among twelve women who had sexually offended with a male co-offender, four had been sexually involved with their fathers in relationships that they described as loving; these four women also described the relationships with their own mates and sexually abused children as loving. Similarly, women who offended against adolescents (all of whom had been sexually abused) seemed to minimize the abuse perpetrated against them in adolescence. They tended to report that their sexual relationships at the age of twelve to fourteen with individuals who were often more than 25 years older were not abusive. The offender's sense of normalcy may often be tainted by her past experiences. Some offenders may view both their own abuse and their offending as relatively normal.

Poor management of emotions such as anger, depression, anxiety, loneliness, rejection and the like may be normal in the dysfunctional environments in which many female sexual abusers spent their early years. Defenses such as denial, rationalization, projection and "fluid reality"[845] may also be normalized in an abusive environment.

Normalizing and assimilating the defenses used by their own offenders or by others in dysfunctional homes may aid victims in becoming offenders. The fusion of negative emotions with sexual activity or with a general disregard of the needs of others may also be relatively normal in some of the offenders' homes of origin.

Other forms of antisocial behavior and other behaviors that allow repeated abuse to occur may be also have been normalized in the psychosocial histories of many offenders. Alcohol or drug abuse may be viewed as relatively normal by women offenders who experienced it as a part of their everyday living experiences as children. They may have incorporated the use of drugs or alcohol as relatively normal strategies for coping or for becoming disinhibited in order to sexually abuse. Disregard for the physical or emotional well-being of others in a variety of forms may also be normalized. Threatening others, manipulating others, behaving under a veil of secrecy, undervaluing the needs of children or women, poor nurturing skills, violence as a means of obtaining needs and so forth may all be relatively normal for some offenders and incorporated into their approach to the world and to children.

Survival

For those who have been chronically abused, and who have no support systems, simple survival may be given priority above the protection of their children from sexual abuse. For those who lack survival skills due to lack of a sense of competency, dependency, emotional distress, social skills insufficient to find or maintain employment and so forth (which may all be related to a history of trauma), it may be more important to cling to a co-offender who will provide resources sufficient for survival than to protect children. For some female sexual abusers, the co-offender may also provide a degree of emotional support, sufficient to prevent suicide or other life-threatening decompensation. To a lesser extent, it is also possible that some female sexual abusers view their victims as possible sources of resources that may aid in survival, for example in cases involving adolescent victims.

Sexual Preoccupation and Sexual Aversion to Adults

Premature and chronic sexualization may contribute to an increased awareness of and interest in the erotic aspects of sexuality. Those who have grown up in highly sexualized environments may place sexual meaning onto everyday events and may over-sexualize relationships. Some of the more chronically abused female sexual abusers report that the pleasant feelings of sexual contact, even when they occurred under abusive circumstances, were among the more positive aspects of their childhood. The premature sexual contact and sexual awareness may contribute to the sexualizing of contact with children on the part of some female sex offenders. Some offenders who were raised in homes in which all of the relationships were sexualized may continue to sexualize relationships inappropriately into adulthood.

Additionally, stimuli associated with early abuse, such as prepubescent bodies, small articles of clothing, young voices or screams may be connected with sexual arousal. These stimuli may have been paired with sexual contact so often as to produce conditioned arousal. This may help to explain why some abusers target those who were the same age as they themselves were at the onset of their own abuse.

When chronic sexual abuse has resulted in aversion to sexual contact with adults, sexual contact with children may be viewed as a means of gratifying sexual needs in a less aversive fashion. Adult features such as the adult penis, voice or approach to sexual activity may also be conditioned not with sexual arousal but with such emotional responses as fear, rage, dissociation, nausea and the like. Children may provide the least threatening and most pleasant form of sexual contact to the severely sexually traumatized abuser.

Lack of Self-Worth

Chronic abuse may result in very low self-esteem for the offender. Many female abusers have undoubtedly been told that their own abuse happened because it was deserved. Both physical and sexual abusers tend to blame their victims for the abuse. Victims may perceive that the abuse would not have happened had they not deserved it. Victims may also experience themselves as peculiar or different because of the sexual or physical abuse itself, resulting in a lower sense of self-worth.

The female sexual abuser's view of herself as worthless, guilty and as less than deserving of basic human dignity, and her view of herself as a sex offender may not be vastly discordant. If she is as bad as she can be, then there is little to be lost by gratifying her needs though sexually offending against children.

Furthermore, if she is offending in the company of a male co-offender, she may lack the esteem to do what is needed to leave and to protect the children against whom she is offending. A lack of self-worth may undermine her sense of competence in being able to manage such areas of life as finances, job responsibilities and creating and managing social support. She may lack the understanding that she is worthy or capable of a better life.

Poor self-esteem may also impact upon the female sexual abuser's ability to form support systems that might assist her to find solutions to problems in ways other than offending. For example, she may lack a social network with whom she might vent, observe adaptive coping strategies, have appropriate sexual relationships or receive other forms of help with the problems that lead to offending.

External Locus of Control

Chronic abuse may undermine a woman's sense of control and power over her environment. The abuse of a child, in part, may assist her to regain a sense of control over some aspect of her surroundings.

Chronic abuse may also result in the woman's lack of a sense of control over her own body. She may lack the sense that she can direct and change her behavior, particularly her sexual behavior, or that she can influence control over her environment. Stirling,[846] for example, points out that some women who have been sexually abused may feel like victims of children's normal sexual interest and have difficulty identifying and enforcing appropriate boundaries.

Women who have been chronically abused may perceive in themselves a chronically ingrained lack of competency in solving problems. After all, if they were persistently and desperately interested in finding a solution to their own abuse and were not able to, then less important, less motivating goals may also seem impossible. Their offending may reflect their lack of ability and experience in solving problems. They may tend to disbelieve that they may impact the world and lack a sense of autonomous control of their own behavior.

Exploring Precursors and Alternatives to Victimizing

Regardless of the method used for treating the female sex offender, she must come away from treatment with an understanding of the specific patterns that led to her offending. She must understand her personal precursors to offending and must have alternatives to the precursors in her repertoire. She must further be able to recognize and alter her patterns of offending as they begin to occur. Precursors to abuse are things which precede the offending and which increase the likelihood of inappropriate sexual behaviors with children taking place.

Precursors to sexual offending might be categorized as follows:

- People
- Emotions
- Situations (places and things)
- Fantasies/sexual arousal
- Justifications
- Thought processes
- Behaviors

In the course of treatment the female sex offender may be helped to identify her precursors to offending in each category. Research to guide this process among female child molesters is in its infancy. Exploration of these categories with the women will be a highly individualized process. Nevertheless, some authors have begun to describe precursors to offending among populations of female sexual abusers. These may be useful in assisting the therapist to help the female sex offender in her own exploration.

People as Precursors

Under the category of people might be included co-offenders and victims, as well as others who may elevate the risk that a specific female sex offender will offend. It is unclear whether some female offenders prefer a specific type of victim, however this warrants exploration in therapy. For example, there is preliminary evidence to suggest that some women offend primarily in (or out of) the family, or primarily with a specific gender or age group. Some authors have noted that some female offenders choose victims who are the same age as they were at the time of their victimizations and that in some cases they identify with the child victim.[847] The possible victim profile should be explored. At the very least, however, female child abusers in treatment should recognize that being in the proximity of their previous victims and, in particular, being alone with them elevates their risk for re-offending.

In some cases, a desire to create a sense of fusion of identity with a child may serve as a precursor to abuse. Welldon[848] stated that "incestuous mothers keep a symbiotic relationship with their child(ren) and do not allow any process of separation/individuation (p. 46)."

Many of the women who molest children do so in the company of a co-offender. Certainly being in the company of a co-offender places them at elevated risk for re-offending. For women who have been co-offenders, it is important that therapy points out that being in the company of the person with whom they sexually offended is a high-risk situation. Similarly, being in the company of another child molester is a high-risk situation. Some offenders may draw a sense of identity from fusion with the identity of an abusive co-offender.

Exploration into the dynamics of the relationship of the female sex offender with her co-offender is likely to be necessary in the cases of women who have offended with a male co-offender. In such cases, it is likely to be important for the female to have an understanding of the "red flags" that signal that a male may be abusive or may be a child molester.

Davin[849] is one of the few researchers to have examined the female sex offenders' perceptions of their relationships with male co-offenders. She found that among female sex offenders who co-offended, many reported that their co-offenders possessed charm and sensitivity in the early stages of the relationships but that, over time, the men became more controlling and abusive. Most were in relationships in which the male co-offender always knew where they were when they were apart from the co-offender. A large number reported that the co-offenders always won disagreements about major issues. Over half reported that the co-offenders would desire sex after battering them.

Female sex offenders who offend in the context of a battering co-offender relationship may benefit not only from an exploration of the signs that a male may be abusive, but also from exploration of the precursors that led to the relationship in the first place. These might include dependency needs, fear, isolation, poor self-esteem and poor survival skills. The offenders may benefit from an exploration of needs that the potential co-offenders met, that made it difficult to extract themselves from the relationship. For those who have offended in a ritualistic or satanic situation, similar exploration of the needs that were met by the group may be useful.

Some women may require assistance in developing practical living skills to help them avoid abusive relationships in the future. Those skills might include employment training, education, job hunting, financial planning, budgeting, leisure skills and locating housing and transportation.

In addition to the exploration of co-offender relationships, in some cases it may be helpful to explore whether other relationships contribute indirectly to the offending and act as precursors. Female child molesters have often been noted to have dysfunctional relationships. It is possible that for some offenders being in the presence of relatives, former abusers, dysfunctional peer groups, drug and alcohol abusers and the like may indirectly contribute to offending. They may indirectly have impact by influencing the thoughts, emotions, situations and so forth of the female offender. For example, a previous abuser may cause an offender to feel angry, aroused, hopeless, in need of physical comfort or anxious, which may in turn lead to offending. Saradjian and Hanks,[850] for example, reported a case in which a female sex offender committed a violent sexual assault following an argument with a brother who had been among the people who sexually abused her.

Problematic relationships may serve as precursors to sexual offending. Lane,[851] for example, found that precipitating events among juvenile female sex offenders often related to parents, family, peers and authority figures. In some cases, relationship problems may serve as precursors to offending. It falls to the female sex offender to identify with her therapist people who engender in the offender the desire to offend and to find ways to manage the relationships or to avoid them.

Many have noted that female child molesters relate with others in the role of either a victim or victimizer. Individuals who provoke these responses in the female sexual abuser may be high-risk individuals for her to spend time with. These may include co-offenders who are not physically abusive, such as co-offenders who are solicited by the female sex offender herself.

Not only exposure to another individual, but identification with another individual may precede offending. Many authors have noted identification with the offender who victimized the female offender in childhood as a defense that contributes to offending.[852] Green and Kaplan[853] also noted that identification with their non-protective mothers was a defense mechanism that contributed to offending among females. It may be the case that for some offenders identification with people who are abusive or identification with those who are ineffectual or easily victimized may serve as precursors to offending.

The lack of the presence of a social support system may also be a precursor for abuse. In particular, a period of time following a divorce or separation may be a high-risk time for some female child molesters. Many authors have found that some female offenders are socially isolated.[854] They may fear relationships or have poor or delayed social skills.[855] Social skills training may be a necessary part of treatment for some, in order to minimize isolation as a precursor to offending. For some offenders, learning active listening skills, assertiveness skills, learning to cope with rejection, learning to develop common interests, set limits and build trust will be important.

Emotional Precursors

Several authors have noted that some female sex offenders may be very dependent in their relationships.[856] Dependency may precede offenses in some cases by contributing to the likelihood that the women will have difficulty extracting themselves from relationships with abusive co-offenders. Larson and Maison[857] noted that some women might avoid taking responsibility because they believe that men prefer them to be dependent rather than self-sufficient and that, if they become self-sufficient, they will not be loved.

Larson and Maison[858] found that free-floating anger was often a motivator for child sexual abuse among imprisoned female sex offenders in treatment. At times the women were actively angry with someone else and, in some cases, were seeking revenge through sexual relations with children. For example, one woman offended against her son to retaliate against her husband for his sexual attraction to their daughter.

Fear of a co-offender may also be a precursor to the abuse of a child. Fear and desire to please a co-offender was noted by Wolfe[859] as a precursor to abuse. Davin[860] noted the fear of abandonment and the fear of death as the most commonly given reasons for participation in the sexual acts by co-offenders.

Some female offenders may feel that they are in love with their victims.[861] They may view their relationships with the victims as love affairs[862] or may feel like a peer to their victims.[863] These feelings of affection or relatedness with the child may serve as precursors to offending.

A variety of other emotions are likely to precede offending on the part of the female sexual abuser although this is an under-researched area. Emotions such as loneliness, anger, depression and anxiety might increase the likelihood of offending in some offenders. It remains for each female sexual abuser to explore with her therapist how her own emotions relate to her offending.

Places and Things, Situational Precursors

In the course of therapy, female child molesters should become able to identify miscellaneous places and things that are associated with offending. For some offenders, abuse may take place in particular places, such as bathrooms or bedrooms. Rosencrans,[864] for example, noted that among cases of maternal incest reported by daughters, 75% had been sexually abused in the bedroom, 58% in the bathroom, 21% in the kitchen and 20% in the living room of the homes. Some offenders have offended in daycare settings. Female sexual abusers should have an understanding of places in which sexual offending is most likely to take place.

Some individuals may use disinhibitors such as drugs or alcohol prior to offending. While it appears that this is not the case for the majority of female sexual abusers, it is likely to be a very important area of exploration for those to whom it applies. Alcohol use during the offense was a factor in roughly 20% of the co-offenders and 17% of the independent offenders studied by Davin.[865] Drugs were a factor during the offense among 30% of co-offenders and 17% of independent offenders. Saradjian and Hanks[866] reported that none of the 36 women whom they studied sexually abused children exclusively when using drugs or alcohol, suggesting that for some women drugs and alcohol are not the primary reason for the offenses.

In some cases, stressful life events may precede sexual offending. For example, separation from a mate sometimes precedes the offending in females. Lane[867] found that school performance and "victimization issues" were often precursors for offending among juvenile females.

Maison and Larson[868] reported that the knowledge of human sexuality among female sex offenders is very limited. This is an area that is likely to be worth exploring in the female sex offender.

Fantasies/Sexual Arousal as Precursors

Fantasies related to love or sexuality or hostility may precede sexual offending in some females. Lane[869] found that among juvenile sex offenders, the fantasies of females included sexual and sexually abusive fantasies, as well as violent or retaliatory fantasies. Often these occurred with masturbation. She also noted that some experienced fantasies of domination (but not of power or force) and that a few acknowledged the intent to inflict harm or sexual humiliation.

Sexual arousal may precede sexual offending for some female child molesters. Davin[870] noted orgasm during the offense for 27% of the independent offenders and five percent of the co-offenders, suggesting sexual desire as a motivation for offending in some cases. Larson and Maison[871] found that for some female sexual abusers, sexual meaning was attached to everyday interaction patterns; offenses occurred in the context of sexually saturated interactions that were often learned in the family of origin.

Some researchers have noted that females may be different in terms of the fantasies that precede offending from the male child molesters. Maison and Larson[872] reported the female sex offenders do not have the compulsive sexual fantasies about children often seen in men, and may be less likely to view sex with children as a means of expressing affection. Woodring[873] noted the absence of power, control and sexual gratification motives by females in contrast to males.

Justifications as Precursors

Among the thoughts that allow sexual abuse are the rationalizations or justifications for abuse. These are just beginning to be documented for female sex offenders.

Lane[874] noted that among juvenile offenders, justifications included making their parents hurt or pay for something that they had done or getting themselves out of an intolerable situation.

In some cases the women may state that their abusive behaviors were not as harmful as their own victimizations.[875] de Young[876] reported that two women abusers who had been severely sexually abused in childhood rated their own experiences as extremely traumatic, yet neither believed that their sons would be harmed by their subsequent sexual contact with them. One reportedly explained that boys are "born knowing more about sex than girls are (p. 68)." The other reported that while her own abuse had been violent, her sexual contact with her son had been loving. Green and Kaplan[877] also noted that female offenders may trivialize the consequences to the victim.

Some female offenders may rationalize that their behaviors are acceptable because the children desire the sexual contact. Some authors have noted that female offenders may project sexual desire onto their victims.[878] Wolfe[879] noted that some female offenders rationalize that they are providing sexual education to their victims.

Some authors, however, have noted that females may have more empathy for their victims than male sex offenders[880]

Thought Processes as Precursors

In addition to specific cognitions, Larson and Maison[881] have identified specific thought processes that are often employed by female offenders. While many may have originally served as defenses in dysfunctional homes, the distortion in thought processes may eventually contribute to the likelihood of offending. Among these thought processes, the authors include being "thoughtless," or having a lack of awareness that allows them to be protected. They also develop a style in which they perceive that they have no impact on their environment and fade into the woodwork as a method of avoidance. The authors also noted rigid dichotomous thinking, so that individuals may be seen as "all good" and, therefore, incapable of abusing. Additionally, they described a fluid manner of perceiving reality and the ability to block reality so that information is denied access to conscious awareness. They noted that female sex offenders may add in bits of reality to a story as they go along. Each of these thought processes has the potential to assist the offender to create a context in which abuse is acceptable. These thought processes may therefore serve as precursors to abuse.

Behaviors as Precursors: Obtaining Victims and Preventing Disclosure

Among the behaviors to be explored in therapy are those that specifically lead to the obtaining of victims who will not disclose. Lane[882] noted that female juveniles offered their potential victims trust and reassurance that they would never be hurt by the offenders. She reported that, to the extent necessary to overcome their inhibitions, the offenders would knowingly objectify their victims. Lane noted that while some threatened their victims to prevent disclosure, some relied on the nature of the relationship, assuming that this would prevent disclosure. However, of note, is that some were prepared to facilitate the disclosure of the victim.

Davin[883] reported that, by the self-report of 30 independent female child molesters, about 27% believed that the child victims were motivated by fear, about 17% believed they were motivated by affection, 17% by pleasure and 30% by "fun" or a game. Thirteen percent told their victims that the sexual abuse was an expression of love. Twenty percent of the independent offenders did not know how they had obtained their victims. Regardless of their victim's perceptions, 27% reported motivating the children by introducing the acts as games, 13% with expressions of love, ten percent with bribes and seven percent by "teaching sex." Threats or force, while they occurred, were less common with this group. A small majority (about 58%) did not attempt to prevent their victims from disclosing. Where such an attempt occurred, most commonly it involved a threat of physical harm to the child.

Davin[884] also reported that of 48 co-offenders, about 70% reported that their victims were motivated by fear. Notably, 23% noted that death threats were used to obtain victim cooperation, 36% noted threats of physical harm to the victim, 18% noted threats of harm to others and 18% threatened abandonment. About eleven percent noted the use of force, about 16% of bribes. Other perceived victim motivations included obligation (about eleven percent), "fun" or perceiving the activity as a game (about nine percent), pleasure (about four percent) and affection (only about two percent). Less common ways in which the women elicited cooperation included threatening the loss of love. Fourteen percent approached the acts as games. Most commonly, the victims of the co-offenders were kept from telling by threatening physical harm or death to the child (about 69% of the women reported this). Other threats were common and only about 13% of the co-offenders denied that the children were prevented from telling about the abuse.

Faller[885] noted that women used threats, pornography and coercion to obtain the cooperation of their victims.

Each female sexual abuser will have her own patterns of obtaining access to her victims and, in some cases, of reducing the likelihood that she will be caught. Female offenders may also have patterns of behavior that culminate in sexual abuse, which should be explored. For some, these may include self-isolating behavior that results in partnering with a co-offender. For some, it may include patterns such as restricting a child's activity and engaging the child in sexually laden discussions. For others, it may include becoming more involved in the social activities of adolescents and engaging a particular teen in "dating" types of activities. The patterns of behavior that culminate in the sexual abuse of the child are likely to be as varied as the female sexual abusers themselves. These patterns should be explored with female sexual abusers in therapy.

Practical Concerns Related to Treatment

Agency Considerations

A practical concern in the treatment of female offenders is that they are a highly specific, resource intensive population in need of long-term treatment and highly specialized care. Because of the multiplicity of problems that they face, effective treatment providers must be highly trained in a wide variety of areas within the mental health field.

At the same time, the population of female sex offenders is an apparently rare population. Few clients are likely to be requesting services in any one facility at any given time. This reduces the financial justification for serving these clients on the part of individuals responsible for keeping mental health treatment centers solvent.

Among the costs involved in setting up a program for female sex offenders are the costs of monitoring the clients to the extent necessary to provide safety. Female sex offenders may require supervision when intermingling with other client populations or separation from other populations. For example, it is unwise to leave an unsupervised female sex offender in a waiting room with children. They may also require supervision when intermingling with each other in the interest of safety.

In some cases, female sex offenders will require their own treatment groups. In many cases, it will be counter-therapeutic to place a female sex offender (especially if she has been severely victimized) into a therapy group of male sexual offenders. In such a group, there is a risk that she will be subtly or overtly victimized, that she will form a relationship with a co-offender or that her or the male offenders' treatment will be impeded by victim-offender dynamics. Similar concerns may also arise in an all-female group, comprised primarily of sexual abuse victims.

Obviously, the extent of these concerns may vary with individual clients and with individual groups. In some cases, a group and an individual may be very well matched in terms of the issues that they are addressing and in terms of their resources for addressing the issues at hand. Establishing safety, however, both of the female offender and potential victims is a primary concern in approaching treatment and should be the deciding factor in merging treatment groups.

These factors raise important considerations in designing programs for female sex offenders. There is a need both for joining female sex offender programs with other programs in the interest of funding and of separating programs in the interest of providing appropriate care. Female sex offenders might best be integrated into programs in which there is an overlap in terms of training for the staff and in terms of the services provided to clients. For example, mental health centers that specialize in treating abuse cases, incest cases, women in prisons and so forth might incorporate the treatment of female sex offenders into the services offered.

The treatment of most female sex offenders is likely to be resource intensive. It may behoove agencies to be well networked with other agencies, such as those providing job training, education, acute care psychiatric hospitalization, emergency housing, legal services, medical services and so on.

Potentially, additional solutions may be found in the development of statewide or national programs specifically for the treatment of female sex offenders. A potential problem with this is the feasibility with which one state or jurisdiction might continually evaluate the services being provided in another area. The treatment of female sex offenders requires sufficient resources in many areas and a competent jurisdiction will want to monitor the provision of such services.

When female sex offenders are treated in a residential setting, there are special areas for clinical attention. Safety and supervision become primary concerns. Unless there are remarkable resources available for supervision, female sex offenders should be housed in separate rooms. It would be unconscionable to board a sex offender in treatment in the bedroom of a multiply sexually abused victim who was also in treatment without extraordinary steps to ensure safety.

Most female sex offenders are both offenders and victims and many dichotomize their relationships into those of victims and offenders, choosing between these two roles in their relationships. Pairing female sex offenders in a bedroom recreates the dynamics of abuse and abusing.

Some female sex offenders tend to sexualize all of their relationships and many have had sexual relationships with women. Placing such women into a situation in which they are undressing, sleeping and sharing private space with another person who has a demonstrated inability to appropriately establish and respect sexual boundaries recreates the dynamics of abuse. In some cases, this may result in abusive sexual or sexualized activities taking place. In other cases, the roles that situation creates for the women may interfere with their ability to benefit from treatment. For some clients, the intimacy involved in sharing a room may create an elevated risk of inducing post-traumatic stress symptoms, dissociative symptoms or other problems.

Similar concerns are likely to arise for many of the females related to the use of the bathroom. As with the bedroom, this area is likely to be associated with abuse for many. Adequate arrangements for privacy must be made if women are to be treated in a residential facility.

If women are housed in a facility with male offenders, intensive supervision and protection become a critical issue. Such an arrangement may not be feasible. Again, housing victims and offenders in close quarters has the potential to recreate the dynamics of abuse, to interfere with treatment and to result in actual victimization.

If treatment is provided to female sex offenders in a residential setting, continuity of care becomes a particularly important issue. Given the difficulties that female sex offenders are often noted to have in forming relationships, abrupt termination of support systems may be destabilizing. It is important for the females in treatment to maintain continuity with the people who care for them while they are in treatment. This should be a consideration in designing the treatment program. If women are promoted to a less restrictive level of care, they should ideally retain at least some contact with the same treatment team initially.

Staff Considerations

Given that many female sex offenders have had trauma inflicted upon them in the context of interpersonal relationships, it becomes important that their therapeutic relationships not continue this cycle. Abrupt termination of therapeutic relationships may reinforce for these women that relationships are painful. Separations from primary therapists may negatively impact their future treatment and may potentially be traumatic. The availability of resources necessary for staff retention, therefore, is an important consideration in developing a successful program for this population.

Because of the multiplicity of problems faced by the female child molester population, there is likely to be a high burnout rate among therapists and other treatment staff in the absence of conditions that actively serve to reduce this. Turnover and the subsequent costs of training new staff have been noted as important considerations by individuals working in the sex offender treatment field.[886]

Those working with female offenders, particularly given this group's traumatic histories and multiplicity of problems, should have access to supervision or case consultation, manageable case loads and sources of agency support. Staff retention should be high on the priority list of those establishing policies for agencies that provide services to female sex offenders. Staff who are well trained, supported and supervised are better able to manage the stress of the work with offenders.[887]

A variety of services to therapists may reduce turnover and burnout and improve the quality of services to the population of female sex offenders. Because of the likelihood that transference, countertransference and general stress-related concerns will arise for therapists working with this population, it is likely to be useful for therapists to have access to supervision, consultation and a support group. On-going training, particularly in areas related to recent research specifically related to female sex offenders, is highly important, as it is only now becoming available. Also important is on-going training in related areas such as post-traumatic stress disorder, personality disorders, abuse and neglect, the management of high risk behaviors and women's issues.

Rewards for working with this population should be equal to the challenges. Therapists working with this population should not model participation in an exploitive environment in which the benefits do not equal the requirements of the position. Salaries, benefits and other rewards such as training should be commensurate with the demands of the position.

Female sex offenders often have histories of pathology, isolation and abandonment in their previous significant relationships. For female sex offenders in residential treatment, relationships with staff who are able to model healthy interactions become a crucial part of the treatment process. Staff members who provide care for several hours per day provide an opportunity for the female offenders to experience relationships that are respectful, assertive and helpful. Of course, this is only true if the staff are well chosen, well trained and not burned out. Because these relationships will be a key part of treatment, efforts towards staff retention, particularly highly skilled staff, are very important. Training for staff working with female sex offenders should be particularly intensive.

Additionally, aftercare following residential treatment is highly important. Plans for aftercare should include a smooth transition of records from the residential placement to the next level of care. Most specifically, a discharge summary should highlight precursors to offending that have been identified and progress towards developing alternatives towards those precursors, so that work can be continued and monitored following discharge. Networking with programs qualified to provide care to this difficult population should occur.

Summary

When initially exploring victimization and patterns of offending, there are several considerations for the therapists. The goal is to walk the line between exploring the trauma and avoiding decompensation that may occur with too direct confrontation. Exploring the trauma initially from a more general, global or factual point of view may be helpful before going into specific details of the client's history, the client's personal perspective or the offender's emotional reactions to trauma and offending.

In cases in which the female sex offender has her own trauma history, the offender's own victimization and its relationship to her offending should be explored. A struggle for identity and belonging, a distorted sense of normalcy, the need for basic survival, sexual preoccupation, sexual aversion to adults, a lack of self-worth and an external locus of control may result from victimization history and contribute to offending.

Each offender's specific precursors to offending must also be explored. Specific emotions, situations, fantasies, justifications, thought processes, interactions with people and behaviors may all increase the likelihood of offending. Offenders must learn to recognize their patterns of offending and to develop and practice alternatives.

Finally, it is important that treatment meet certain basic standards of care. The most important consideration is providing a safe environment for the offenders. Retaining a knowledgeable and well-supported staff and providing an appropriate continuum of care is also important.

Notes ───────────────────

[842] Turner & Turner (1994)
[843] Saradjian & Hanks (1996)
[844] Saradjian & Hanks (1996)
[845] Larson & Maison (1987)
[846] Stirling (1994)
[847] Green & Kaplan (1993)
[848] Welldon (1996)
[849] Davin (1999)
[850] Saradjian & Hanks (1996)
[851] Lane (1991)
[852] Green & Kaplan (1993)
[853] Green & Kaplan (1993)
[854] Lane (1991)
[855] Maison & Larson (1995)

[856] Hislop (1999); Larson & Maison (1987); Wolfe (1985)
[857] Larson & Maison (1987)
[858] Larson & Maison (1989)
[859] Wolfe (1985)
[860] Davin (1999)
[861] Larson & Maison (1989)
[862] Wolfe (1985)
[863] Larson & Maison (1989)
[864] Rosencrans (1997)
[865] Davin (1999)
[866] Saradjian & Hanks (1996)
[867] Lane (1991)
[868] Maison & Larson (1995)
[869] Lane (1991)
[870] Davin (1999)
[871] Larson & Maison (1989)
[872] Maison & Larson (1995)
[873] Woodring (1995)
[874] Lane (1991)
[875] de Young (1982)
[876] de Young (1982)
[877] Green & Kaplan (1993)
[878] Green & Kaplan (1993); Wolfe (1985)
[879] Wolfe (1985)
[880] Matthews (1994); Ray & English (1995)
[881] Larson & Maison (1987)
[882] Lane (1991)
[883] Davin (1999)
[884] Davin (1999)
[885] Faller (1987)
[886] Mathews (1997)
[887] Mathews (1997)

References

Allen, C. (1990). Women as perpetrators of child sexual abuse: Recognition barriers. In A. Horton, B. Johnson, L. Roundy & D. Williams (Eds.). *The incest perpetrator: A family member no one wants to treat.* (pp. 108-125). Newbury Park, CA: Sage Publications.

Allen, C. (1991). *Women and men who sexually abuse children: A comparative analysis.* Orwell, VT: The Safer Society Press.

Allen, C. & Lee, C. (1992). Family of origin structure and intra/extrafamilial childhood sexual abuse victimization of male and female offenders. *Journal of Child Sexual Abuse, 1*(3), 31-45.

Apfelberg, B., Sugar, C. & Pfeffer, A. (1944). A psychiatric study of 250 sex offenders. *American Journal of Psychiatry. 100*, 762-770.

ATCOM, Inc. (1980). The child comes of age: Confronting the challenges of the '80s. New York: *The TODAY Newsletters*, ATCOM, Inc.

Bachmann, K., Moggi, F. & Stiremann-Lewis, F. (1994). Mother-son incest and its long- term consequences: A neglected phenomenon in psychiatric practice. *The Journal of Mental and Nervous Disorders, 182*(12), 723-725.

Banerjee, G. (1950/1955, 1959). *Sex delinquent women and their rehabilitation.* Bombay: The Tata Institute of Social Sciences.

Banning, A. (1989). Mother-son incest: Confronting a prejudice. *Child Abuse and Neglect, 13*, 563-570.

Barnett, S., Corder, F. & Jehu, D. (1990). Group treatment for women sex offenders against women. *Groupwork, 3*(2), 191-203.

Barry, M. & Johnson, A. (1958). The incest barrier. *Psychoanalytic Quarterly, 27*, 485- 500.

Bass, A. (July 7, 1991). A touch for evil. *Boston Globe Magazine.* pp. 12, 18, 21-25.

Becker, J. (1998). The assessment of adolescent perpetrators of childhood sexual abuse. *The Irish Journal of Psychology, 19*(1), 68-81.

Bender, L. & Blau, A. (1937). The reaction of children to sexual relations with adults. *American Journal of Orthopsychiatry, 7*, 500-518.

Benward, J. & Densen-Gerber, J. (1979). Incest as a causative factor in antisocial behavior: An exploratory study. *Contemporary Drug Problems, 4*(3), 303-339.

Berendzen, R. & Palmer, L. (1993). *Come here: A man overcomes the tragic aftermath of child sexual abuse.* New York: Villiard Books.

Berry, G. (1975). Incest: Some clinical variations on a classical theme. *Journal of American Academy of Psychoanalysis, 3*(2), 151-161.

Berry, M. & Johnson, A. (1958). The incest barrier. *Psychoanalytic Quarterly. 27*, 485-500.

Briggs, F. & Hawkins, R. (1995). Protecting boys from the risk of sexual abuse. *Early Child Development and Care, 110*, 19-32.

Brockman, B. & Blugrass, R. (1996). A general psychiatric approach to sexual deviation. In I. Rosen (Ed.). *Sexual deviation (3rd ed.).* (pp. 1-42). New York: Oxford University Press.

Browne, A. & Finkelhor, D. (1986). Impact of child sexual abuse: A review of the research. *Psychological Bulletin, 99*(1), 66-77.

Burgess, A.W., Hazelwood, R., Rokous, F., Hartman, C. & Burgess, A.G. (1988). Serial rapists and their victims: Reenactment and repetition. *Annals of the New York Academy of Sciences, 528*, 277-280.

Burns, N., Williams, L. & Finkelhor, D. (1988). Victim impact. In D. Finkelhor, L. Williams & N. Burns (Eds.). *Nursery crimes: Sexual abuse in day care.* (pp. 114-137). Newbury Park, CA: Sage Publications.

Butler, S. (1978). *Conspiracy of silence: The trauma of incest.* Volcano, CA: Volcano Press.

Cameron, P., Coburn, W., Larson, H., Proctor, K., Forde, N. & Cameron, K. (1986). Child molestation and homosexuality. *Psychological Reports, 58*, 327-337.

Campbell, J. & Carlson, K. (1995). Training and knowledge of professionals on specific topics in child sexual abuse. *Journal of Child Sexual Abuse, 4*(1), 75-86.

Carlson, E. (1997). *Trauma assessments: A clinician's guide.* New York: The Guilford Press.

Catanzarite, V. & Combs, S. (1980). Mother-son incest. *Journal of the American Medical Association, 243*(18). 1807-1808.

Chasnoff, I., Burns, W., Schnoll, S., Burns, K., Chissum, G. & Kyle-Spore, L. (1986). Maternal-neonatal incest. *American Journal of Orthopsychiatry, 56*(4), 577-580.

Chatham, C. (1992, Spring). Female sex offenders. Unpublished clinical research paper. College of St. Catherine, University of St. Thomas.

Chideckel, M. (1935). *Female sex perversions: The sexually aberrated woman as she is.* New York: Eugenics.

Coleman, J. (1994). Satanic cult practices. In V. Sinason (Ed.). *Treating survivors of Satanist abuse.* (pp. 242-253). New York: Routledge.

Colver, S. (1994). Cutting the cord: The resolution of a symbiotic relationship and the untwisting of desire. In V. Sinason (Ed.). *Treating survivors of Satanist abuse* (pp. 131-135). New York: Routledge.

Committee on Sexual Offences Against Children and Youth (Canada) (1984, August). *Sexual offenses against children. (Vol. 1).* Canada: The Minister of Justice and Attorney General of Canada, The Minister of National Health and Welfare, Ottawa, Canada: Canadian Government Publishing Centre.

Committee on Sexual Offences Against Children and Youth (Canada) (1984, August). *Sexual offenses against children. (Vol. 2).* Canada: The Minister of Justice and Attorney General of Canada, The Minister of National Health and Welfare, Ottawa, Canada: Canadian Government Publishing Centre.

Condy, S. (1985). Parameters of heterosexual molestations of boys. Unpublished doctoral dissertation, California School of Professional Psychology-Fresno, Fresno, CA.

Condy, S., Templer, D., Brown, R. & Veaco, L. (1987). Parameters of sexual contact of boys with women. *Archives of Sexual Behavior, 16*(5), 379-394.

Conte, J. & Schuerman, J. (1987). Factors associated with an increased impact of child sexual abuse. *Child Abuse and Neglect, 11*, 201-211.

Cooklin, A. & Barnes, G. (1994). The shattered picture of the family: Encountering new dimensions of human relations, of the family and of therapy. In V. Sinason (Ed.). *Treating survivors of Satanist abuse.* (pp. 120-130). New York: Routledge.

Cooper, A., Swaminath, S., Baxter, D. & Poulin, C. (1990). A female sex offender with multiple paraphilias: A psychologic and endocrine case study. *Canadian Journal of Psychiatry, 35*, 334-337.

Cooper, I. & Cormier, B. (1982). Inter-generational transmission of incest. *Canadian Journal of Psychiatry, 27*, 231-235.

Cooper, I. & Cormier, B. (1990). In R. Blugrass & P. Bowden (Eds.). *Principles and practice of forensic psychiatry.* (pp. 749-765.). New York: Churchill Livingston.

Courtois, C. (1979). The incest experience and its aftermath. *Victimology: An International Journal, 4*, 337-347.

Crewdson, J. (1988). *By silence betrayed: Sexual abuse of children in America.* Boston: Little, Brown and Company.

Cupoli, J. & Sewell, P. (1988). One thousand fifty-nine children with a chief complaint of sexual abuse. *Child Abuse and Neglect, 12*, 151-162.

Davin, P. (1993). The best kept secret: A study of female sex offenders. Unpublished doctoral dissertation. The Felding Institute.

Davin, P. (1999). Secrets revealed: A study of female sex offenders. In E. Bear (Ed.). *Female sexual abusers: Three perspectives.* Brandon, VT: The Safer Society Press.

De Francis, V. (1969). *Protecting the victims of sex crimes committed by adults.* Denver: American Humane Association.

DeJong, A., Hervada, A. & Emmett, G. (1983). Epidemiological variations in childhood sexual abuse. *Child Abuse and Neglect, 7*, 155-162.

de Young, (1982). *The sexual victimization of children.* Jefferson, NC: McFarland & Company.

Dolan, B. (1991, October 7). My own story. *Time Magazine*, p. 47.

Dunbar, T. (1993). Women who sexually molest female children. Unpublished doctoral dissertation. University of Southern California, Los Angeles, CA.

Dunbar, T. (1999). Women who sexually molest female children. In E. Bear (Ed.). *Female sexual abusers: Three perspectives.* Brandon, VT: The Safer Society Press.

Elliott, A. & Peterson, L. (1993, July). Maternal sexual abuse of children: When to suspect it and how to uncover it. *Postgraduate Medicine, 94*(1), 169-180.

Elliot, M. (Ed.). (1994). *Female sexual abuse of children.* New York: The Guilford Press.

Erickson, P. & Rapkin, A. (1991). Unwanted sexual experiences among middle and high school youth. *Journal of Adolescent Health, 12,* 319-325.

Etherington, K. (1997). Maternal sexual abuse of males. *Child Abuse Review, 6,* 107- 117.

Evert, K. & Bijkerk, I. (1987). *When you're ready: A woman's healing from childhood physical and sexual abuse by her mother.* Walnut Creek, CA: Launch Press.

Faller, K. (1987). Woman who sexually abuse children. *Violence and Victims, 2*(4), 263- 276.

Faller, K. (1988). The spectrum of sexual abuse in daycare. An exploratory study. *Journal of Family Violence, 3*(4), 283-298.

Faller, K. (1989). Characteristics of a clinical sample of sexually abused children: How boy and girl victims differ. *Child Abuse and Neglect, 13,* 281-291.

Faller, K. (1995). A clinical sample of women who have sexually abused children. *Journal of Child Sexual Abuse, 4*(3), 13-29.

Farber, E., Showers, J., Johnson, C., Joseph, J. & Oshins, L. (1984). The sexual abuse of children: A comparison of male and female victims. *Journal of Clinical Child Psychology, 13*(3), 294-297.

Feeney, S. (1994, October). Unspeakable acts: Women like you commit them, too. *Mirabella, 6*(5), 96-99.

Fehrenbach, P. & Monastersky, C. (1988). Characteristics of female adolescent sexual offenders. *American Journal of Orthopsychiatry, 58*(1), 148-151.

Feinauer, L. (1989). Comparison of long-term effects of child abuse by type of abuse and by relationship of the offender to the victim. *The American Journal of Family Therapy, 17*(1), 48-56.

Finkelhor, D. (1979). *Sexually victimized children.* New York: The Free Press.

Finkelhor, D. (1984). *Child sexual abuse: New theory and research.* New York: The Free Press.

Finkelhor, D. (1986). *A sourcebook on child sexual abuse.* Beverly Hills: Sage Publications.

Finkelhor, D., Hotaling, G., Lewis, I. & Smith, C. (1990). Sexual abuse in a national survey of adult men and women: Prevalence, characteristics, and risk factors. *Child Abuse Neglect, 14*, 19-28.

Finkelhor, D. & Russell, D. (1984). Women as perpetrators: Review of the evidence. In D. Finkelhor (Ed.). *Child sexual abuse: New theory and research.* New York: The Free Press.

Finkelhor, D. & Williams, L. (1988). Perpetrators. In D. Finkelhor, L. Williams & N. Burns (Eds.). *Nursery crimes: Sexual abuse in day care.* (pp. 27-69). Newbury Park, CA: Sage Publications.

Forbes, J. (1992). Female sexual abusers: The contemporary search for equivalence. *Practice, 6*(2), 102-111.

Forward, S. & Buck, C. (1978). *Betrayal of Innocence.* New York: Penguin Books.

Freel, M. (1995). *Women who sexually abuse children.* Social Work Monographs, Norwich: University of Hull, Monograph 135.

Friedrich, W., Urquiza, A. & Beilke, R. (1986). Behavior problems in sexually abused young children. *Journal of Pediatric Psychology, 11*(1), 47-57.

Fritz, G., Stoll, K & Wagner, N. (1981, Spring). A comparison of males and females who were sexually molested as children. *Journal of Sex and Marital Therapy, 7*(1), 54-59.

Fromuth, M. (1983). The long term psychological impact of childhood sexual abuse. Unpublished doctoral dissertation, Auburn University: Auburn, Alabama.

Fromuth, M. & Burkhart, B. (1987). Childhood sexual victimization among college men: Definitional and methodological issues. *Violence and Victims, 2*(4), 241-253.

Fromuth, M. & Conn, V. (1997). Hidden perpetrators: Sexual molestation in a nonclinical sample of college women. *Journal of Interpersonal Violence, 12*(3), 456- 465.

Froning, M. & Mayman, S. (1990). Identification and treatment of the sexually abused male. In M. Hunter (Ed.). *The sexually abused male: Application of treatment strategies (vol. 2).* (pp. 199-224). New York: Lexington Books.

Gebhard, P., Gagnon, J., Pomeroy, W. & Christenson, C. (1965). *Sex offenders: An analysis of types.* New York: Harper and Row.

Glasser, M. (1990). Paedophilia. In R. Blugrass & P. Bowden (Eds.). *Principles and practice of forensic psychiatry.* (pp. 739-748). New York: Churchill Livingston.

Goldman, L. (June 25-26, 1993). Female sex offenders: Societal avoidance of comprehending the phenomenon of women who sexually abuse children. Paper presented at The National Institute of Mental Health Meeting on Female Sex Offenders, Bethesda, MD.

Goldstein, E. (1992). Sexual abuse in families: The mother-daughter relationship. *Issues in Ego Psychology, 15*(1), 63-64.

Gomes-Schwartz, B., Horowitz, J. & Cardareelli, A. (1990). *Child sexual abuse: The initial effects.* Newbury Park: Sage Publications.

Goodwin, J. & DiVasto, P. (1979). Mother-daughter incest. *Child Abuse and Neglect, 3*, 953-957.

Goodwin, J., McCarthy, T. & DiVasto, P. (1981). Prior incest in mothers of abused children. *Child Abuse and Neglect, 5*, 87-95.

Grayson, J. (1989, Summer). Female sex offenders. *Virginia Child Protection Newsletter*, pp. 5-7, 11-13.

Green, A. & Kaplan, M. (1994, September). Psychiatric impairment and childhood victimization experiences in female child molesters. *Journal of American Academy of Child and Adolescent Psychiatry, 33*(7), 954-961.

Grier, P., Clark, M. & Stoner, S. (1993). Comparative study of personality traits of female sex offenders. *Psychological Reports, 73*, 1378.

Groth, N. (1979a). *Men who rape: The psychology of the offender*. New York: The Plenum Press.

Groth, N. (1979b). Sexual trauma in the life histories of rapists and child molesters. *Victimology: An International Journal, 4*(1), 10-16.

Groth, N. & Burgess, A. (1980). Male rape: Offenders and victims. *American Journal of Psychiatry, 137*(7), 806-810.

Groth, N. & Loredo, C. (1981). Juvenile sexual offenders: Guidelines for assessment. *International Journal of Offender Therapy and Comparative Criminology, 25*(1), 31-39.

Hale, R. & Sinason, V. (1994). Internal and external reality: Establishing parameters. In V. Sinason (Ed.). *Treating survivors of Satanist abuse.* (pp. 274-284). New York: Routledge.

Harper, J. (1993). Prepubertal male victims of incest: A clinical study. *Child Abuse and Neglect, 17*, 419-421.

Haugaard, J. & Emery, R. (1989). Methodological issues in child sexual abuse research. *Child Abuse and Neglect, 13*, 89-100.

Herman, J. (1979). *Trauma and recovery*. New York: Basic Books.

Hewitt, S. (1990). The treatment of sexually abused preschool boys. In M. Hunter (Ed.). *The sexually abused male.* (pp. 225-248). New York: Lexington Books.

Higgs, D., Canavan M. & Meyer, W. (1992, February). Moving from defense to offense: The development of a female sex offender. *Journal of Sex Research, 29*(1), 131-140.

Hindman, J. (1989). *Just before dawn*. Onterio, Oregon: AlexAndria Associates.

Hislop, J. (1994). Female child molesters. Unpublished doctoral dissertation, California School of Professional Psychology-Fresno, Fresno, CA.

Hislop, J. (1999). Female child molesters. In E. Bear (Ed.). *Female sexual abusers: Three perspectives*. Brandon, VT: The Safer Society Press.

Holubinskyj, H. & Foley, S. (1986). Escape or rescue: Intervention in a case of mother/daughter, with an adolescent girl. *Australian Journal of Sex, Marriage & Family, 8*(1), 27-31.

Hudson, A. (1995). Personality assessment of female sex offenders: A cluster analysis. Unpublished doctoral dissertation, University of Oklahoma.

Hunt, P. & Baird, M. (1990). Children of sex rings. *Child Welfare, 69*(3), 195-207.

Hunter, J., Lexier, L, Goodwin, D., Browne, P. & Dennis, C. (1993). Psychosexual, attitudinal, and developmental characteristics of juvenile female sexual perpetrators in a residential treatment setting. *Journal of Child and Family Studies, 2*(4), 317-326.

Hunter, M. (Ed.). (1990). *The sexually abused male: Prevalence, impact and treatment. Vol. 1.* New York: Lexington Books.

Jackson, M. (1986, September 3). PHASE extends to female sex abusers. *Ramsey County Review*, p. 1.

James, B. & Nasjleti, M. (1983). *Treating sexually abused children and their families*. Palo Alto, CA: Consulting Psychologists Press, Inc.

Johansen, D. (1990). Distinguishing sexually abused children from nonabused children on the basis of sexual behavior. Unpublished doctoral dissertation. Milwaukee, Wisconsin: Marquette University.

Johnson, R. & Shrier, D. (1987). Past sexual victimization by females of male patients in an adolescent medicine clinic population. *American Journal of Psychiatry, 144*(5), 650-652.

Johnson, T. (1989). Female child perpetrators: Children who molest other children. *Child Abuse and Neglect, 13*(4), 571-585.

Justice, B. & Justice, R. (1979). *The broken taboo: Sex in the family*. New York: Human Sciences Press.

Kasl, (1990). Female perpetrators of sexual abuse: A feminist view. In M. Hunter (Ed.). *The sexually abused male: Application of treatment strategies (vol. 1).* (pp. 259-274). New York: Lexington Books.

Kaufman, A., Divasto, P., Jackson, R., Voorhees, D. & Christy, J. (1980). Male rape victims: Noninstitutional assault. *American Journal of Psychiatry, 137*(2), 221-223.

Kaufman, K., Wallace, A., Johnson, C. & Reeder, M. (1995, September). Comparing female and male perpetrators' modus operandi: Victims' reports of sexual abuse. *Journal of Interpersonal Violence, 10*(3), 322-334.

Kempe, R. & Kempe, C. H. (1984). *The common secret: Sexual abuse of children and adolescents.* New York: W.H. Freeman and Company.

Kendall-Tackett, K. & Simon, M. (1987). Perpetrators and their acts: Data from 365 adults molested as children. *Child Abuse and Neglect, 11,* 237-245.

Kercher, G. & McShane, M. (1985). Characterizing child sexual abuse on the basis on a multi-agency sample. *Victimology: An International Journal, 9*(3-4), 364-382.

Kinsey, A., Pomeroy, W. & Martin, C. (1948). *Sexual behavior in the human male.* Philadelphia: W.B. Saunders.

Knight-Ridder News Service (March 15, 1998). Ex-teacher who had child by boy is pregnant again. *The Virginian-Pilot.* pp. A1-A9.

Knopp, F. & Lackey, L. (1987). *Female sexual abusers: A summary of data from 44 treatment providers.* Orwell, VT: The Safer Society Press.

Knopp, F. & Stevenson, W. (1990). *Nationwide survey of juvenile & adult sex-offender treatment programs.* Orwell, VT: The Safer Society Press.

Korbin, J. (1986). Childhood histories of women imprisoned for fatal child mal-treatment. *Child Abuse and Neglect, 10,* 331-338.

Korbin, J. (1990). Child sexual abuse: A cross-cultural view. In R. Oates (Ed.). *Understanding and managing child sexual abuse.* (pp. 42-58). Philadelphia: Harcourt Brace Jovanovich, Publishers.

Krug, R. (1989). Adult male report of childhood sexual abuse by mothers: Case descriptions, motivations and long-term consequences. *Child Abuse and Neglect, 13,* 111-119.

Kubo, S. (1959, July). Researches and studies on incest in Japan. *Hiroshima Journal of Medical Sciences, 8*(1), 99-159.

Landis, J. (1956). Experiences of 500 children with adult sexual deviation. *Psychiatric Quarterly Supplement, 30,* 91-109.

Lane, S. (1991). Special offender populations. In G. Ryan & S. Lane (Eds.). *Juvenile sexual offending: Causes, consequences and correction.* (pp. 299- 332). Lexington, MA: Lexington Books.

Langmade, C. (1983). The impact of pre- and postpubertal onset of incest experiences in adult women as measured by sex anxiety, sex guilt, sexual satisfaction and sexual behavior. Unpublished doctoral dissertation. Rosemead School of Psychology, Biola University, La Mirada, CA.

Larson, N. & Maison, S. (1987). *Psychosexual treatment program for female sex offenders: Minnesota Correctional Facility—Shakopee.* St Paul, MN: Meta Resources.

Lawson, C. (1991). Clinical assessment of mother-son sexual abuse. *Clinical Social Work Journal, 19*(4), 391-403.

Lawson, C. (1993). Mother-son sexual abuse: Rare or underreported? A critique of the research. *Child Abuse and Neglect, 17,* 261-269.

Lawson, W. (1984). Depression and crime: A discursive approach. In M. Craft & A. Craft (Eds.). *Mentally abnormal offenders.* Philadelphia: Bailliere Tindale.

Lidz, R. & Lidz, T. (1969). Homosexual tendencies in mothers of schizophrenic women. *The Journal of Nervous and Mental Disease, 149*(2), 229-235.

Lloyd, C. (1987, February). Working with the female offender: A case study. *British Journal of Occupational Psychology, 50*(2), 44-46.

Longdon, C. (1994). A survivor and therapist's viewpoint. In M. Elliot (Ed.). *Female sexual abuse of children.* New York: The Guilford Press.

Lukianowicz, N. (1972). Other types of incest. *British Journal of Psychiatry, 120,* 308- 313.

Macchietto, J. (1998). Treatment issues of adult male victims of female sexual aggression. In P. Anderson & C. Struckman-Johnson (Eds.). *Sexually aggressive women: Current perspectives and controversies.* (p. 187-204). New York: The Guilford Press.

MacHovec, F. & Wieckowski, E. (1992). The 10FC: Ten-factor continua of classification and treatment criteria for male and female sex offenders. *Medical Psychotherapy, 5,* 53-64.

Maison, S. & Larson, N. (1995). Psychosexual treatment program for women sex offenders in a prison setting. *Nordisk Sexologi, 13,* 149-162.

Maltz, W. & Holman, B. (1987). *Incest and sexuality: A guide to understanding and healing.* Lexington, MA: Lexington Books.

Margolin, L. (1986). The effects of mother-son incest. *Lifestyles: A Journal of Changing Patterns, 8*(2), 104-114.

Margolin, L (1991). Child sexual abuse by nonrelated caregivers. *Child Abuse and Neglect, 15*, 213-221.

Margolin, L. & Craft, J. (October, 1989). Child sexual abuse by caretakers. *Family Relations, 38*(4), 450-455.

Margolis, M. (1977). A preliminary report of a case of consummated mother-son incest. *Annual Psychoan, 5*, 267-293.

Margolis, M. (1984). A case of mother-adolescent son incest: A follow-up study. *Psychoanalytic Quarterly, 53*, 355-385.

Marvasti, J. (1986). Incestuous mothers. *American Journal of Forensic Psychiatry, 7*(4), 63-69.

Masters, R. (1963). *Patterns of incest.* New York: The Julian Press.

Mathews, F. (1997). The adolescent sex offender field in Canada: Old problems, current issues, and emerging controversies. *Journal of Child and Youth Care, 11*(1), 55-62.

Mathews, R., Hunter, J. & Vuz, J. (1997). Juvenile female sexual offenders: Clinical characteristics and treatment issues. *Sexual Abuse: A Journal of Research and Treatment, 9*(3), 187-199.

Mathews, R., Matthews, J. & Speltz, K. (1989). *Female sexual offenders: An exploratory study.* Orwell, VT: The Safer Society Press.

Mathis, J. (1972). *Clear thinking about sexual deviations.* Chicago: Nelson-Hall Company.

Matthews, J. (1994). Working with female sexual abusers. In M. Elliot (Ed.). *Female sexual abuse of children.* New York: The Guilford Press.

Matthews, J., Mathews, R. & Speltz, K. (1991). Female sexual offenders: A typology. In M. Patton (Ed.). *Family sexual abuse: Frontline research and evaluation.* (pp. 199-219). Newbury Park, CA: Sage Publications.

Mayer, A. (1983). *Incest: A treatment manual for therapy with victims, spouses and offenders.* Holmes Beach, FL: Learning Publications.

Mayer, A. (1992). *Women sex offenders: Treatment and dynamics.* Holmes Beach, FL: Learning Publications.

McCarty, L. (1986). Mother-child incest: Characteristics of the offender. *Child Welfare, 65*(5), 447-458.

McMullen, R. (1990). *Male rape: Breaking the silence on the last taboo.* Boston: GMP Publishers Limited.

Meiselman, K. (1978). *Incest: A psychological study of causes and effects with treatment recommendations.* San Francisco: Jossey-Bass.

Mellor, C., Farid, N. & Craig, D. (1988, August). Female hypersexuality treated with cyproterone acetate. *American Journal of Psychiatry, 145*(8), 1037.

Merx, K. (August 9, 1998). Sex with teacher took boy's youth. *The Detroit News.*

Mezey, G. & King, M. (1987). Male victims of sexual assault. *Medicine, Science and the Law, 27*(2), 122-124.

Miletski, H. (1995). *Mother-son incest: The unthinkable broken taboo.* Brandon, VT: The Safer Society Press.

Mitchell, J. & Morse, J. (1998). *From victims to survivors: Reclaimed voices of women sexually abused in childhood by females.* Washington, D.C.: Accelerated Development.

Motiuk, L. & Belcourt, R. (1996). Profiling the Canadian federal sex offender population. *Forum on Corrections Research, 8*(2), 3-7.

Mrazek, P., Lynch, M. & Bentovim, A. (1987). Recognition of child sexual abuse in the United Kingdom. In P. Mrazek & C.H. Kempe (Eds.). *Sexually abused children and their families.* New York: Pergamon Press.

Myers, K. (1992). The experiences of adult women who, as children, were sexually abused by an older, trusted female: An exploratory study. Unpublished masters thesis. Northhampton, MA: Smith College School for Social Work.

Nasjleti, M. (1980). Suffering in silence: The male incest victim. *Child Welfare, 59*(5), 269-275.

Neisser, U. (1997, May). Jane Doe's memories: Changing the past to serve the present. *Child Maltreatment, 2*(2), 123-125.

News Sentinel Fort Wayne Indiana (November 18, 1996). Woman charged in sexual assault. p. 7A.

Nielsen, T. (1983, November). Sexual abuse of boys: Current perspectives. *The Personnel and Guidance Journal*, pp. 139-142.

Norris, J. (1991). *Henry Lee Lucas: The shocking true story of America's most notorious serial killer.* Kensington Publishing Company.

O'Connor, A. (1987). Female sex offenders. *British Journal of Psychiatry, 150,* 615-620.

Ogilvie, B. & Daniluk, J. (1995, July/August). Common themes in the experiences of mother-daughter incest survivors: Implications for counseling. *Journal of Counseling & Development, 73,* 598-602.

Okami, P. (1991). Self-reports of "positive" childhood and adolescent sexual contacts with older persons: An exploratory study. *Archives of Sexual Behavior, 20*(5), 437- 457.

Paiser, P. (1992). Relational experiences of women survivors of female-perpetrated childhood sexual abuse. Unpublished doctoral dissertation. Boston: Massachusetts School of Professional Psychology.

Palmer, R., Bramble, D., Metcalfe, M., Oppenheimer, R. & Smith, J. (1994). Childhood sexual experiences with adults: Adult male psychiatric patients and general practice attenders. *The British Journal of Psychiatry, 165*(5), 675-679.

Parrot, A. (1998). Meaningful sexual assault prevention programs for men. In P. Anderson & Struckman-Johnson (Eds.). *Sexually aggressive women: Current perspectives and controversies.* (pp. 205-223). New York: The Guilford Press.

Peluso, E. & Putnam, N. (1996, January). Case study: Sexual abuse of boys by females. *Journal of American Academy of Child and Adolescent Psychiatry, 35*(1), 51-54.

Petrovich, M & Templer, D. (1984). Heterosexual molestation of children who later become rapists. *Psychological Reports, 54*(3), 810.

Pierce, L. & Pierce, R. (1987). Incestuous victimization by juvenile sex offenders. *Journal of Family Violence, 2*(4), 351-364.

Plummer, K. (1981). Pedophilia: Constructing a sociological baseline. In M. Cook & Howells (Eds.). *Adult sexual interest in children.* (pp. 225-250). New York: Academic Press.

Pothast, H. & Allen (1994). Masculinity and femininity in male and female perpetrators of child sexual abuse. *Child Abuse and Neglect, 18*(9), 763-767.

Quintano, J. (1992). Case profiles of early childhood enema abuse. *Treating Abuse Today, 2*(5), 11-22.

Ramsey-Klawsnik, H. (1990, April). Sexual abuse by female perpetrators: Impact upon children. Paper presented at the 1990 National Symposium on Child Victimization, "Keepers of the Children," Atlanta, GA.

Raphling, D., Carpenter, B. & Davis, A. (1967). Incest: A genealogical study. *Archives of General Psychiatry, 16*, 505-511.

Ray, J. & English, D. (1995). Comparisons of female and male children with sexual behavior problems. *Journal of Youth and Adolescence, 24*(4), 439-451.

Reinhart, M. (1987). Sexually abused boys. *Child Abuse and Neglect, 11*, 229-235.

Rentoul, L. & Appleboom, N. (1997). Understanding the psychological impact of rape and serious sexual assault of men: A literature review. *Journal of Psychiatric and Mental Health Nursing, 4*, 267-274.

Renvoize, J. (1982). *Incest: A family pattern.* London: Routledge & Kegan Paul.

Rinsley, D. (1978). Borderline psychopathology: A review of aetiology, dynamics and treatment. *The International Review of Psychoanalysis, 5*, 45-54.

Risin, L. & Koss, M. (1987). Sexual abuse of boys: Prevalence, and descriptive characteristics of childhood victimizations. *Journal of Interpersonal Violence, 2*(3), 309-323.

Rist, K. (1979). Incest: Theoretical and clinical views. *American Journal of Orthopsychiatry, 49*(4), 680-691.

Rosencrans, B. (1993, June 25-26). Unpublished comments. National Institute of Mental Health meeting on female sex offenders.

Rosencrans, B. (1997). *The last secret: Daughters sexually abused by mothers.* Brandon, VT: The Safer Society Press.

Rowan, E., Langelier, P. & Rowan, J. (1988). Female pedophiles. *Corrective and Social Psychiatry and Journal of Behavior Technology Methods and Therapy, 34*(3), 17-20.

Rowan, E., Rowan, J. & Langelier, P. (1990). Women who molest children. *Bulletin of the American Academy of Psychiatry and the Law, 18*(1), 79-83.

Roys, D. & Timms, R. (1995). Personality profiles of adult males sexually molested by their maternal caretakers: Preliminary findings. *Journal of Child Sexual Abuse, 4*(4), 63-77.

Rudin, M., Zalewski, C. & Bodmer-Turner, J. (1995, August). Characteristics of sexual abuse victims according to perpetrator gender. *Child Abuse and Neglect, 19*, 963- 973.

Russell, D. (1983). The incidence and prevalence of intrafamilial and extrafamilial sexual abuse of female children. *Child Abuse and Neglect, 7*, 133-146.

Russell, D. (1986). *The secret trauma: Incest in the lives of girls and women.* New York: Basic Books.

Ryan, G. Miyoshi, T., Metzner, J., Krugman, R. & Fryer, G. (1996, January). Trends in a national sample of sexually abused youth. *Journal of the Academy of Child and Adolescent Psychiatry, 35*(1), 17-25

San Diego Union-Tribune. (October 27, 1996). Mom faces prison in child-sex case. p. A7.

Saradjian, J. & Hanks, H. (1996). *Women who sexually abuse children: From research to clinical practice.* New York: John Riley and Sons.

Sarrel, P. & Masters, W. (1982). Sexual molestation of men by women. *Archives of Sexual Behavior, 11*(2), 117-131.

Scavo, R. (1989). Female adolescent offenders: A neglected treatment group. *Social Casework, 70*(2), 114-117.

Schoenewolf, G. (Winter, 1991). The feminist myth about sexual abuse. *The Journal of Psychohistory, 18*(3), 331-343.

Schultz, L. & Jones, P. (1983). Sexual abuse of children: Issues for social services and health professionals. *Child Welfare, 62*(2), 99-108.

Seghorn, T., Prentky, R. & Boucher, R. (1987). Childhood sexual abuse in the lives of sexually aggressive offenders. *Journal of American Academy of Child and Adolescent Psychiatry, 26*(2), 262-267.

Sgroi, S. & Sargent, N. (1994). Impact and treatment issues for victims of sexual abuse by female perpetrators. In M. Elliot (Ed.). *Female sexual abuse of children.* New York: The Guilford Press.

Sheldon, V. & Sheldon, R. (1989). Sexual abuse of males by females: The problem, treatment modality, and case example. *Family Therapy, 16*(3), 249-258.

Sheldrick, C. (1991). Adult sequelae of child sexual abuse. *British Journal of Psychiatry, 158* (suppl. 10), 55-62.

Shengold, L. (1980). Some reflections on a case of mother/adolescent son incest. *International Journal of Psychoanalysis, 61,* 461-476.

Shrier, D. & Johnson, R. (1988). Sexual victimization of boys: An ongoing study of an adolescent medicine clinic population. *Journal of the National Medical Association, 80*(11), 1189-1193.

Silber, A. (1979). Childhood seduction, parental pathology and hysterical symptomatology: The genesis of an altered state of consciousness. *International Journal of Psychoanalysis, 60,* 109-116.

Simari, C. & Baskin, D. (1982). Incestuous experiences within homosexual populations: A preliminary study. *Archives of Sexual Behavior, 11*(4), 329-344.

Smith, H. & Israel, E. (1987). Sibling incest: A study of the dynamics of 25 cases. *Child Abuse and Neglect, 11,* 101-108.

Sonkin, D. (1992). *Wounded boys, heroic men: A man's guide to recovering from child sexual abuse.* Stamford, CT: Longmeadow Press.

Spencer, M. & Dunklee, P. (1986). Sexual abuse of boys. *Pediatrics, 78*(1), 133-138.

Stevens, E. (1993). Women survivors' stories. In M. Elliot (Ed.). *Female sexual abuse of children.* New York: The Guilford Press.

Stevenson, M. & Gajarsky, W. (1991). Unwanted childhood sexual experiences relate to later victimization and male perpetration. *Journal of Psychology and Human Sexuality, 4*(4), 57-70.

Stirling, A. (1994). *From generation to generation: Understanding sexual attraction to children.* Tiburon, CA: The Printed Voice.

Sugar, M. (1983). Sexual abuse of children and adolescents. *Adolescent Psychiatry, 11,* 199-211.

Summit, R. (1983). The child sexual abuse accommodation syndrome. *Child Abuse and Neglect, 7,* 177-193.

Swink, K. (1989, March). Therapeutic issues for women survivors of maternal incest. Presented at the Association for Women in Psychology National Conference, Newport, Rhode Island.

Travin, S., Cullen, K. & Protter, B. (1990). Female sex offenders: Severe victims and victimizers. *Journal of Forensic Sciences, 35*(1), 140-150.

Tsai, M., Feldman-Summers, S. & Edgar, M. (1979). Childhood molestation: Variables related to a differential impact of psychosexual functioning in adult women. *Journal of Abnormal Psychology, 88,* 407-417.

Turner, M. & Turner, T. (1994). *Female adolescent sexual abusers: An exploratory study of mother-daughter dynamics with implications for treatment.* Brandon, VT: The Safer Society Press.

U.S. Department of Health, Education and Welfare, Public Health Service, Center for Disease Control (12/13/85). Adolescent sex offenders— Vermont, 1984. *Morbidity and Mortality Weekly Report, 34*(9), 738-741.

Vanderbuilt, H. (1992, February). Incest: A chilling report. *Lear's,* pp. 49-77.

Vedros, D. (March 13, 1999). Personal communication.

Wahl, C. (1960). The psychodynamics of consummated maternal incest: A report of two cases. *Archives of General Psychiatry, 3,* 188-193.

Wakefield, H. & Underwager, R. (1991). Female sexual abusers: A critical review of the literature. *American Journal of Forensic Psychology, 9*(4), 43-69.

Walker, N. & McCabe, S. (1973). *Crime and insanity in England.* Edinburgh: Edinburgh University Press.

Walters, D. (1975). *Physical and sexual abuse of children: Causes and treatment.* Bloomington: Indiana University Press.

Weber, F., Gearing, J., Davis, A. & Conlon, M. (1992). Prepubertal initiation of sexual experiences and older first partner predict promiscuous sexual behavior of delinquent adolescent males—unrecognized child abuse? *Journal of Adolescent Mental Health, 13,* 600-605.

Weinberg, S. (1955). *Incest behavior.* Secaucus, NJ: Citadel Press.

Weir, I. & Wheatcroft, M. (1995). Allegations of children's involvement in ritual sexual abuse: Clinical experience of 20 cases. *Child Abuse and Neglect, 19*(4), 491-505.

Welldon, E. (1996). Female sex offenders. *Prison Service Journal, 39*(107), 39-47.

Wilkins, R. (1990, May). Women who sexually abuse children: Doctors need to become sensitised to the possibility. *British Medical Journal, 300,* 1153-1154.

Williams, L. & Farrell, R. (1990). Legal response to child sexual abuse in daycare. *Criminal Justice and Behavior, 17*(3), 284-302.

Wolfe, F. (1985, March). Twelve female sexual offenders. Paper presented at "Next steps in research on the assessment and treatment of sexually aggressive persons (paraphiliacs)." St. Louis, Mo.

Woodring, H. (1995, August). An MMPI study of incarcerated female sex offenders. Unpublished master's thesis. Bucknell University.

Wulffen, E. (1934). *Woman as sexual criminal.* New York: American Ethnological Press.

Yorukoglu, A. & Kemph, J. (1966). Children not severely damaged by incest with a parent. *Journal of the American Academy of Child Psychiatry, 5*(1), 111-125.

Zaidi, L. & Gutierrez-Kovner, V. (1995, June). Group treatment of sexually abused latency-age girls. *Journal of Interpersonal Violence, 10*(2), 215-228.

Ziotnick, C., Begin, A., Shea, M., Pearlstein, T., Simpson, E. & Costello, E. (1994, November/December). The relationship between characteristics of sexual abuse and dissociative experiences. *Comprehensive Psychiatry, 35*(6), 465-470.

Index

About the Author

Dr. Hislop has worked with physically and sexually abused children and adults, as well as child abusers and sex offenders, in a variety of settings. She is currently affiliated with a Children's Advocacy Center at the Children's Hospital of The King's Daughters in Norfolk, Virginia, and is in private practice in Virginia Beach, Virginia. She has served as an adjunct faculty member for Old Dominion University and Saint Leo University in Norfolk, Virginia.

Her previous publication in the field of sexual abuse, *Female Sexual Abusers: Three Views*, was a collaborative effort with other researchers, available through the Safer Society Press. She also wrote *Coping with Rejection* for adolescents which was listed among the best books for teenagers by the New York Public Library.